ELEVATE
SCHOOL-BASED
PROFESSIONAL LEARNING

JOELLEN KILLION | WILLIAM A. SOMMERS | ANN DELEHANT

Solution Tree | Press a division of
Solution Tree

555 North Morton Street
Bloomington, IN 47404
800.733.6786 (toll free) / 812.336.7700
FAX: 812.336.7790

email: info@SolutionTree.com
SolutionTree.com

Visit **go.SolutionTree.com/leadership** to download the free reproducibles in this book.

Printed in the United States of America

Library of Congress Cataloging-in-Publication Data

Names: Killion, Joellen, author. | Sommers, William A., author. | Delehant,
     Ann M., author.
Title: Elevate school-based professional learning / Joellen Killion,
     William A. Sommers, Ann Delehant.
Description: Bloomington, IN : Solution Tree Press, [2022] | Includes
     bibliographical references and index.
Identifiers: LCCN 2022028299 (print) | LCCN 2022028300 (ebook) | ISBN
     9781954631397 (Paperback) | ISBN 9781954631403 (eBook)
Subjects: LCSH: Learning. | Professional development for teachers. | Team
     learning approach in education. | Teachers--In-service training. |
     Teachers--Training of. | School improvement programs.
Classification: LCC LB1060 .K544 2022 (print) | LCC LB1060 (ebook) | DDC
     371.3/6--dc23/eng/20221102
LC record available at https://lccn.loc.gov/2022028299
LC ebook record available at https://lccn.loc.gov/2022028300

Solution Tree

Jeffrey C. Jones, CEO
Edmund M. Ackerman, President

Solution Tree Press

President and Publisher: Douglas M. Rife
Associate Publisher: Sarah Payne-Mills
Managing Production Editor: Kendra Slayton
Editorial Director: Todd Brakke
Art Director: Rian Anderson
Copy Chief: Jessi Finn
Senior Production Editor: Sarah Foster
Content Development Specialist: Amy Rubenstein
Copy Editor: Evie Madsen
Proofreader: Charlotte Jones
Text and Cover Designer: Abigail Bowen
Associate Editor: Sarah Ludwig
Editorial Assistants: Charlotte Jones and Elijah Oates

ACKNOWLEDGMENTS

We are grateful to the many people in our personal and professional lives who have been our mentors, teachers, and colleagues. Some we are fortunate enough to call both friend and colleague. We especially want to acknowledge Shirley Hord, who has been a force in each of our lives. She has been a constant voice in our ears for scholarship, integrity, professional learning, and leading change. We each have countless memories of the debates, discussions, and deliberations with her individually and collectively. She made each of us a better educator.

To the teachers, teacher leaders, coaches, principals, central office staff, professional association leaders and members, union leaders, regional and state or ministry leaders and policy makers, and consultants with whom we have worked over the years, thank you for being our learning partners. Students in schools you have touched are the fortunate beneficiaries of your visionary and dedicated work.

Solution Tree Press would like to thank the following reviewers:

John D. Ewald
Education Consultant
Frederick, Maryland

Caitlin Fox
College of Education Instructor
Reed Deer College
Red Deer, Alberta, Canada

Laura Hesson
Washington County School District
     Board Member
Washington County School District
St. George, Utah

Louis Lim
Vice-Principal
Richmond Green Secondary School
Richmond Hill, Ontario, Canada

Peter Marshall
Education Consultant
Burlington, Ontario, Canada

Rick Pease
Principal
Edmonton Public Schools
Edmonton, Alberta, Canada

Visit **go.SolutionTree.com/leadership** to download the free reproducibles in this book.

TABLE OF CONTENTS

Reproducibles are in italics.

PART 1
Understanding School-Based Professional Learning

CHAPTER 1
Discovering Why School-Based Professional Learning Works

CHAPTER 5

Planning School-Based Professional Learning 89

CHAPTER 6

Implementing and Supporting the Plan. 115

ABOUT THE AUTHORS

Joellen Killion is a leadership and learning consultant residing in Lakeway, Texas. She serves as the senior advisor and a senior consultant for Learning Forward. Joellen champions educator learning as the primary pathway to student success. Joellen leads, facilitates, and contributes to initiatives related to examining the link between professional learning and student learning. She has over forty years of experience in planning, designing, implementing, and evaluating professional learning in schools, school systems, state, ministry, and regional education agencies, international schools, and professional associations.

Joellen is a member of Learning Forward, American Educational Research Association, Phi Delta Kappa, and the Association for Supervision and Curriculum Development. She presents at many international and U.S.-based educational conferences and has presented at thirty-seven consecutive Learning Forward conferences on her work and research in curriculum, professional learning, coaching, and leadership. She received merit recognition for her work with Adams 12 Five Star Schools and the National Staff Development Council or Learning Forward. She initiated Learning Forward's Coaches Academy and led the development, research, and implementation of the Standards for Professional Learning, and the design and implementation of comprehensive professional learning systems for the Common Core State Standards curriculum.

Joellen is the author of *What Works in the Middle: Results-Based Staff Development*; *What Works in the Elementary School: Results-Based Staff Development*; *What Works in the High School: Results-Based Staff Development*; *Assessing Impact: Evaluating Professional Learning*; and *The Feedback Process: Transforming Feedback for Professional Learning*. She is coauthor of *The Learning Educator: A New Era in Professional Learning*; *Becoming a Learning School*; *Taking the Lead: New Roles for Teachers and School-Based Coaches*; and *Coaching Matters*. She has contributed to many articles, chapters in professional publications, workbooks, training manuals, and monographs, including *The SAGE Handbook of Mentoring and Coaching in Education*.

Joellen has an undergraduate degree from the University of Michigan in classical studies and has completed master's degrees in communication, educational leadership, and advanced studies from the University of Colorado. Her studies include facilitation, evaluation, and coaching through professional programs.

To learn more about Joellen's work, follow @jpkillion on Twitter.

William A. Sommers, PhD, of Austin, Texas, is a learner, teacher, principal, author, leadership coach, and consultant. He has come out of retirement multiple times to put theory into practice as a principal in high schools and middle schools. He has worked in inner-city schools, as well as in high-socioeconomic-status suburban districts. Bill has been a consultant for cognitive coaching, adaptive schools, brain research, poverty, habits of mind, conflict management, and classroom-management strategies. He is a Marshall Goldsmith–certified Stakeholder Centered Coach.

Bill served on the boards of trustees of the National Staff Development Council (now Learning Forward) for five years and as president for one year. He is the former executive director for Secondary Curriculum and Professional Learning for Minneapolis Public Schools and has been a school administrator for over thirty-five years. He has also been a Senior Fellow for the Urban Leadership Academy at the University of Minnesota. Bill has served as an adjunct faculty member at Texas State University, Hamline University, University of Saint Thomas, Saint Mary's University, Union Institute, and Capella University. In addition, he has been a program director for an adolescent chemical-dependency treatment center and on the board of a halfway house for twenty years.

Bill has coauthored ten books: *Living on a Tightrope: A Survival Handbook for Principals*; *Being a Successful Principal: Riding the Wave of Change Without Drowning*; *Reflective Practice to Improve Schools: An Action Guide for Educators*; *A Trainer's Companion: Stories to Stimulate Reflection, Conversation, Action*; *Energizing Staff Development Using Film Clips: Memorable Movie Moments That Promote Reflection, Conversation, and Action*; *Leading Professional Learning Communities: Voices From Research and Practice*; *Guiding Professional Learning Communities: Inspiration, Challenge, Surprise, and Meaning*; *The Principal's Field Manual: The School Principal as the Organizational Leader*; *Habits of Mind: Teacher's Companion*; and *Nine Professional Conversations to Change Our Schools: A Dashboard of Options*. He has also coauthored chapters in several other books.

To learn more about Bill's work, visit Learning Omnivores (https://learningomnivores.com), or follow @BillSommers8 on Twitter.

Ann Delehant is the owner of Delehant and Associates, an education consulting practice. She is an experienced facilitator, learning leader, and agent of systemwide change. Ann's work focuses on developing, supporting, and coaching leaders at all levels, building collaborative cultures, and facilitating systems change.

Ann is a senior consultant for Learning Forward. For nearly thirty years, she was a member of The Dolan Team, a labor-management consulting firm that specialized in deep systemic change. She also served on the faculty of the University of Pennsylvania Center for Educational Leadership and held many positions at the Rochester City School District, including coordinator of the Cooperation, University, Business, and Education (CUBE) Program, grant writer, and director of staff development.

Ann served as a trustee of the National Staff Development Council (now Learning Forward) and was a founding member of Learning Forward New York. She received the National Staff Development Council's Distinguished Service Award in 1996. Ann is the lead author of *Making Meetings Work*. She coauthored *A Systemic Approach to Elevating Teacher Leadership* as well as a chapter in the third edition of *Powerful Designs for Professional Learning*.

Ann graduated from Carlow College (now Carlow University) in Pittsburgh, Pennsylvania, with a bachelor's degree (communication and education). She has master's degrees from Arizona State University (communication), Canisius College in Buffalo, New York (counselor education), and Brockport State University (school and district administration). She also continued studies in adult learning at the University of Rochester.

To learn more about Ann's work, visit her website (https://anndelehant.com), or follow @AnnDelehant on Twitter.

To book Joellen Killion, William A. Sommers, or Ann Delehant for professional development, contact pd@SolutionTree.com.

INTRODUCTION

I am always doing what I can't do yet in order to learn how to do it.
—VINCENT VAN GOGH

Imagine the power of learning tied directly to the work educators do each day.

▶ Learning that is relevant because it focuses on issues that emerge in practice

▶ Learning that is driven by inquiry and continuously refined

▶ Learning that is immediately applicable to practice

▶ Learning that is sustained over time and shared within the community

This type of learning energizes and engages educators to learn and grow. This is *school-based professional learning*.

To elevate the role of professional learning in a school and ensure it results in educator and student learning, it is essential to build leaders' understanding about professional learning and how it contributes to educators' practice and student learning. Both teacher leaders and school and system administrators who facilitate, coordinate, manage, or lead professional learning, share responsibilities for tasks related to planning, implementing, and sustaining professional learning. To accomplish this work, leaders must have foundational knowledge and advocate for high-quality, effective professional learning that ensures every educator learns, so every student succeeds.

> School-based professional learning immerses educators in their learning in their work context—with their students, curriculum, resources, and daily practice.

The essential point of school-based professional learning is that it immerses educators in their learning in their work context—with their students, curriculum, resources, and daily practice. In addition, as teachers and staff become more conscious of what works and what doesn't, learning with others provides a transformational learning experience that leads to dramatic results for students. The following three scenarios of school-based professional learning demonstrate the power of having a repertoire of teaching strategies: (1) from struggling to success, (2) from apathy to engagement, and (3) from a few teachers to many.

From Struggling to Success

A third-grade teacher, new to the grade level, grappled with the mathematics curriculum. When she shared her confusion with her grade-level team and the school's mathematics coach, she discovered other teachers were similarly confused. Her willingness and vulnerability to share her questions resulted in the assistant principal scheduling a biweekly, two-hour facilitated learning experience for interested teachers.

The teachers shared their questions and samples of student work, read the research, studied the curriculum and learning progressions, and designed and trialed various ways to answer their questions. During each biweekly meeting, teachers shared analyzed data collected from the trials, examined student errors, and synthesized what they were learning. Together, they clarified learning intentions and success criteria for the next unit and explored how to integrate what they were learning into instructional planning. By expanding and sharing knowledge, skills, and applications, this collaborative process accelerated learning for all the teachers.

From Apathy to Engagement

The seventh-grade team struggled to engage its students. The school's instructional coach met with the team multiple times to explore ways to increase engagement, yet teachers questioned the efficacy of nearly every recommendation. Therefore, the principal and coach met to explore alternatives for the team. Together, they read about a professional learning design in which teachers observed students throughout the school day. The team worked with the coach to identify students with varying levels of academic success, scheduled their observations, and created an observation guide with the other seventh-grade teams in the school. The principal coordinated class coverage for teachers who observed their designated students unobtrusively.

The principal and coach then helped the team analyze the data and debrief the observations. The experience allowed teachers to conduct an ethnographic study that led them to identify viable ways other teachers engage their students. In the end, the seventh-grade team identified three practices they committed to use during the next month, gathered data, and measured engagement again at the end of the month. As a result, student engagement and achievement in team members' classrooms increased 20 percent during the marking period.

From a Few Teachers to Many

Two high school teachers, one social studies and one music, were part of a district team that participated in a regional conference on project-based learning (PBL). When they returned to their respective schools, they shared their eagerness with the school's leadership team to bring together interested teachers to learn more about how to integrate PBL into their classroom curricula. As a result, the principal agreed to host an after-school meeting of interested teachers.

Twenty-two teachers attended the meeting and agreed to form a study group to learn more. They designed a plan to interview teachers applying PBL in high schools across the United States, studied sample PBL units and student work, and read multiple articles about the effectiveness of and approaches to implementing PBL. The team met weekly during their early release time to learn together, unpack what they discovered, and share possibilities for implementing PBL in their classrooms.

After some experimentation with PBL units and armed with data indicating student success, the teachers presented what they were learning to the whole faculty to help spread the practices to more classrooms. Fifteen additional teachers expressed interest in learning more. The larger team split into three work groups to continue their experimentation and data gathering. At the end of the semester, the team met with school leaders to propose schoolwide implementation of PBL during the following school year.

Transformative Cultures

In each scenario, teachers, along with instructional support staff and administrators, joined to explore and address issues in their school. By doing so, they could personalize and situate their learning in their unique context. As evident in these scenarios, *school-based professional learning* empowers educators to build collective efficacy, extend and refine their practice, and influence results. These scenarios exemplify what experts in educational leadership Eleanor Drago-Severson and Jessica Blum-DeStefano (2017) identify as *transformative cultures*. This form of school-based professional learning addresses the learning needs of individual educators, but it also extends to other team members with the potential of influencing the whole school community.

The teachers in the three scenarios, all learners, also exhibited three traits leadership coaches Marshall Goldsmith and Sal Silvester (2018) cite as important for change.

1. They demonstrated the courage to name and confront real issues by gathering data to identify critical areas and designing new approaches to solve the problems.

2. They exhibited the humility to listen, learn from multiple sources, and be open to possibilities.

3. They used discipline to implement new ways of professional practice and follow through with monitoring and measuring their effectiveness.

School-based professional learning is essential for addressing the unique needs of a school and its staff and the shifting priorities of the existing community and culture. The goal is to elevate and accelerate the learning of staff who directly influence student learning. School communities continually grapple with challenges related to students' success. Because school staff receive local, state, and federal resources to address students' educational needs, they have a concomitant responsibility to use those resources in ways that will produce immediate and long-term results. Transforming professional learning practices to be more efficient and effective will achieve the desired results.

However, when professional learning is disconnected from educators' daily work and their specific school context, the learning may not transfer to practice. This is a long-standing challenge. Coauthors Bruce R. Joyce and Beverly Showers (2002) caution educators that not all professional learning transfers to the workplace. In addition, professional learning that focuses only on knowledge or skill development is inadequate. In *The Knowing-Doing Gap*, experts in organizational behavior Jeffrey Pfeffer and Robert Sutton (2000) set out to understand why the "knowing-doing problem—the challenge of turning knowledge about how to enhance organizational performance into actions consistent with that knowledge" exists (p. 4). They stress while knowledge is important, it is insufficient to produce long-term change (Pfeffer & Sutton, 2000). In addition, veteran educators Pete Hall and Alisa Simeral (2008) claim this transfer may be a greater problem in education than in any other profession.

About This Book

Effective professional learning focuses on the overarching goals of a school and its system and aligns with school-improvement plans. This book addresses nesting goals and actions to create intentional and focused professional learning that aligns resources and effort level to accelerate adult learning in schools and allows individuals to have choice and voice in the content and structure of learning for student success.

We designed this book for preK–12 educators and the central office staff who support them. It answers three overarching questions: (1) What is school-based professional learning? (2) Why is school-based professional learning needed to tackle challenges in student learning? and (3) How does school-based professional learning work? The book also offers foundational knowledge, supporting research, and tools to guide implementation.

Each chapter includes five elements: (1) foundational knowledge, (2) research, (3) leadership tips, (4) reflection questions, and (5) tools for implementation (reproducibles at the end of each chapter). Teacher teams, school leadership teams, or whole faculties can study chapters to empower them to create their own system of school-based professional learning.

School system leaders also can use this book to develop the capacity of school-based leadership teams to design, implement, and evaluate professional learning. Even university and school system–based leadership development program faculty and students can use this text to develop their capacity to manage and facilitate professional learning. Finally, the book can inform school board members and trustees about the complex, rigorous work of school-based professional learning.

Chapter 1 (page 9) establishes the rationale for why professional learning at the school level accelerates the application of learning, personalizes the learning process for the school's specific needs, and builds collective responsibility for student and educator learning.

Chapter 2 (page 27) explores the roles and responsibilities of district staff, school administrators, school leadership teams, teacher leaders, and coaches. It identifies each role's unique and overlapping responsibilities, emphasizes how collaborative planning facilitates the essential staff support, and guides them to monitor and assess progress.

Chapter 3 (page 53) explores how to create a team of leaders and prepare them for the work of continuous, school-based professional learning. It explains how to use data to establish clear and compelling reasons for the work and to connect the work with school and district priorities.

Chapter 4 (page 75) explains which data is necessary to analyze. It introduces the theory of change as a tool for planning and organizing the work and engaging stakeholders, and it identifies how to develop the essential knowledge, attitudes, skills, aspirations, and behaviors (KASABs) necessary to achieve the goals. It guides leaders to plan for assessing progress by identifying indicators of success. Finally, it establishes structures for ongoing collaboration.

Chapter 5 (page 93) outlines the learning designs at the individual and team levels that support ongoing learning in a school. It introduces implementing the professional learning communities (PLCs) process, choosing a coaching style, and building talent density across the staff. It guides team leaders to consider multiple protocols and processes for designing learning and for facilitating rapid cycles of improvement within teams across the school. Finally, it also incorporates processes for lateral learning across teams in the school.

Chapter 6 (page 119) emphasizes the critical nature of ongoing sustained support to achieve high levels of mastery with new learning and structures. These include coaching individuals and teams, coaching administrators, peer coaching, learning walks schoolwide and across schools, and other processes that build efficacy and mastery with new practices. In addition, the chapter offers guidance on how to integrate performance assessment or evaluation with ongoing reflection within teams to build shared adult and student accountability for results.

Chapter 7 (page 151) focuses on formal and informal ways of assessing and evaluating professional learning within teams and schoolwide. It outlines the evaluation process steps, offers examples of ways to evaluate rapid cycles of improvement and annual plans for school improvement. Finally, it suggests an evaluation framework and explains how school leadership teams use formative and summative evaluations to make ongoing adjustments to accelerate results.

Chapter 8 (page 173) describes ways to celebrate, report, and use the findings to make improvements. It offers recommendations on different ways of communicating, engaging key stakeholders in periodic review sessions, building trust with stakeholders, and sharing within buildings and across districts to encourage cross-site learning.

Chapter 9 (page 183) focuses on building safety and trust to engage in public reflection about team and individual efforts to support professional learning. It offers protocols to use with various teams and stakeholders, processes for after-action analyses, and tools for reviewing strengths and opportunities in the work. In addition, it uses a constructivist approach centered in the feedback process to engage every role-specific group to identify what worked, what didn't work, and the next steps for forward movement.

Chapter 10 (page 199) looks at common challenges such as resistance, complacency, compliance, conflict, leadership gaps, and so on. This chapter identifies these challenges and offers some guidance on addressing them.

This book guides leaders and team members through the process of school-based professional learning that directly aligns to the unique needs of a school. Furthermore, it unlocks the potential for each school to achieve success for all students and educators.

We are eager to partner with you on the journey of discovery and learning designed to create success for each student and educator in your school.

PART 1

Understanding School-Based Professional Learning

CHAPTER 1

Discovering Why School-Based Professional Learning Works

A man should live thinking he might die tomorrow but learn as if he would live forever.

—MAHATMA GANDHI

An old cartoon educators shared in the early 1990s depicts a teacher at the gates of hell. Over the gates a sign reads, "Welcome to the in-service." This cartoon aptly characterizes many teachers' negative perceptions of in-service training and their beliefs about professional learning. However, district and school leaders can move teachers past the passive experience of receiving information to an active, teacher-generated learning experience. Research confirms active engagement in professional learning leads to success in adult learning (Audisio, Taylor-Perryman, Tasker, & Steinberg, 2022; Garet, Heppen, Walters, Parkinson, Smith, Song, et al., 2016; Garrett, Zhang, Citkowicz, & Burr, 2021).

> **Applying learning in the classroom is what leads to real understanding, depth of practice, and professional transformation.**

This chapter explores *why* learning in school is more beneficial to educators and students than learning outside school, and then introduces the school-based professional learning cycle. First, we, the authors, acknowledge learning outside school can provide foundational knowledge and exposure to experts, which then initiates school-based professional learning. Most educators value learning new skills and increasing their knowledge, but the lack of transfer back to the job after participating in training outside the school frustrates them. This frustration might be because applying learning in the classroom is what leads to real understanding, depth of practice, and professional transformation. Focusing professional learning at the school and in the classroom increases the focus on areas of learning most closely aligned with the school's student and educator learning needs.

This chapter delves into the power of learning at the heart of the work and working in the community. Then, it explains the importance of school-based professional learning and the research that supports it. Finally, the chapter presents the school-based, seven-step professional learning cycle to help leaders break down the tasks for planning, implementing, evaluating, and sustaining professional learning. The seven-step professional learning cycle is further developed in chapters 3 through 9.

Learning at the Heart of the Work

Learning at the heart of the work increases the likelihood that the learning is relevant, timely, and desired. When student learning isn't up to par, the first step isn't sending staff out of the school to learn; it is discovering what is happening in the day-to-day student classroom experience. The farther interventions are from the classroom, the less likely they will generate change in classroom practice. An analogy for this is when a tire is flat, you change the tire or replace it; you don't repair the motor. Therefore, to leverage professional practice to change student learning, you first work at the heart of the teaching and learning process. While it may be necessary to shore up, repair, or even replace aspects of the entire school system, working as close to the heart of the teaching and learning system just makes sense.

Transformative learning occurs in communities whose members commit to holding students' interests at the forefront of their work and identifying and addressing those issues in constructive ways. As cofounder of Netflix Reed Hastings and business expert Erin Meyer (2020) write in their book, *No Rules Rules*, increasing talent density is critical to continuous progress: "Talented people make one another more effective" (p. 7). Ongoing conversations within the system initiate and sustain continual learning.

To understand why school-based professional learning works, look at an example of a district adopting a new integrated curriculum for mathematics preK–12. In a typical process, after district leaders purchase the curriculum, they distribute instructional materials to schools and implement overview sessions for teachers, teacher leaders, coaches, and principals right before the beginning of the school year. Next, the real work of implementing a new curriculum begins as teachers use the curriculum in the classroom.

Using school-based professional learning, teachers learn the new curriculum so they can effectively and efficiently address student learning needs, make informed decisions on adapting or supplementing the curriculum, and monitor and assess progress daily. This collective experience of learning the new curriculum helps teachers build one another's fluency and address challenges. Together, teachers can celebrate success, acknowledge challenges, and discover situationally appropriate solutions. All of this happens within the day-to-day work in a school, at its heart.

Working in the Heart of a Community

As authors, we base our approach to professional learning on positive deviance work (Pascale, Sternin, & Sternin, 2010). The fundamental assumption driving positive deviance is the solution to every problem exists in people in the community who discover ways to successfully address the issue (positive deviants). Pascale and colleagues (2010) applied the principles of positive deviance to their work with Save the Children (https://savethechildren.org) to help eradicate childhood malnutrition in post-war Vietnam villages and to other deeply rooted social issues around the globe.

The process involved engaging community members in identifying the problem using local data, setting specific, measurable outcomes, finding and studying the positive deviants, and engaging them to spread their practices throughout the community. In this way, the entire community found solutions to childhood malnutrition and built their capacity to address other issues in their environment. Working in the heart of the community was essential to solve its problems successfully (Pascale et al., 2010).

Similarly, working at the heart of teaching and learning may more quickly generate long-lasting results because those responsible for implementing them have been deeply involved in the process and are committed to the results.

Understanding the School-Based Professional Learning Difference

"At school, everyone's job is to learn." This tagline served as a rallying cry for the National Staff Development Council (now Learning Forward; https://learningforward.org) to emphasize the importance of educator learning in advancing student learning. In the United States and other countries, national agencies and local school systems have invested in professional learning to strengthen student learning. Examples include federally funded mathematics, science, and technology initiatives of the 1990s and 2000s and Florida's statewide implementation of reading coaches. Unfortunately, these efforts often result in new programs that are time limited based on the funding duration.

At school, everyone's job is to learn.

For example, in the United States, considerable funding through grants was dedicated to mathematics, science, and technology professional learning during the early 2000s. A typical example is a university-based summer program where teachers participated in courses to extend their content knowledge and expand their content-specific pedagogical practice. However, when teachers returned to their schools, they lacked the same physical equipment or other resources necessary to implement what they learned and also found their curricula often misaligned. In addition, teachers often implemented national curriculum initiatives in the United Kingdom with insufficient resources.

Therefore, it isn't the traditional one-off, large-scale professional development that makes a substantial difference in educator practice and student learning. Instead, school-based, classroom- and school-focused learning that aligns closely with the curriculum, engages educators to collaborate on a narrow range of related topics, and uses active learning processes to model the learning processes that accelerate student learning.

Considering Research to Support School-Based Professional Learning

Why does school-based professional learning work? There are three main reasons.

1. Authentic learning in context requires immersion in the context where a teacher applies learning.

2. The context influences a teacher's ability to apply new learning, receive support during various stages of implementation, and find and address problems of practice.

3. Sustaining new learning to mastery requires deep levels of engagement, agency, and efficacy generating a strong commitment and a sense of responsibility and ownership.

The following sections look at these reasons one at a time.

Authentic Learning in Context

If you want to learn to sail, you can choose to read a book or watch videos about operating a sailboat. However, learning to sail requires being in the boat to feel how the wind and water affect the boat's course and adjust the sail accordingly.

Similarly, although workshops, conferences, reading, or training are invaluable for building knowledge, they typically occur outside the school where educators apply the learning. Therefore, educators strive to translate the learning for use in their classrooms, with their students, within their content areas.

Joyce and Showers (2002) and researchers Bruce R. Joyce, Marsha Weil, and Emily Calhoun (2015) report only 10 to 15 percent of educators who participate in professional development that presents theory and modeling practice apply their learning to solve problems in their school. Only when the learning integrates coaching of the practice in school will applying that learning increase dramatically to 80 to 90 percent (Joyce & Showers, 2002; Joyce et al., 2015).

To bridge the learning-doing gap, learning and development specialists in private and public sectors turn to virtual simulations. For example, at Midwestern State University in Wichita Falls, Texas, the nursing school immerses students in laboratories equipped with computerized mannequins that simulate patient behaviors. Students learn by recording and analyzing each behavior with their instructors.

Similarly, instructional coaches work with teachers in their classrooms to note interactions between teachers and students and offer real-time interventions or engage teachers to analyze those interactions. In addition, leadership coaches partner with administrators to surface assumptions that drive their leadership practice and potentially interfere with adopting new practices.

One factor interfering with the broader implementation of school-based professional learning is the lack of deep understanding of learning. The traditional notion of learning as a process of filling an empty vessel is a misconception about the design of professional learning and its potential for impact (Killion, 2019). For many, learning is a process of conveying information based on the assumption that if teachers have information, they will be able to act on it. Yet information alone is insufficient; it may serve as the foundation for action, however, it is unlikely to promote action. Researchers offer the following definitions of learning.

- ▶ *Learning* is a process through which experiences cause a permanent change in knowledge and behavior (Woolfolk, Winne, & Perry, 2012).

- ▶ "*True* [italics added] learning . . . happens when the learner is an *active* [italics added] participant in constructing knowledge and in constantly thinking about how new information confirms or challenges previously existing beliefs and ideas" (Katz & Dack, 2013, p. 27). Associate professors in adult education Gaynell Green and Glenda H. Ballard (2010) suggest this model of learning is successful because it encompasses factors of adult learning theory and practice such as ownership, modeling, teamwork, and the application of course-based teaching strategies.

- ▶ *Experiential learning*, which occurs in the situation, involves a direct encounter with the phenomenon educators are studying rather than merely thinking about the encounter or considering it (Brookfield, 2013; Dewey, 2009; Kolb, 1984; Schön, 1983).

- ▶ Simply acquiring or transmitting content alone cannot transform an individual; rather, transformation occurs when an individual interfaces with the content in a direct experience and reflects on learned concepts (Kolb, 1984).

When leaders understand learning as a process of transmitting information without opportunity for practice, coaching, and extended study, little long-term change will occur in classroom instruction. When leaders recognize learning requires understanding, application in simulated and authentic situations, and refinement over time, they can design learning experiences that lead to sustained change in instructional practice. Sustained change in classroom practice has a greater likelihood of impacting student learning.

Contextual Influences

A learner's willingness to learn and apply learning depends on the context in which learning occurs. The three conditions for a productive learning environment from the research are (1) psychological and emotional safety, (2) community, and (3) leadership support.

Psychological and Emotional Safety

Two closely related factors influence learning: (1) psychological safety and (2) emotional safety. "Psychological safety describes people's perceptions of the consequences of taking interpersonal risks in a particular context such as a workplace" (Edmondson & Lei, 2014, p. 23). A closely related construct, emotional safety, "is the 'knowing' of what we're feeling; the ability to be able to identify our feelings and then take the ultimate risk of feeling them" (Huysman, 2014).

When learners feel supported and safe, they are more open to identifying what they want to know or don't, to take risks, and to change. When they feel others judge them, learners may be reticent to ask for assistance or acknowledge the reasons to learn or change. Their sense of support and safety directly results from leaders' actions in the school and the trust among teachers and among teachers and administrators.

In studies of professional learning communities (PLCs) in the United States, Denmark, and Singapore, researchers find trust fosters openness, confidence, critical discussions, willingness to question existing practices, collaboration to build competencies, and engagement in actions to build a collective level of engagement in the PLC (Anderson, 2016; Hallam, Smith, Hite, Hite, & Wilcox, 2015; Ning, Lee, & Lee, 2016).

Researcher Pamela R. Hallam and colleagues (2015) highlight the role of leader trust in teacher learning and collaboration and in teachers' trust in one another. When practices, values, and contexts align to support collective learning, teachers are more satisfied in their work and more open to continuous learning. Ultimately, teachers have more success in meeting their students' learning needs.

In separate reviews of the literature on the effectiveness of professional learning, Norwegian University of Science and Technology researchers and professors May Britt Postholm (2018) and Kåre Hauge (2019) identify leadership and trust as factors influencing teacher engagement in the effectiveness of professional learning. Educational consultant Michael Fullan (2007) posits that "professional learning in context is the only education that ultimately changes classroom practices" (p. 153). Another review of research on professional learning cites strong evidence that professional development is best when embedded in the teachers' specific subject areas (Wei, Darling-Hammond, Andree, Richardson, & Orphanos, 2009). These studies emphasize the importance of school culture, collaboration, and shared learning to make a difference in learners' perception of their learning experiences and in their willingness to take risks when implementing them.

Community

Schools where teachers are members of strong teacher communities have higher student achievement (Bryk, Sebring, Allensworth, Luppescu, & Easton, 2010). In a random trial study of teachers' professional development, researchers note that site-based teacher teams positively influence teacher engagement with new instructional practices (Garet, Porter, Desimone, Birman,

& Yoon, 2001). According to educational researcher Hilda Borko (2004), participation and discourse practices contribute to teacher learning by encouraging professional critique, reflection, and collaboration. A strong connection exists between teacher participation in communities of practice and improved classroom teaching.

In his seminal work *Communities of Practice*, Etienne Wenger (1998) outlines three elements to create and sustain strong communities of learners, where learners become active members of a collaborative team to learn together, study, refine their practice, and examine results for themselves and students. Coauthors Anthony S. Bryk, Louis M. Gomez, Alicia Grunow, and Paul G. Mathieu (2015) apply the following fundamental principles in their work on networked improvement communities in schools.

1. **Mutual engagement:** Individuals have the ability to interact with one another.

2. **Negotiated meaning:** Ensure individuals have a common language and probe for specific meaning. Too often, educators don't clarify first, then pursue ways to learn.

3. **Shared repertoire:** Individuals learn, then share that learning throughout the school culture. This process is—*what happens here, leaves here*—the reverse of the Las Vegas slogan.

In a random trial study of teachers' professional development, researchers note that site-based teacher teams positively influence teacher engagement with new instructional practices (Garet et al., 2001). According to Borko (2004), participation and discourse practices contribute to teacher learning by encouraging professional critique, reflection, and collaboration. A strong connection exists between teacher participation in communities of practice and improved classroom teaching.

Chapter 6 (page 119) includes further information on the attributes of a professional culture that supports educator learning at school.

Leadership Support

The role of principals in teacher learning and establishing conditions to support learning influences teacher learning. In a study of teacher peer excellence groups, researchers examine the role of principals in supporting teacher learning (Cravens, Drake, Goldring, & Schuermann, 2017). Teacher peer excellence groups use an iterative cycle of collaborative teacher lesson planning, peer observation, peer feedback, lesson revisions teachers lead and own, and principals' support. Results show principal leadership is a key condition for teachers to feel comfortable with the deprivatizing practice, especially when principals provide flexibility and support to teacher leaders. Deprivatizing practice opens classroom doors, makes individual teacher practice visible and transparent, and fosters learning with and from one another's work. It requires vulnerability and risk taking on the part of learners, yet it creates purposeful collaboration.

Consultant, researcher, and author Eric J. Feeney's (2016) mixed-methods case study identifies open communication with the principal, shared decision making, learning structures, and autonomy in decision making as factors that support professional development. In contrast, school-context factors, often connected to administrative actions, such as lack of time, accountability pressures, lack of communication, and lack of shared vision and values, hinder teacher development.

Opportunities to Sustain New Learning to Mastery

Gaining foundational knowledge does not necessarily translate into practice. Instead, new knowledge transforms into practice through continuous-improvement cycles: opportunities to review and reflect on practice; engage in feedback processes with coaches, peers, and supervisors; and identify successes and upgrades (Bailey & Jakicic, 2017; Bryk, et al., 2015; DuFour, DuFour, Eaker, Many, & Mattos, 2016). These cycles of continuous improvement help sustain new learning to mastery.

Educational researchers Linda Darling-Hammond, Maria E. Hyler, and Madelyn Gardner (2017) report professional learning with the most significant impact on student learning has the following qualities.

- Sustained over time
- Focuses on the content teachers are responsible for teaching
- Engages adult learners actively in the learning process
- Models the pedagogical processes teachers integrate into their practice
- Provides support with coaching from knowledgeable others
- Provides opportunities for teachers to reflect on practice with peer review

In this way, each teacher is responsible for every other teacher's success in a way that creates shared ownership for every student's success and sustains professional learning.

Increasing Educator Learning

In education, the focus is mainly on student learning. As seen in the previous section, student learning depends on educator learning. This is not a novel idea. Former director of Harvard's Principals' Center Roland S. Barth (1990) wrote, "The most crucial role of the principal is as *head learner*" (p. 46). In 1997, in an opinion in *Education Week*, Barth redoubled his message, stating:

> The most important responsibility of every educator is to provide the conditions under which people's learning curves go off the chart. Whether one is called a principal, a teacher, a professor, a foundation official, or a parent, our most vital work is promoting human learning. That's what it means to be an educator. Learning on the part of younger people called students, of older people called teachers, and, above all, our own learning. To paraphrase Vince Lombardi, "In schools, learning isn't everything; learning is the *only* thing."

Modeling and participation by lead administrators and lead staff are key to increasing adult learning. It takes all staff to engage in learning for long-term change. The more adult learning in a school, the more student learning. Teachers engage in continuous learning to refine their instructional practices and stay current with curriculum and content. Administrative and instructional leaders in a school signal what's important by the time they spend on tasks and relationships. If the *killer Bs* (budgets, boundaries, and busses) take most of an administrator's time, how do the *three Cs* (communication, collaboration, and coaching) rank in importance?

Exploring the School-Based Professional Learning Cycle

Since time is a limited resource, the school-based professional learning cycle helps leaders break down the tasks for planning, implementing, evaluating, and sustaining professional learning. This iterative process occurs multiple times at all levels, from leadership teams to small grade-level or department teams, over a school year.

Teams work together to carry out the professional learning cycle. Throughout the process, several types of teams work simultaneously. The first team is the leadership or professional learning team. This is a schoolwide team with primary responsibility for making decisions about school-based professional learning. Ideally, this team includes representation of appointed or elected school administrators and teacher and support leaders, representing the full spectrum of school's staff from classroom teachers and resource or specialized staff to support staff in all roles. It may include representatives from parents and community organizations, the district office, and students.

This team effectively and efficiently works together using an agreed-on process over a sustained period, preferably a school year or longer. Team members commit to learning about effective professional learning, making decisions aligned with the needs of the school's students and staff, and using meeting processes such as an agenda, designated decision-making models, set meeting times, and clearly delineated authority.

Other teams working together on professional learning are made up of school staff and appropriate administrators, resource staff, and others who have responsibility for a particular group of students such as a grade-level or department team. Team members come together as an ad hoc group for a specific purpose, such as increasing student engagement or refining formative assessment practices, or who have responsibility for a particular function in the school, such as the facilities team or student support team that includes specialized resource personnel.

These teams work together as learning partners. They support one another's growth and development, implement and refine their practice, engage in problem solving to address challenges, and contribute information to the school's leadership team about their professional learning needs, successes, progress, and challenges. These teams also commit to using a collaborative, productive, and efficient process to share the common purpose of strengthening adult practice for the benefit of student success.

Figure 1.1 (page 17) provides an overview of the process. The following sections elaborate on each step further, and subsequent chapters delve deeply into the process.

Step 1: Analyze

Planning professional learning at the school or team level always begins with student data illuminating student learning needs. Then, using the data, the leadership team or teacher team identifies and addresses gaps likely to have the most significant impact on students' overall success. They then prioritize gaps based on which make the most difference in student success.

For example, focusing on *inferring* in literacy may more likely accelerate students' reading performance than focusing on *vocabulary*. Likewise, focusing on *problem solving* in mathematics may be more critical than *operations*. Of course, vocabulary and operations are essential. However, it is a matter of prioritizing what becomes the content for professional learning.

In addition to addressing gaps, the leadership (or teacher) team examines staff data, including members' input, to identify educator learning needs related to the prioritized student needs. This shift moves away from the "what-do-you-want from professional learning interest survey" to a needs-based focus. In this way, the identified student needs informed decisions about the professional learning content. Following the examination of data, the team considers the school's context, including areas such as the school's experience with change through professional learning, leadership and staff stability, resources, and community support. Chapter 3 (page 53) discusses step 1.

1 ANALYZE

- Gather and analyze student and educator data.
- Study the school context.

2 PREPARE

- Review and write vision, mission, and values.
- Develop school-improvement goals and benchmarks.
- Write goals and outcomes.
- Prepare theory of change for professional learning.
- Plan for evaluation.

7 REFLECT

- Review findings.
- Prioritize next actions based on findings.
- Celebrate and integrate successes.
- Set new goals.

SCHOOL-BASED PROFESSIONAL LEARNING CYCLE

6 REPORT AND CELEBRATE

- Share successes.
- Share challenges.
- Report findings.
- Celebrate learning, successes, and mistakes.
- Celebrate individual and collective effort.

3 PLAN

- Study the research.
- Write professional learning plan as a logic model.
- Study and select learning designs.
- Ensure resources for success.
- Plan implementation supports.

5 MONITOR AND MEASURE

- Provide ongoing support.
- Collect data on implementation and impact.
- Refine practice based on evidence.
- Evaluate impact on students and adults.

4 IMPLEMENT AND SUPPORT

- Learn individually and collectively.
- Apply learning in practice.
- Coach application.
- Analyze application using evidence.
- Adjust practice.

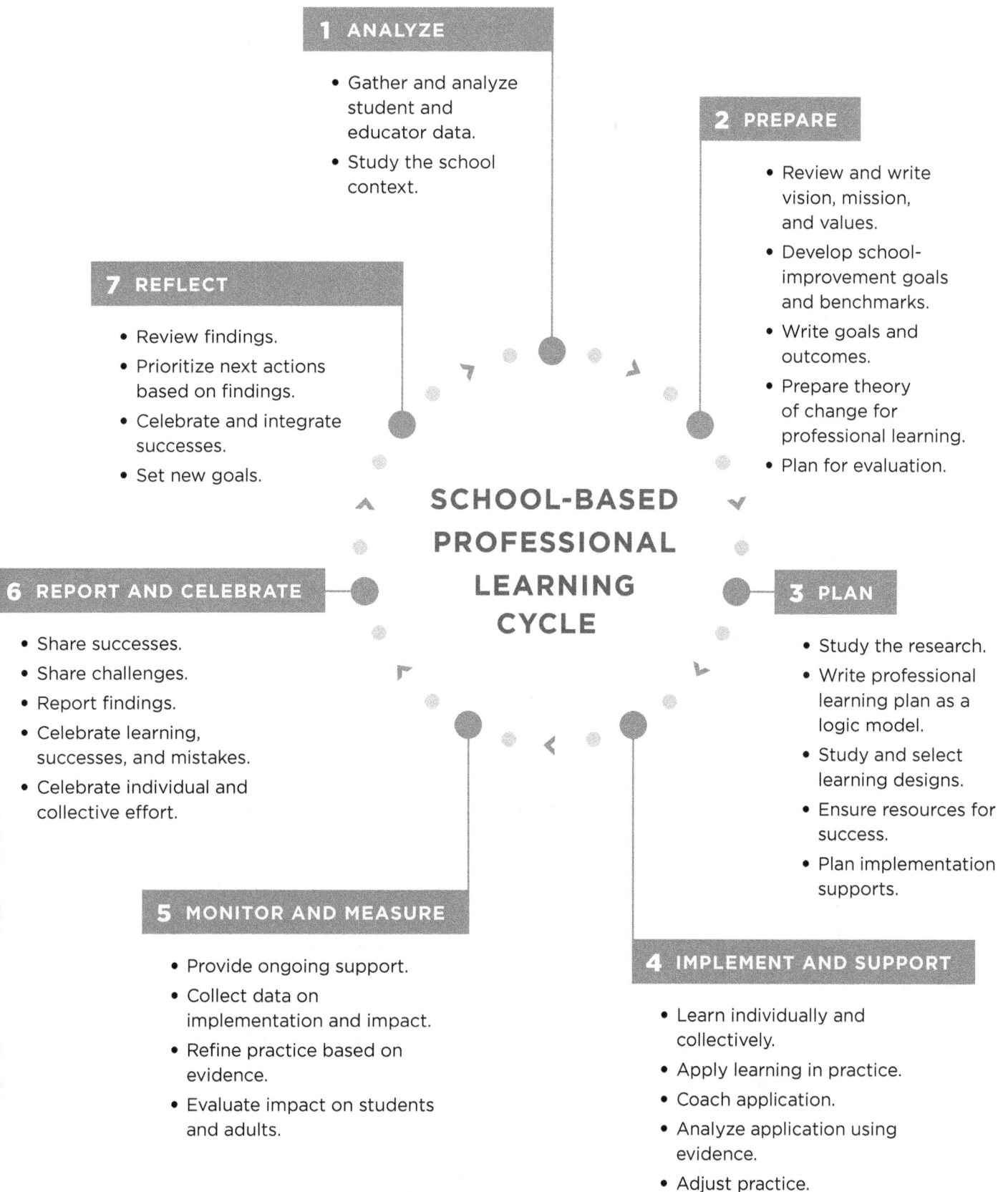

FIGURE 1.1: School-based professional learning cycle.

Step 2: Prepare

The leadership team begins preparing for the design work using analyzed data about students, staff, and the school context. Next, the team reviews the school's vision, mission, and values and rewrites them if necessary. These key elements serve as the agreed-on drivers for the collective work of a school's staff. A school's *vision* describes what it aspires to achieve. Its *mission* explains its function—what it does to achieve the vision. The *values* establish the foundational beliefs on which the school's work rests.

Then, the team members study research and evidence about how similar schools have made changes and what types of professional learning are successful in the identified areas. With research in hand, the school leadership (or teacher) team writes the school-improvement goals and benchmarks for success. Finally, the team develops the theory of change and logic model for the changes, especially those in practice, necessary to achieve the results. These two detailed tools help the team conceptualize how they will bring about the change and create a tool for managing the process. Chapter 4 (page 75) discusses step 2.

Step 3: Plan

Based on the broader plan and clear goals and outcomes, the leadership (or teacher) team members analyze the factors that influence the learning design and how it supports learning. Next, they study research and best practices to develop the professional learning plan and choose the designs most likely to achieve goals. Finally, they consider ways to weave the necessary implementation supports to facilitate applying learning to practice into the plan. Chapter 5 (page 93) discusses step 3.

Step 4: Implement and Support

With solid design work in hand, the school leaders oversee the implementation work. This work includes learning processes (acquiring, exploring, expanding, and refining knowledge, attitudes, and skills) and applying the learning to practice. This recursive and iterative work occurs individually and collectively. Learners learn, apply their learning, engage in coaching, analyze their practice with evidence, and adjust practice. Chapter 6 (page 119) discusses step 4.

Step 5: Monitor and Measure

Learning is a continuous process and requires frequent opportunities to review practice using evidence to adjust accordingly. The continuous cycle of practice, review, and adjustment gives practitioners visible evidence of the impact of their efforts so they can assess what works and what doesn't. After multiple rapid and repeated cycles of practice, review, and adjustment, the learners and the leadership (or teacher) team evaluates its results. Members essentially ask two questions: What is working?" and "What isn't working?" Chapter 7 (page 151) discusses step 5.

Step 6: Report and Celebrate

Sharing successes, challenges, and even failures is a part of the learning process. Reporting on the work (efforts, progress, and results) is a core responsibility of professional learning and leadership teams. Members also celebrate their work and acknowledge the collective and individual efforts that made a difference in the team's progress. Chapter 8 (page 173) discusses step 6.

Step 7: Reflect

Using their experience (evidence from rapid and repeated cycles) and the evaluation, learners and the leadership team members examine their findings, determine and prioritize next steps, and celebrate and integrate what works well into routine practice. They make these decisions before they begin the entire professional learning cycle again. The findings from the evaluation of one cycle of professional learning become the first step of a new cycle, which reinforces the recursive nature of professional learning. Chapter 9 (page 183) discusses step 7.

Conclusion

Learning is a continuous process for adults and students. When adults learn, students learn. This continuous process of learning establishes the driver, the *why* for professional learning. Barth (1990) notes, "A key to improving schools within, then, lies in improving the interactions among teachers and between teachers and principals" (p. 28). The *how* is bringing staff together to expand their practice repertoire and agility to meet the diverse learning needs of students. The *what* is content directly applicable to the work at hand—the knowledge, attitudes, skills, and practices necessary to attract and embrace learners at all levels. As the adults learn multiple ways to extend learning and apply the content they are learning, they widen their repertoire of practices and, in turn, positively affect student learning.

Planning, implementing, and sustaining learning includes a series of core tasks made up of seven smaller subtasks: (1) analyze, (2) prepare, (3) plan, (4) implement and support, (5) monitor and measure, (6) report and celebrate, and (7) reflect. The process occurs in rapid, repeated cycles over time. It's continuous and recursive, and it explores the *why, how,* and *what* for professional learning. Administrators and teachers are significant contributors who model professional learning for others. Their efforts influence others' willingness to learn and create a safe space for others to apply new learning. Working together, a school's staff creates the conditions that make learning a priority for educators and students.

Leadership Tips

School leaders can take practical steps to determine how staff engages in learning, models continuous learning, and explains the purpose of school-based professional learning. The following tips will help you get started.

- ▶ Engage the school's leadership team in a deep reading of the introduction (page 1) and chapter 1 (page 9) using a text-analysis protocol. See the reproducible "Introduction to Elevate School-Based Professional Learning" (page 21).

- ▶ Conduct an internal review of how staff currently engages in learning at school. See the reproducible "Assessing the Current State of School-Based Professional Learning" (page 22).

- ▶ Establish a schoolwide professional learning leadership team or charge the existing school leadership team with making data-informed decisions about school-based professional learning. See the reproducible "Decision Making About School-Based Professional Learning" (page 24).

▶ Write a leadership team position statement, purpose statement, or proposition that explains the purpose of school-based professional learning to share with staff.

▶ Model continuous learning by sharing your learning goals broadly—why you are learning, what you are learning, and how you are integrating that learning into your practice.

Reflection Questions

1. What percentage of time does staff spend in school-based professional learning compared to district-based professional learning or other out-of-school learning? What might account for these differences?

2. As you think about how staff in your school collaborate, describe the types of collaborative work. What portion of that collaboration can you characterize as learning? What makes it learning?

3. How would you explain the purpose of school-based professional learning to parents or guardians?

4. As you review the process for school-based professional learning, which parts of the process are strengths, and which are opportunities for ongoing development? How might you celebrate the successes and focus on developing other areas?

5. How do you advocate for school-based professional learning with decision and policy makers, such as school board members and trustees?

Introduction to Elevate School-Based Professional Learning

This tool guides the leadership team to discuss the introduction (page 1) of *Elevate School-Based Professional Learning* and provides an overview of the book's content.

PURPOSE   To familiarize the school's professional learning team with the introduction (page 1) and chapter 1 (page 9)

PRODUCT   The professional learning team's understanding of the purpose and structure of *Elevate School-Based Professional Learning*

PARTICIPANTS   Professional learning team, school leadership team, or other decision-making body responsible for professional learning in the school

MATERIALS   A copy of *Elevate School-Based Professional Learning* for each team member

TIME   One hour

PREPARATION   Provide the book in advance and invite members to read the introduction (page 1)

PROCESS   **Step 1**
Share the purpose of the meeting with the team and introduce the book.

Step 2
Use a text-response protocol (see the next bullet point) to read and discuss the introduction (page 1). (Twenty minutes)

Step 3
Assign or invite each team member or a pair of team members to choose one chapter to skim (it is not necessary to include all chapters) to report the following information.

- The highlights of this chapter are . . .
- This chapter will contribute to the team's work related to professional learning by . . .
- One question I have related to this chapter is . . .
- One intriguing idea I read is . . .

Step 4
Invite members to report out on their chapters. Here are some ideas for reporting out on their reading.

Team members might do the following.

- Make a list of key ideas from the introduction (page 1) and each chapter.
- Create a mind map of each chapter.
- Prepare a brief presentation to share with the entire staff about the key ideas from their reading.
- Engage in an affinity process to cluster key ideas from the introduction (page 1) and chapter 1 (page 9).
- Create a visual representation of the key ideas from their reading.

Assessing the Current State of School-Based Professional Learning

This tool guides leadership teams in assessing the current state of school-based professional learning.

PURPOSE To guide the school's leadership team, principal, school-based professional learning team, or teacher team in assessing the current state of school-based professional learning

PRODUCT A list of findings on the alignment between the past year's professional learning and the school's improvement plan and goals, team learning goals, and individual professional learning goals

PARTICIPANTS Professional learning team, school leadership team, and staff representatives

MATERIALS Data about the previous year or current year-to-date professional learning and meeting agenda

TIME Two hours

PREPARATION Prepare the data from the previous year in either print or electronic format so participants can access and use the data during the meeting.

PROCESS **Step 1**
Invite staff to submit data or construct a data set to complete the data chart.

Step 2
Use the following chart to assess school-based professional learning from the previous school year or current year to date.

Step 3
Review data about past years' or current year-to-date professional alignment with school goals, student learning needs, and staff learning needs.

Step 4
Calculate the percentage of time staff devoted to each level of professional learning alignment: aligned with school goals, aligned with identified student learning needs, or aligned with identified staff learning needs.

Step 5
Establish the desired level of alignment for school-based professional learning: align with school goals, aligned with student learning needs, or aligned with staff learning needs.

Assessment of School-Based Professional Learning

Title of Schoolwide or Team-Based Professional Learning	Time Spent	Goals and Outcomes	Alignment With . . . (Use Rating Scale)		
			School Goals	Identified Student Learning Needs	Identified Staff Learning Needs

Rating scale: 3 = high or direct link; 2 = mostly aligned; 1 = slightly aligned; 0 = no alignment

Decision Making About School-Based Professional Learning

Leadership teams can use this tool to clarify or prepare a process for making decisions about school-based professional learning.

PURPOSE To review, evaluate, adjust, and develop a process for decision making about school-based professional learning

PRODUCT A charge statement regarding decisions about schoolwide and team-based professional learning

PARTICIPANTS School leadership team, including representatives of teachers, and support and administrative staff

MATERIALS
- Meeting agendas
- Current professional learning decision-making process
- List of questions to guide data analysis
- List of charge statement elements

TIME Three hours

PROCESS **Step 1**

Review the current process for decision making about school-based professional learning, including schoolwide, team-based, individual workshops, book studies, coaching, inquiry cycles, PLC-related topics, and so on. Consider the full range of learning experiences and how decisions are made about them.

Step 2

Ask participants the following questions to query their understanding of the current process for making decisions about professional learning.
- "What is working regarding staff engagement in decisions about their professional learning? What evidence supports these findings?"
- "What aspects of the decision-making process about professional learning merit revision or clarification based on the data?"

Step 3

Write a charge statement regarding decisions about professional learning. A *charge statement* includes the following elements.
- Names of participants, including the selection process, tenure of term, representation
- Purpose of the team
- Scope of decisions and responsibilities (data gathering, communication with stakeholders, representation of stakeholders, oversight for implementation, evaluation of effects, and so on)
- Frequency and length of meetings
- Level of decision making such as final decisions, recommendation (and to whom), and so on
- Timelines for decisions

PROCESS
(cont.)

Step 4

Share the charge statement for review with the whole staff. Before finalizing the process for making decisions about professional learning, share the draft charge statement with the faculty for their input, questions, and suggested revisions.

Step 5

Using the input from staff, the leadership team revises the charge statement as appropriate. In some cases, it will be helpful to repeat step 4 for another review by the staff or staff representatives to ensure the revisions reflect staff suggestions. Once completed, post the final charge statement for all staff to access and use.

CHAPTER 2

Sharing Responsibility for School-Based Professional Learning

Execution beats luck.
Consistency beats intensity.
Curiosity beats smart.
Kind beats clever.
Together beats alone.

— SHANE PARRISH

Effective school-based professional learning requires the commitment and effort of many stakeholders. This chapter explores the roles and responsibilities of the school-based and district-level staff who contribute to the success of professional learning. District leaders (including curriculum and professional learning coordinators, federal programs directors, special education resource staff, human resources staff, and so on), school leaders (including school administrators, school leadership and professional learning teams, teacher leaders, and coaches), classroom teachers, instructional support staff, noninstructional staff, and students and families share responsibility for educator learning. Because many share the work of educating students, the more engaged people are in making decisions about their work and the more ownership and effort they feel make success likely (Landry, 2020). Students and staff benefit when these key stakeholders collaborate to plan, implement, coordinate, and evaluate professional learning.

To make professional learning as relevant and successful as possible, all staff share in the work associated with planning, implementing, and evaluating professional learning.

The primary responsibility of all members of the education community is *learning*. Therefore, to make schools effective and efficient, primarily focus on learning for all staff. To make professional learning as relevant and successful as possible, all staff engage in the work associated with planning, implementing, and evaluating professional learning. The following sections outline the roles and responsibilities of all stakeholders. In addition, the reproducibles "Checklist of Roles and Responsibilities" (page 37) and "Roles for School-Based Professional Learning" (page 43) help clarify roles. Table 2.1 (page 28) summarizes some roles and responsibilities for school-based professional learning.

TABLE 2.1: Roles and Responsibilities for School-Based Professional Learning

Stakeholder	Roles and Responsibilities
Teachers and instructional support staff	• Take an active role in learning with, from, and on behalf of one another about issues related to their content area and grade level, their students, their instruction, and areas of responsibility. • Share leadership of their PLCs.
Teacher leaders and instructional coaches	• Develop a culture of collaborative professional learning linked directly to teaching and learning. • Facilitate PLCs.
Principals	• Work actively with teachers and teacher leaders to develop the structure, support system, and culture of collaborative professional learning linked directly to teaching and learning. • Ensure teams have adequate resources, time, and strategies to improve teaching and learning. • Provide data each team requests.
Supervisors	• Ensure teams have adequate resources and strategies to improve teaching and student learning. • Work actively with teachers and teacher leaders to provide the structure, support, and culture for collaborative professional learning linked directly to teaching and student learning.
District administrators	• Support schools in creating collaborative professional learning opportunities that align with school and district goals. • Ensure school staff have resources for their work. • Provide data, expertise, and resources about content areas, instruction, assessment, and professional learning. • Support developing local professional learning plans that reflect the needs of schools, teams, and individuals and support collaborative learning.
School- and district-based professional learning committees	• Develop a school or district professional learning plan that reflects the needs of schools, teams, and individuals and supports collaborative learning. • Use site plans to drive district supports. • Serve as local experts about research, district regulations, and state policies. • Ensure all staff have access to high-quality collaborative professional learning.
Professional learning facilitators	• Model collaborative professional learning and integrate these strategies into all work. • Support and focus on the needs of individuals, teams, and schools. • Provide support and follow-up to enhance the ongoing transfer of learning to practice and results for students.

Source: Adapted from Killion & Roy, 2009.

Roles and Responsibilities of School-System Staff

In times of change, leaders double down on the school district's vision, mission, and values. When leaders define and focus on vision, mission, and values, they help all stakeholders, employees, and community members uphold the driving principles and grounding beliefs to maintain stability. In turbulent or changing times in education learning and equity, leaders help educators, students, and community members to trust in one another's ability to pull through and emerge successfully. Therefore, students are ready for their future, not their educators' past. The following are some responsibilities of school-system leaders.

- ▶ Advocate for continuous learning and school-based professional learning with decision and policy makers.

- ▶ Seek support for the time, budget, and staff to support professional learning.

- ▶ Inform decision and policy makers about the work and its alignment with the school-system priorities.

- ▶ Explain the link between educator learning and student success.

- ▶ Prepare site leaders, including administrators and teacher leaders, to lead in changing times.

Because school-based staff interact with parents, guardians, and community members, they benefit from learning how to facilitate conversations about what and how schools prepare students for success after high school. School administrators also influence building staff flexibility and agility with learning and teaching repertoires. In addition, district leaders are responsible for directing site leader learning to strengthen the leaders' capacity in these areas.

District leaders also cultivate and model what change expert and coauthors Victoria Boyd and Shirley M. Hord (1994) label *professional learning communities* (PLCs) in their groundbreaking work (see also Hord, 1997a, 1997b, 2004). In a PLC, the emphasis is on achieving high levels of learning by building a collaborative culture and focusing on results (DuFour et al., 2016; Hord & Sommers, 2008). In true PLCs, all members in a school or district work in collaborative teams and commit to the growth and development of one another to ensure learning for all.

District leaders determine the parameters and expectations for collective responsibility, establish high expectations for collaborative learning, and work to tap the expertise of all community members. In addition, district leaders are lead learners in the district who engage site leaders in learning how to be lead learners in their schools. Site leaders then model effective PLC processes with their staff, who, in turn, model and establish learning communities with students. As a result, students (directly and indirectly) gain the employable skills of collaboration and joint work, and the ability to build strong communities.

Roles and Responsibilities of School Administrators

In the school, the quality of teaching has the most direct impact on student learning, and school leadership has the second most influence on students' academic success (Leithwood & Seashore-Louis, 2012; Grissom. Egalite, & Lindsay, 2021). Researchers Jason Grissom, Anna Egalite, and Constance Lindsay (2021) conclude, "Across six studies of data from more than 22,000 principals in four states and two urban school districts, principals matter substantially. We find that a

1 standard deviation increase in principal effectiveness increases the typical student's achievement by 0.13 standard deviations in math and 0.09 standard deviations in reading" (p. xiii).

According to researchers, professors, and coauthors Kenneth Leithwood and Karen Seashore-Louis (2012) in *Linking Leadership to Student Learning*, these influences are more significant in high-poverty schools. Because high-poverty schools have higher staff turnover rates and students whose academic needs are often greater than their low-poverty peers, teachers and administrators experience increased pressure to build success.

In addition, according to Grissom and colleagues (2021), leadership practices that have a particularly strong influence on student achievement include the following:

- Engaging in instructionally focused interactions with teachers
- Building a productive school climate
- Facilitating productive collaboration and professional learning communities
- Managing personnel and resources strategically (p. xvi)

When school administrators model and facilitate learning designs staff can transfer to their work, it builds their repertoire and encourages them to use those processes with students. For example, integrating pedagogical processes such as Socratic seminars, cooperative structures, or project-based learning (PBL) into professional learning gives teachers a sense of how those instructional methods affect learning. In addition, the leaders' experiences with these methods may increase teachers' use of similar methods in their classrooms.

School administrators also provide structures that support the transfer of the learning into classrooms by monitoring and facilitating coaching, peer visits, collaborative planning, and ongoing professional learning to enhance professional growth, rather than mere acquisition of knowledge and skills.

A helpful resource for identifying strategies for learning is author William A. Sommers's (2021) *Creating Talent Density*, which "offers suggestions for what you can do to increase the group's effectiveness and enhance the culture of learning for all staff" (p. xxvii). Having resources available that delineate processes to facilitate professional learning make the work easier. Chapter 4 (page 75) explores more about various designs for professional learning.

In addition to modeling and facilitating learning for staff, school administrators reshape the school culture so it is conducive to learning and provides a safe space for students and staff. School administrators make risk taking risk free in a safe environment.

A *safe environment* is socially, physically, and emotionally safe and encourages and sustains innovative thinking and shared expertise among colleagues. One way to increase psychological safety for learning is to celebrate learning from missteps as well as successes. In addition, school administrators can create a space that makes learning a daily routine for educators. Finally, administrators, with teacher support, use student work as evidence of success and leverage student results to engage in conversations about how to address instructional practices that increase student success.

Inviting diverse perspectives and voices into decision-making conversations, analyzing trends and actions from multiple perspectives, facilitating rapid cycles of improvement, and setting clear expectations are actions that model and communicate learning and equity are essential to student and staff success (Bryk, 2020; Bryk et al., 2015). These actions cultivate norms for collaborative, blame-free risk taking and failing forward, cultivate trust among staff, open lines of communication for productive discourse, build and monitor PLCs, and challenge assumptions and beliefs that contradict the school or district's vision, mission, and values.

Embedding learning and modeling into the routine daily work of a school makes the crucial work of continuous inquiry an everyday expectation rather than an occasional event. School administrators have ample opportunities to model and facilitate learning and build a learning-focused culture schoolwide—in individuals, department or grade-level meetings, and community meetings. School administrators who shift their priorities from managing the killer Bs (budgets, boundaries, and busses) to creating opportunities for everyone to learn, make space for learning to be the driver of success.

One of the most significant responsibilities of school administrators is to cultivate leadership capacity in others. All leaders, especially administrators, seek to identify those with a desire or potential to serve as leaders, facilitate and support professional learning for those who aspire to lead, provide authentic opportunities for aspiring leaders to apply leadership, and coach them to implement leadership skills (Killion, Harrison, Colton, Bryan, Delehant, & Cooke, 2016). Additionally, by making their leadership practices transparent, they model leadership for others and engage them in conversations about nuanced behaviors related to leadership practices.

Roles and Responsibilities of Teacher Leaders and Instructional Coaches

Teacher leaders and instructional coaches have significant responsibilities in shaping professional learning and school culture. Leadership is not only the responsibility of those with positional authority but also of all who manage, coordinate, oversee, facilitate, and engage in professional learning. Teacher leaders and instructional coaches face unique pressures because of their position in the school hierarchy.

As educational consultants Robert Garmston and Carolyn McKanders (2022) remind educators in *It's Your Turn: Teachers as Facilitators—A Handbook*, *facilitating* is to ease the group's work and not to influence its outcome. Garmston and McKanders (2022) describe this dilemma, emphasizing the heightened need for knowledge and skill:

> Demands on facilitators are a problem in any facilitated group but are especially difficult in groups in which the person is also a member. A predictable request is "Tell us what you think." To give your opinion violates a central premise of facilitation . . . teacher-facilitators must be impartial and unaligned with any specific position. This is possible if armed with the necessary knowledge. (p. xii)

Teacher leaders and instructional coaches clarify their roles, explicitly stating whether they are serving as consultants advising or directing the actions of others, or coaches facilitating others to determine their actions. Teachers who have full- or part-time classroom roles and engage in professional learning have a substantial responsibility to make decisions about their learning in their districts, schools, and teams. Actions matter more than titles when it comes to professional learning.

Joellen Killion and colleagues (2016) further note:

> Leadership roles for teachers have traditionally been narrowly defined or lacked flexibility, and many require that teachers who choose leadership must decide to leave teaching for administration. . . . Advancing their careers while remaining in the role of teacher is what many teacher leaders want and their students and the profession deserve. (p. 5)

As leaders, staff in these roles share many of the same responsibilities as school administrators and district leaders. In addition, they serve as lead learners who model continuous learning. Killion and colleagues (2016) continue, "Teacher leadership requires a clear statement of purpose and clearly defined outcomes and designated roles aligned with the outcomes to be more than just another panacea for fixing schools" (p. 10).

The roles of teacher leaders and instructional coaches include the following.

- ▶ Facilitate learning for others or engage in it as a partner.
- ▶ Foster a safe environment to encourage flexibility and agility in instruction.
- ▶ Facilitate collaboration in collaborative teams.
- ▶ Make their leadership work transparent to others to cultivate leadership skills in all staff.

Teacher leaders and instructional coaches are particularly responsible for fostering psychological and emotional safety in a team and in schoolwide meetings. They work to establish and adhere to norms that support safety and trust. In addition, teacher leaders create structures for teamwork to ensure equity and collaboration among members. Finally, they watch for and address behaviors that hinder a sense of belonging and safety in teams and encourage behaviors that promote inclusion, safety, and respect.

Expert in human interaction Amy C. Edmondson (2019) urges leaders and coaches to address the following negative behaviors.

- ▶ Judging those who make mistakes as less competent or experienced
- ▶ Ostracizing those who act or think differently than the majority
- ▶ Avoiding asking for help or acknowledging one's own needs

Positive behaviors Edmondson (2019) encourages include the following.

- ▶ Taking risks to do something unfamiliar or uncomfortable
- ▶ Honoring individuals, their efforts, and contributions
- ▶ Sharing and applying expertise to solve problems
- ▶ Engaging in candid conversation by asking questions, sharing feedback, seeking help, and being open about needs and challenges
- ▶ Collaborating with mutual respect and shared goals
- ▶ Experimenting to discover what works, recognizing that it is a process of trial and error
- ▶ Reflecting to critically analyze results and actions for the purpose of learning how to improve

When teacher leaders, coaches, or cocurricular advisors facilitate teamwork, they teach, practice, model, and assess psychological and emotional safety among staff. One way to establish safety is to assess for it in teams. Teacher leaders and instructional coaches help teams create, monitor, and assess a sense of team. They ask members to share perspectives, discuss the status, and identify options for strengthening how well the team functions, including how members interact, how safe they feel, and how effective and efficient their work is.

Another critical responsibility of teacher leaders and instructional coaches is *managing up*. Leadership development consultant Mary Abbajay (2018) defines *managing up* as a "deliberate effort to increase cooperation and collaboration in a relationship between individuals who often have different perspectives and uneven power levels. . . . Managing up is about you taking charge of your workplace experience" (p. 1). In addition, *managing up* is a responsibility of all leaders in a school system, especially those who interact most frequently with staff, who work most closely with students.

The superintendent can manage up to the board of education; district leaders can manage up to the superintendent; principals can manage up to district leaders; and so on. So, everyone works in systems that include people who report to leaders, people leaders report to, and peers with roles at the same level in the organization.

Managing up occurs when leaders do the following.

- ▶ Share information, perspective, and thinking.

- ▶ Make recommendations with appropriate evidence and reasoning.

- ▶ Identify issues that need attention.

- ▶ Engage in decision making and problem solving.

- ▶ Inquire about supervisor reasoning.

- ▶ Serve as another set of eyes and ears for the supervisor.

Reverse mentoring is another responsibility of learning leaders. In *Rookie Smarts*, leadership researcher Liz Wiseman (2014) advances the concept of learning from those whom leaders supervise or teach. Novices may have talents, skills, and knowledge more experienced staff do not share. Someone new to a teaching position, for example, may be fluid with technology and have new energy. Sharing expertise in a safe environment in which every member shares—regardless of experience level—enhances the practice of every member of the community.

Roles and Responsibilities of Teachers and Instructional Support Staff

Teachers' learning experiences matter most as they are in the classroom every day. Therefore, they want to be a part of the decision-making process:

> Those who are going to be implementing changes in their classrooms, schools, and districts, because of professional learning need to be involved in determining exactly how the professional learning will be constructed. Gone are the days when someone "higher up" decides what teachers should be doing in terms of professional learning. Gone are the days when "buy-in" is needed because someone "higher up" has determined how to develop others . . . and wants them to like what's happening to them. (Delehant & Easton, 2015, p. 33)

To be a part of the decision-making process, teachers and instructional support staff share multiple responsibilities for extending learning cycles in schools and classrooms. Their primary responsibilities include the following.

- ▶ Tap into what they are experiencing each day.

- ▶ Learn from those experiences.

- ▶ Use the newly acquired understanding to design learning for students.

- ▶ Evaluate the effects of their actions.

This continuous-learning cycle requires teachers and instructional support staff (such as teacher assistants, specialized resource staff who work with designated students, and others) to apply the school-based professional learning cycle so student learning drives staff learning. They also analyze data about student learning, set goals, design learning experiences, implement those learning experiences, monitor and measure results using multiple forms of formative and summative assessments, reflect on the learning and results, and use what they learned as they enter the next cycle, as the next scenario demonstrates.

SCHOOL-BASED PROFESSIONAL LEARNING IN PRACTICE
The Continuous-Learning Cycle

Teachers and instructional support staff have multiple opportunities to engage in the continuous-learning cycle. For example, suppose a middle school world language teacher implements an instructional unit about verb tenses. As she facilitates a sorting task with students, she notices native English-speaking students struggle more with the differentiation among tenses than English learners.

After some thought, she adapts her examples to make them more relevant to students' previous lessons. She notes that using examples drawn from students' immediate experiences aided their understanding. She plans to share her discovery with colleagues at the next team meeting and ask if others had similar experiences. When a teacher shares a discovery like this, it extends and expands the instructional repertoire of her team.

Another responsibility of teachers and instructional support staff is to share what they learn with one another to extend and enrich everyone's instructional repertoire. When team members hold themselves accountable for drawing learning from every experience and sharing it with others, they spread knowledge and influence practice.

The key to sharing is to share the learning, the evidence that led to the learning, the adaptations made, and the results. By continually drawing from one another's experiences and reflecting on their potential for others' situations, the community of learners becomes a living laboratory in which all members share responsibility for the success of every student.

Sharing also increases accountability for the success of the whole community. It builds collective efficacy among team members, where individual success contributes to the entire community's success. This principle is a fundamental premise of positive deviance (see chapter 1, page 9) rather than to one's individual success.

A final responsibility of teachers and instructional support staff is to adopt a continuous-learner mindset. Educators commit to being continuous learners, not for compliance requirements of governing agencies, but as a core value they hold. That value guides how teachers and instructional support staff engage in their work and with one another. Those with a continuous-learner mindset realize every experience is an opportunity to learn, confirm or disprove what they know, and discover new questions to ask.

Roles and Responsibilities of Noninstructional Staff

Schools and school systems have many employees whose work indirectly connects to students, such as office assistance, food services, custodial, transportation, and other staff. These noninstructional staff make vital contributions to the functioning of a school or school system. They also share responsibilities for professional learning, including the following.

- ▶ Commit to continuous learning to strengthen their performance.
- ▶ Stay current with issues related to the school or school system.
- ▶ Advocate for the vision, mission, and values of the district and school in the community.

Noninstructional staff often live in the school or school-system community and have frequent interactions with other community members. As employees, they represent the school or school system and demonstrate their support for the school's or school system's vision, mission, and values through their actions. They also recognize and value learning as a part of their career growth and development, and seek and demand opportunities for continuous learning.

Roles and Responsibilities of Students and Families

If learning is the primary focus for district and school staff, it also is for students and families. In *Execution: The Discipline of Getting Things Done*, business consultants and coauthors Larry Bossidy and Ram Charan (2002) acknowledge that robust dialogue—the kind that reveals reality through openness, candor, and informality—incubates most innovations and inventions. Unfortunately, top-level leadership often restricts this type of dialogue and rarely involves the staff and students and their families. Student and family responsibilities include the following.

- ▶ Seek and accept opportunities to participate in dialogue and decision making.
- ▶ Share information and perspectives about themselves.
- ▶ Acquire and process information about the school, curriculum, instructional processes, operations, and policy.

These interactions allow organizations to gather and understand information, and use it to make decisions with community input.

Students and families also can engage in reverse mentoring of staff about their unique needs, learning preferences, and supports necessary for success. They are primarily responsible for helping educators understand their cultures and offer relevant ways to support culturally responsive learning. Groundbreaking psychologist and best-selling author Maysa Akbar (2020), in *Beyond Ally*, encourages open conversations about culture so teachers, administrators, families, and students learn with and from one another. Akbar (2020) says, "I encourage you to enter into this journey with humility, an open mind, and a loving heart. It is OK to be a student and to learn the right way" (p. xxxiii).

For example, after reading several brief articles about microaggressions, family members and students discuss their experiences with microaggressions (in and out of school) with educators (De La Rosa, S., 2021; Miller & Miskimon, 2021). Family members and students join in an open, honest, and safe space with the common purpose of learning together how to create the best learning experiences for all students. They approach their work as equals who share responsibility for student success.

Conclusion

A Swahili saying, *Mikono mingi kazi haba*, means, *Many hands make light work* (Center for African Studies, n.d.). If many people cooperate to achieve what otherwise is too much for one person, it becomes easy when many people share the effort. In the work of professional learning, many people contribute to its success. Regardless of role, each stakeholder in the education community has responsibilities to shape the learning for self and others. Chief among their responsibilities is a commitment to and engagement in continuous learning. When every stakeholder makes learning for students and adults the primary focus, students benefit.

Leadership Tips

School leaders can help create a successful culture by defining responsibilities, creating norms to foster learning, and making leadership practices transparent. The following tips will help you get started.

- ▸ Define the responsibilities of all stakeholders in student success.

- ▸ Create norms that foster learning, risk taking, and applying learning throughout the school system.

- ▸ Address interruptions or interferences quickly and decisively.

- ▸ Cultivate a culture with high expectations for collective responsibility and collaboration among educators. See the reproducible "Staff Perception of Their Engagement in Decisions About Professional Learning" (page 45).

- ▸ Make leadership practices transparent.

Reflection Questions

Who are the most responsible persons for professional learning in your school system? What are their roles and responsibilities?

1. How do all stakeholders, including staff, administrators, students, families, and community members, learn about their roles and develop the competencies to fulfill them?

2. How do leaders communicate and develop roles and responsibilities among stakeholders?

3. What interferes with the success of any stakeholder group to meet expectations?

4. How do leaders address those interferences?

5. What procedures are in place for monitoring, assessing, and facilitating growth related to stakeholder roles and responsibilities?

Checklist of Roles and Responsibilities

This tool guides professional learning stakeholders to examine how their roles and responsibilities contribute to school-based professional learning.

PURPOSE To assist district and school stakeholders in assessing the current state of roles and responsibilities related to school-based professional learning

PRODUCT A summary of current perceptions of roles and responsibilities related to school-based professional learning

PARTICIPANTS Stakeholders or representatives of stakeholder groups

MATERIALS Survey, survey results, and questions to analyze survey results

TIME Two hours to prepare the survey, distribute the survey, analyze results, and prepare a report

PREPARATION **Step 1**
Adapt the responsibilities in the following lists to include district and school policies and guidelines regarding roles and responsibilities in professional learning.

Step 2
Determine which options to use to gather data.

- Option one: Ask representatives of all stakeholder groups to respond regarding all stakeholder responsibilities.
- Option two: Ask representatives or all stakeholders in a group to respond to their specific roles and responsibilities.

PROCESS **Step 1**
Create online or paper surveys from the following charts (beginning on page 38) and adapt as appropriate to reflect your specific district and school policies and guidelines related to professional learning. Each chart includes common responsibilities.
Add or delete items to reflect a district or school's particular professional learning responsibilities. Gather responses from a representative sample of stakeholders.

Step 2
Distribute the surveys to all stakeholders and gather data.

Step 3
Compile results as a percent of respondents checking each area.

Step 4
Ask the following questions and discuss results.

- "Which area has the most significant discrepancy between current and desired state?"
- "Which areas have the most significant level of agreement between current and desired state?"
- "For areas with the most significant discrepancy, what are the expected roles and responsibilities in current policies and guidelines?"

PROCESS
(cont.)

- "For areas with the most significant discrepancy, what might contribute to the discrepancies?"
- "What areas are not listed that you want to add to each stakeholder group's current expected responsibilities?"
- "How can policies and guidelines be changed to align with or support the desired state?"
- "How do you use these results to strengthen the overall professional learning system?"

Roles and Responsibilities: District Staff

In the appropriate column, please check each task that is a current or a desired responsibility of this role group.

	Current State	Desired State
1. Establish district policies for professional learning.		
2. Clarify state statutes and regulations related to professional learning for school leaders.		
3. Share requirements for provisional and permanent certification for all educators, and maintain all records for human resources.		
4. Scan the environment for the seeds of change, emerging trends, and indicators.		
5. Support the school leaders as they deal with unpredictability.		
6. Maintain focus on the district and school vision, mission, values, goals, and students' futures.		
7. Ensure a focus on diversity, equity, and inclusion.		
8. Prepare site leaders to lead.		
9. Onboard new site administrators and teacher leaders.		
10. Mentor new educators.		
11. Cultivate and model collaborative work for staff and students.		
12. Ensure educators have access to the important community, staff, and student data.		
13. Support school-based professional learning.		
Add other responsibilities in current district or school policies or guidelines here.		

Roles and Responsibilities: School Administrators

In the appropriate column, please check each task that is a current or a desired responsibility of this role group.

	Current State	Desired State
1. Model and facilitate learning that staff can transfer to their work using learning designs.		
2. Create conditions to support learning for staff and students.		
3. Provide opportunities for coaching, peer visits, collaborative planning, and ongoing professional learning.		
4. Shape the school culture to ensure it is conducive to learning and provide a safe space for learning and risk taking.		
5. Explore problems, issues, or differences of practice together to improve and transform actions.		
6. Create opportunities for team teaching, collaborative planning, and collaborative action research.		
7. Create a space for learning for all.		
8. Read and share essential articles from professional journals, and participate in and share highlights from learning experiences.		
9. Establish a growth-based feedback process with staff.		
10. Lead with data dialogue.		
11. Develop leadership opportunities for staff and students.		
12. Decide how to decide.		
13. Build relationships with families; recognize and celebrate families.		
14. Gather data from community members, families, and staff, and use the data to guide improvements.		
Add other responsibilities in current district or school policies or guidelines here.		

Roles and Responsibilities: Teacher Leaders, Instructional Coaches, and Cocurricular Advisors

In the appropriate column, please check each task that is a current or a desired responsibility of this role group.

	Current State	Desired State
1. Serve as lead learners to model learning.		
2. Facilitate learning with others.		
3. Foster a safe environment to encourage flexibility and agility in instruction.		
4. Accelerate collaboration among collaborative team members and make leadership work transparent to cultivate leadership skills in all staff.		
5. Encourage psychological and emotional safety in team and schoolwide meetings.		
6. Establish and adhere to norms that support safety and trust.		
7. Create structures for teamwork that ensure equity and collaboration among members.		
8. Address behaviors that hinder a sense of belonging and safety.		
9. Manage difficult conversations.		
10. Keep the team's focus on the team's goals and critical questions of learning; make sure all voices are heard.		
11. Remind the group of its commitments to fairness, openness, and respect.		
12. Help teams monitor, assess, and address a sense of team.		
13. Share information, perspective, and thinking; identify issues needing attention.		
14. Engage in decision making and problem solving.		
15. Learn from those you coach or teach.		
Add other responsibilities in current district or school policies or guidelines here.		

Roles and Responsibilities: Students and Families

In the appropriate column, please check each task that is a current or a desired responsibility of this role group.

	Current State	Desired State
1. Seek and accept opportunities to participate in the dialogue and decision making; share information and perspectives about yourselves and your child.		
2. Communicate unique needs, learning preferences, and necessary supports for success for your child.		
3. Share information about your culture to support learning.		
4. Work to build positive and productive school-home relationships throughout the year.		
5. Learn about the curricula.		
6. Ensure your child completes assignments, spends time reading each day, and goes to school ready to learn.		
7. Help your child understand the value of learning; be a positive role model for your child to shape the child's opinions and attitudes about learning.		
8. Involve yourself in your child's education.		
Add other responsibilities in current district or school policies or guidelines here.		

Roles for School-Based Professional Learning

This tool guides professional learning stakeholders to clarify their roles and responsibilities.

PURPOSE To develop with stakeholders an understanding of their responsibilities for school-based professional learning (While you may adapt the roles and responsibilities, this reproducible can be a starting point for clarifying roles and responsibilities and holding all stakeholders accountable for their contributions.)

PRODUCT A district- and school-specific chart of roles and responsibilities for school-based professional learning (see the following chart)

PARTICIPANTS Representatives of all stakeholders

MATERIALS This model document, current district policy about professional learning, and other district or school guidelines about responsibilities related to professional learning

TIME Two hours for study and development of a school-specific document

PREPARATION Share the chart and supporting documents for participants to review before the meeting.

PROCESS **Step 1**

Meet with representatives of each stakeholder group together or in separate groups. Meeting together has the advantages of building a systemwide perspective for shared responsibility and accountability for decisions and actions that relate to professional learning. They might review the chart before moving to step 2.

Step 2

Invite stakeholders to use the chart to create a district- and school-specific table that delineates roles and responsibilities for all staff and external partners. Table 2.1 (page 28) is an example. (See the following blank version for your use.) Stakeholders answer the following questions.

- What tasks delineated in each role group are we currently doing?
- Which tasks are not a part of the responsibilities of each role?
- What tasks do we want to add to the responsibilities of each role to create a comprehensive professional learning system?
- How do we formalize these roles and responsibilities so stakeholders are familiar with and prepared for their responsibilities?
- How will we monitor and adjust roles as necessary or at least annually?
- How do we communicate regularly about the roles and responsibilities to all stakeholders?

Stakeholder	Roles and Responsibilities for School-Based Professional Learning
Teachers and instructional support staff	
Teacher leaders and instructional coaches	
Principals	
Supervisors	
District administrators	
School- and district-based PLCs	
Professional learning facilitators	

Reference

Killion, J., & Roy, P. (2009). Becoming a learning school. Oxford, OH: National Staff Development Council.

Staff Perception of Their Engagement in Decisions About Professional Learning

This tool is a quick survey to gather staff perceptions about their engagement in decisions about professional learning.

PURPOSE   To assess staff perceptions about how they contribute to decisions about professional learning

PRODUCT   Survey results to serve as both baseline data and progress indicators

PARTICIPANTS   All stakeholders

MATERIALS   The survey (see step 2)

TIME   One hour to review, study, and adapt the survey; ten minutes to complete the survey; and two hours to review and analyze the survey results and determine necessary actions

PREPARATION   Study the survey and adapt it as necessary for the specific school; prepare and disseminate the survey; and compile survey results.

PROCESS   **Step 1**
Gather the team currently responsible for making decisions about school-based professional learning.

Step 2
Review this sample survey and adjust as necessary.

Sample survey questions with a four- or five-point Likert scale response (SurveyMonkey, n.d.b).

- I have an active role in decisions about schoolwide professional learning.
- I have an active role in decisions about team-based professional learning.
- I have an active role in decisions about my professional learning.
- I want more opportunities to be involved in decisions about schoolwide professional learning.
- I want more opportunities to be involved in decisions about team-based professional learning.
- I want more opportunities to be involved in decisions about my professional learning.
- My school uses my professional learning needs to make decisions about professional learning in the school.
- My professional learning needs are being met through school-based professional learning.
- The professional learning I experience at school strengthens my performance.
- The professional learning I experience at school strengthens students' performance.

Step 3
Distribute the survey.

PROCESS **Step 4**
(cont.) Aggregate responses.

Step 5
Analyze the data to determine the following.

- Patterns of responses
- Strengths
- Opportunities
- Outliers

Step 6
Hypothesize the reasons for the patterns and outliers.

Step 7
Determine needed actions.

PART 2

Working Through the School-Based Professional Learning Cycle

CHAPTER 3

Analyzing Data to Design School-Based Professional Learning

A journey of a thousand miles begins with a single step.

—LAO TZU

For professional learning, educators strive to understand their current reality (or where they are now), what the present and emerging needs are, and what the rationale is for moving forward. Analyzing data about students, educators, and the school context is a pivotal part of this step. Understanding the starting point also includes determining who to involve in the work and the scope of their engagement and authority. This chapter explores these questions and offers resources to guide school leadership and professional learning teams to undertake these tasks. Often, planning professional learning begins by distributing an annual needs assessment, asking teachers to identify their learning needs. Unfortunately, the resulting diverse list of teacher interests may not address student needs. Therefore, a better way to begin planning school-based professional learning is by analyzing student, educator, and school-context data.

Start this process by using data to ruthlessly assess current reality. In *Powerful Designs for Professional Learning*, coauthors Ann Delehant and Lois Brown Easton (2015) state:

> Data illuminate critical needs, reveal the "pain" in the system—what worries people most. Data highlight the challenges that the system faces as well as the assets the system can build upon. Data analysis is an exciting opportunity to discern what might drive individual, team, and system improvements. (p. 33)

When used to peel away layers of possibilities, data expose what is not obvious, especially when you place juxtaposing data sets side by side. As Bryk (2020) writes, "When a problem is complex and resources are constrained, data-based insights can help improvers discern where to target their efforts" (p. 54). The advantage of data analysis for planning professional learning is the learning can respond specifically to student and educator needs, build shared expertise among faculty, and create significant equity in students' opportunities to learn.

When used to peel away layers of possibilities, data exposes what is not obvious, especially when you place juxtaposing data sets side by side.

This chapter explores maintaining safety when analyzing data and how to identify, select, and analyze data. Then, it discusses analyzing the school context and narrowing the focus on the highest priorities.

Maintaining Safety When Analyzing Data

Educators often fear others will judge or blame them for student results and educator learning needs (Ball, 2015; Dam, Janssen, & van Driel, 2020). Unfortunately, this fear may relate to past experiences with others using the data punitively rather than constructively. In addition, analyzing data may seem threatening to educators who perceive their practice as already accomplished, are unwilling to acknowledge the need for continuous learning and growth, and lack confidence and efficacy in data analysis and use. Teachers and administrators equally share a sense of trepidation about the analysis of educator data. (Ball, 2003, 2015; Lasater, Albiladi, Davis, & Bengtson, 2020). In *Chief Joy Officer: How Great Leaders Elevate Human Energy and Eliminate Fear*, author and process, teamwork, and organizational design expert Richard Sheridan (2018) reminds educators, "Fear does not make bad news go away. Fear makes bad news go into hiding" (p. 104). Therefore, data analysis requires courage and vulnerability.

Data analysis occurs best when strong norms for maintaining safety while taking risks are in place, with protocols for guiding the process, and dedicated time to analyze data collaboratively to determine next actions. Teachers feel more comfortable with the process and are more willing to set aside anxiety about data analysis when norms for interaction establish a blame-free environment, a focus on understanding and using data (rather than on finding fault), and finding practical solutions to identified challenges. For example, the following norms may be helpful for teams examining data at the macro level (system- or schoolwide) or at the micro level (individual or classroom).

- ▸ Focus on what the data tell you and ask hard questions about the data.
- ▸ Focus on what actions to take and desired results.
- ▸ Remain judgment and blame free.
- ▸ Think creatively and comprehensively to consider all possibilities.
- ▸ Listen fully and prepare your response after someone speaks.
- ▸ Maintain confidentiality.
- ▸ Be a part of the solution.

Vulnerability and courage require educators to trust one another, believe they can identify and address issues, and hold one another's best interests in mind. Educators earn trust by demonstrating they are trustworthy.

Understanding Data Analysis

When teams prepare to analyze data for professional learning, they begin by identifying which data to examine and for what purpose. Consultants Cindy Harrison and Chris Bryan (2008) describe five types of data conversations that occur in school. All can inform decisions about professional learning. Table 3.1 (page 51) summarizes the types of data conversations, data the conversations focus on, who is involved, the conversation topics, and how often the conversations occur.

TABLE 3.1: Types of Data Conversations

Type of Data Conversation	Data Used	Who Is Involved	Conversation Topics	Frequency
School-Improvement Team Conversations	• State assessments • District benchmarks	• School-improvement team • Entire staff	• Patterns of student achievement • Needs for schoolwide programs (instructional, curricular, professional development, and so on) • Needs for additional knowledge and skills for staff	• Twice per year
Teacher-Supervisor and Teacher-Coach Conversations	• State assessments • Benchmark exams • End-of-course assessments • Classroom assessments • Common assessments	• Teacher plus administrator or coach (or both)	• Growth of students • Overall student proficiency • Instructional strategies to meet student learning needs	• Two or three times per year
Department and Grade-Level Team Conversations With Focus on Individual Student Interventions	• Student performance on classroom and common assessments • Discipline records • Student work	• Core teams • Grade-level teams	• Diagnosis of individual knowledge and skills • Next steps for students • Grouping students for instruction and intervention • Pyramid of interventions	• Once per month or more often
Department and Grade-Level Team Conversations With Focus on Instructional Strategies	• State assessments • Benchmark assessments • Common assessments • Unit assessments	• Grade-level or content-area groups	• Growth of students • Patterns in proficiency • Instructional strategies • Assessment strategies	• Once per week to once every six to eight weeks
Student Goal-Setting Conversations	• Student work • Grades • State assessments • Common assessments • Benchmark assessments	• Teacher and individual students	• Goal setting • Strategies for success • Celebrations of learning	• Once a week to once a month

In schools, data are everywhere, yet schools are notoriously data rich and information poor, also known as *DRIP*. While large amounts of data exist from multiple sources, the availability of useful data and the use of the data to inform practice may be limited. Basing decisions about professional learning on data rather than teachers' interests means professional learning addresses the specific areas needing attention.

Educators are familiar with using data to identify school goals for annual school-improvement plans, write professional-growth goals, measure progress and successes, and adjust instruction. These same data are also the basis for planning professional learning.

Selecting Data

Because data are prevalent in schools, choosing appropriate data to analyze for professional learning planning is essential. Analyze data likely to contribute to understanding the current state, such as common assessment data, daily formative assessment results, and end-of-unit assessment. Not all data add value in the analysis process or serve the purpose of building an understanding of the current state of student learning needs, subsequent educator learning needs, and school context. In *Data Analysis for Continuous School Improvement*, Victoria L. Bernhardt (2018), executive director of the nonprofit Education for the Future Initiative, recommends four categories of data to understand schools and drive change processes.

1. Student achievement data (not just test scores), including high-stakes, end-of-year assessments, common assessments, and student work products

2. Demographics such as gender, ethnicity, race, family background, primary and secondary language, specialized support programs, and free or reduced-priced lunch eligibility

3. Perceptions, such as individuals' opinion about climate, culture, and safety collected from surveys of students, families, and staff

4. Processes that make up the learning conditions, drive change, and often result in the current state of achievement and perceptions

However, Bernhardt (2018) does not include data about educators or the school context in this list. Data from multiple sources and in multiple forms are essential (Learning Forward, 2022). Data that create a rich portrayal of the status of student learning, educator attributes, and school context contribute to sound decision making.

When selecting data, ensure the data do the following.

- ▶ Explain what the data represent
- ▶ Represent a span of time to account for outliers and examine trends over time
- ▶ Portray the full spectrum of reality to understand the variances
- ▶ Derive from various types of assessments, including high-stakes, end-of-course, benchmark, and informal classroom assessments
- ▶ Come in different forms, including qualitative and quantitative
- ▶ Are available in formats everyone can analyze
- ▶ Are displayed clearly with accurate labels and titles

Analyzing Data

The process of data analysis is like a treasure hunt. Educators follow a map, usually a data-analysis protocol or process, such as the "Data-Driven Dialogue Note-Catcher" (page 64), to make discoveries about their students, their instruction, themselves, and the school context. After identifying and selecting appropriate data to analyze, the next step is to identify missing data that can add useful information for understanding root causes and when seeking to fill gaps with additional data. For example, it may be necessary to seek additional data for elementary school students regarding their engagement in preschool programs and the types of programs they attended. Or it may be necessary to add the number of years the students have been in the district to middle school student-data analysis. The process continues with analyzing data to find trends in successes and gaps between what educators expect or desire and what occurs, and also narrowing the focus to identify specific learning needs of students and the corresponding learning needs of educators. However, it is crucial to acknowledge, as business consultants and coauthors Christopher J. Frank and Paul F. Magnone (2011) remind educators in *Drinking From the Fire Hose*, "Data is a means to an end. It is the supporting character. Too often it takes center stage" (p. 207).

The following overarching questions guide the data-analysis process. The following sections address more specific questions related to particular data sets of relevance specifically to students and faculty.

- ▸ What data sources are available to determine our current state?
- ▸ What is our current state regarding student success, adult learning, and culture for continuous learning?
- ▸ What do the data tell us?
- ▸ What are the root causes?
- ▸ What issues are schoolwide, affect grade levels or departments, or affect individual classrooms?
- ▸ How do we upskill staff to implement the professional learning cycle and engage in professional learning to strengthen results?

Data analysis involves searching for patterns, trends, outliers, highs, and lows across the whole school, within groups, and among individuals. This level of analysis allows educators to understand what is happening overall in terms of student and educator learning, and what differences occur among groups. Grouping students and educators by characteristics allows educators to understand specific needs emerging for each group and provides insights into how to adjust learning.

When educators examine their own and their students' variations, they gain a deeper understanding of how to differentiate their practice to address the learning needs of each student to maintain high standards for all students. While data analysis takes time, building capacity increases fluidity and comfort with the process. The more educators engage in data analysis, the more they will enjoy the discovery process and find it easier to accomplish.

Analyzing Student Data

To understand how students are performing, educators analyze multiple forms of data by answering key questions. Frank and Magnone (2011) state, "Asking the right question is the key to finding the indispensable answer in the mountain of information" (p. xv).

The following questions guide the student data-analysis process. When answering the questions, probe for the evidence that supports the responses. A finding is stronger if several data points support it and weaker if it has fewer supporting data points.

- What types of data are we examining?

- What does each data set represent, measure, or demonstrate? What *can't* we learn from each data set?

- What types of data are missing? How will we either gather the missing information or compensate for its absence?

- In what content strands are students meeting or exceeding the standard? What is the scope (schoolwide, grade level, or class) of these successes? What evidence supports this?

- In which specific knowledge and skills in the strand are students meeting or exceeding the standard? What evidence supports this?

- How do these successes vary by student group and scope (schoolwide, grade level, or class)? What evidence supports this?

- In what types of expression of learning (original text, illustration, short- or long-answer, multiple choice, oral response, and so on) are students most successful?

- How do these successes in types of expression vary by student group and scope (school-wide, grade level, or class)? What evidence supports this?

- How does the type of expression of learning affect the results? What evidence supports this?

- In which content strands are students not meeting the standard? What evidence supports this?

- How do these gaps vary by student group and scope (schoolwide, grade level, or class)?

- In which specific knowledge and skills in the strand are students not meeting the standards? What evidence supports this?

- Which student groups are not meeting the standard in each content strand? What is the scope (schoolwide, grade level, or class) of these gaps? What evidence supports this?

- How does the type of expression of learning influence the gaps for each student group?

- What specific knowledge and skills in each content strand will we address for all student groups? For some student groups?

- What might be potential contributors to the current student results we can address?

- Which of the potential contributors, if we address them, will have the most significant overall impact on student success in the course or grade level?

- What other factors, such as social-emotional, sense of safety and belonging, or relational trust with adults and peers, influence student learning results?

- What will teachers do differently to address those areas in their instruction and relationships with students and one another?

- What else do we want to know about the students' learning, instruction, and ourselves that would be helpful? How might we gather data to inform us about these areas?

- What patterns are we finding in the data for the whole group and various student groups?

- What are the major conclusions or statements of finding we can draw from the data analysis? Specify the data that support each.

Types of student data to analyze might include the following.

- Attendance (daily, hourly, day-of-the week, and so on)

- Academic performance (high stakes, common formative, daily formative, and so on)

- Parental engagement, climate surveys (student, student groups, parent, community, staff, and so on)

- Cocurricular activities

- Discipline referrals

- Social circles

When educators give the data-analysis process the attention and time it deserves, it offers opportunities for investigation and discovery. Therefore, take time to be methodical and consider the data from multiple perspectives by asking and answering a wide array of questions about various types of data. The more information drawn from data analysis, the more teachers and administrators understand the current state and what is contributing to it. With an expanded understanding of how they arrived at the current state, educators can make more informed decisions about how to impact the future.

Analyzing Faculty Data

Once they analyze student data, educators shift their focus to analyzing educator data using a protocol like the one in the previous section (just replace *students* with *educators* where appropriate). For example, educator data might include experience levels, career pathways, preparation programs, history with change initiatives, and demographics. By analyzing their own knowledge and practice, faculty can identify their strengths and opportunities.

Data analyzers replace student content standards with educator performance standards. In this way, they focus on the criteria for accomplished practice a school system established to support growth and measure performance. For example, school systems expect educators to use knowledge of their students' backgrounds, families, and communities to create a culturally responsive classroom environment and design instruction.

The following questions are helpful for guiding the analysis of educator data. Probe for evidence when answering these questions.

- What types of data are we examining regarding educators in the school?

- What does each data set represent, measure, or demonstrate? What *can't* we learn from each data set?

- What types of data are missing? How will we either gather the missing information or compensate for its absence?

- As we look at student data, what patterns do we see regarding corresponding educator (teacher, coach, administrator) learning needs? What evidence supports this?

- How do those patterns vary by educator group?

- In what areas of performance standards are educators (teachers, administrators, coaches) meeting or exceeding the standard? What is the scope (schoolwide, grade level, or level of experience) of these successes? What evidence supports this?

- ▸ In what areas of student content standards are educators' students meeting or exceeding standards? What is the scope (schoolwide, grade level, or class) of these successes? What evidence supports this?

- ▸ How do these successes vary by educator group and scope (schoolwide, grade level, or department)? What evidence supports this?

- ▸ In which performance areas are educators demonstrating a need for extension or refinements? What evidence supports this?

- ▸ How do these needs vary by educator group and scope (experience level, schoolwide, grade level, or department)?

- ▸ What specific knowledge and skills in each performance standard relate to student performance results? What is the relationship?

- ▸ What might be potential contributors to the current educator status that we can address?

- ▸ Which of the potential contributors, if we address them, will have the most significant overall impact on educator success?

- ▸ What other factors, such as social-emotional, sense of safety and belonging, or relational trust, influence educator learning needs?

- ▸ What patterns are we finding in the data for the whole group and various educator groups?

- ▸ What are the major conclusions or statements of finding we can draw from the data analysis? Specify the data that support each.

The following example illustrates the importance of data analysis.

SCHOOL-BASED PROFESSIONAL LEARNING IN PRACTICE
Data Analysis

When coauthor William A. Sommers was a junior high school principal in Owatonna, Minnesota, the mathematics scores were trending downward. Therefore, he engaged the staff in examining the unique case variations. When the staff examined the data by case, Somali students' variations stood out. Looking at averages would not have uncovered that data. As a result, teachers did not change the mathematics curriculum. Instead, they found ways to teach Somali students based on their specific needs. When teachers started applying those strategies, scores began to rise.

Based on their analysis of student work and data, teachers gain insights into their strengths and opportunities for their own learning. Strengths occur when areas such as the following align with adopted content standards and student learning needs.

- ▸ Teachers' content knowledge

- ▸ Design and rigor of instruction and assessment

- ▸ Time invested in units of study

- ▸ Resources used

- ▸ Forms of expression of learning

- ▸ Methods to reteach and extend learning

Areas of opportunity that student performance indicate represent misalignment in some aspects of the learning process. During this process, educators' clarity and honesty are crucial to discovering reasons for the variation in student performance related to students themselves, curriculum, resources, instruction, and teaching methodology. Some possibilities include the following.

- ▸ Teachers do not have a common content base and, therefore, interpret the standards differently.

- ▸ Teacher instructional agility varies, or the level of rigor and learning experiences they facilitate vary.

- ▸ Students enter the class with different background knowledge or at different places along the learning progression, and the instruction doesn't address these differences.

- ▸ Teachers are more comfortable teaching native English-speaking students than students with different levels of English proficiency.

- ▸ A new teacher trying to understand the theory underlying the mathematics curriculum may continue to struggle unless the mathematics coach can provide the appropriate level of support.

Using Data to Find Opportunities

Consider how finding areas of opportunity leads to increased student performance. In this fictional scenario, high school biology teachers want to plan their first-semester professional learning based on the previous year's data; end-of-course results from the past three years; end-of-unit assessments and formative data from several units from the previous year; and sample student work from a few units from the previous year. The teachers spread the data sets across multiple lab tables and address several questions to guide their observation.

First, they notice successes in each set of data. For example, the teachers notice students did well with recall-type questions on the formative assessments. They find the same pattern on the end-of-course and end-of-unit assessments from the past three years. Finally, they notice students' highest results occur on the natural selection and evolution, and structure and function areas.

Next, the teachers look for gaps in student learning in areas where they expect students to perform better. They look first at the low scores on the past year's end-of-course assessment and then compare that with the previous three years' results. Then, they list areas in which students scored below proficient and look at each unit's assessment results from the previous year and note the low-score areas. By pulling ten copies of student work to see if the same trend appears, they notice students seem to recall information. However, they struggle with higher-order questions on matter and energy in organisms and ecosystems, and inheritance and variation of traits, two areas in which recall information is less prevalent.

Teachers also notice all the work and assessments they are examining require students to read and write in English. Very few samples involve visual representation, diagramming, modeling, or other forms of expression. They note this, wondering if anywhere in their learning process students have opportunities to express learning in ways not grounded in linguistic capability.

Next, they look for discrepancies, areas within their data sets where there are wide ranges of differences. Unsurprisingly, the areas of greatest discrepancy are the same areas with lower scores overall.

When teachers look more closely at the data, they discover that male Asian students perform better than any other group, and English learners perform well below other groups.

The biology teachers draw several conclusions from their data analysis that help inform their decisions about their first-semester professional learning. For example, they learn that student performance varies by language level, the type of thinking teachers ask students to do, how students express their learning, and content strands. Now, the teachers are ready to identify which areas of their practice to enrich, narrow the list, and prepare to move to the second step of the school-based professional learning cycle.

The teachers also want to investigate how the form of expression influences student success and are eager to set up some mini action–research cycles to explore that question more deeply. By holding teachers responsible for finding and addressing their own change efforts (rather than imposing them from on high), the administrators allowed these biology teachers to become owners and operators of their own efforts, increasing their responsibility and accountability to one another and their students.

In this fictional example, teachers use a variety of data to identify the successes and opportunities in their classrooms. They discover their decisions influence student performance, and they can modify their instruction to affect student performance. By studying the content strands more deeply to understand what they expect students to know and do, integrating more questions and tasks that require higher-order thinking, and differentiating the ways in which students express their learning in linguistic and nonlinguistic ways, all students will have more opportunities for success. These areas are the logical focus for the teachers' continued professional learning and collaboration to achieve the goal they want—to elevate student success in their classrooms.

Analyzing School Context

Context matters. It influences one's mindset, sense of safety, and level of willingness to succeed. Context also affects the agency and efficacy of community members. In terms of data analysis, trying to analyze data without considering context is inadequate. Therefore, as educators examine student data and their own learning needs, they must consider the context of the school. A tool such as "Survey for Assessing School Culture" (page 67) is useful for gathering information about staff perception of the school culture. Both structural and psychological factors make up the school context.

Structural factors include instructional materials; space and equipment for professional learning; access to experts and knowledgeable others to stretch staff content knowledge, pedagogical practice, and relational competence; time in the school-day schedule and calendar year for professional learning; and support for transferring learning to practice and ongoing refinement. These factors also include policies and expectations for learning the performance standards outline.

Psychological factors include the beliefs, values, norms, communication patterns, and symbolic behaviors that communicate the value of professional learning. The culture of learning, risk taking, and administrative support for learning—from budget to beliefs—all influence the depth and degree of learning teachers are likely to experience. When the principal advocates professional learning by describing her learning to others and seeks their input on her professional growth goals and application of learning, teachers in the school do more to push their learning. Sheridan (2018) reminds educators, "Our leaders and aspiring leaders must be active learners" and readers (p. 210).

When the culture promotes psychological safety for teachers to acknowledge their own learning needs, teachers will be more open to learning. When instructional support from peers and coaches is available for teachers, they will likely tap into those supports and expand their practice. When the school's overall vision, mission, and values emphasize success for every student through stakeholders' collective responsibility, shared accountability, and collaboration, educators turn to one another to meet expectations.

Sometimes, structural and psychological factors need attention. In the previous biology team example, two teachers with the most seniority told the assistant principal the three newer teachers on the team did not respect or honor their years of experience. The assistant principal met with the team several times to facilitate discussions that led to creating new working agreements among team members, including greater trust and respect, and more direct and honest communication. The team requested and received two half-days of release time for professional collaboration for learning for the first semester of the school year in addition to their weekly team meetings.

The following questions help guide the analysis of context data. Invite staff to share the evidence they are using to formulate an answer.

- ▶ What types of data are we examining regarding educators in the school?

- ▶ What does each data set represent, measure, or demonstrate? What *can't* we learn from each data set?

- ▶ What types of data are missing? How will we either gather the missing information or compensate for its absence?

- ▶ As we look at schoolwide climate or culture data, what patterns do we see in terms of corresponding educator (teacher, coach, administrator) learning needs? What evidence supports this?

- ▶ How do those patterns vary by educator group?

- ▶ In what areas of the school climate and culture are we meeting or exceeding our expectations? What is the scope (schoolwide, grade level, or level of experience) of these successes? What evidence supports this?

- ▶ In what areas of the school climate and culture are we not meeting or exceeding our expectations? What is the scope (schoolwide, grade level, or level of experience) of these successes? What evidence supports this?

- ▶ How do these gaps vary by educator group and scope (experience level, schoolwide, grade level, or department)?

- ▶ What might be potential contributors to the current school-context conditions we can address?

- ▶ Which of the potential contributors, if we address them, will have the greatest overall impact on school-context conditions?

- ▶ What other factors, such as social-emotional, sense of safety and belonging, or relational trust, influence the school-context conditions?

- ▶ What patterns are we finding in the data for the whole group and various educator groups?

- ▶ What are the major conclusions or statements of finding we can draw from the data analysis? Specify the data that supports each.

Just as analyzing student data takes time and attention, so does analyzing school-context data. It is likely that conclusions staff draw from the data will inform decisions about the fit of potential interventions. Because schools vary on many factors, it is important to understand the characteristics that make each school distinct from others. For example, a school with a large percent of experienced staff will need a different type of professional learning design than one with more novice teachers. Taking time to uncover information about each school's culture, staff, history with change, leadership, community relationships, and district support will be useful when making decisions about how to address the identified needs. Tools like the "Here's What, So What, Now What?" protocol (page 69) focus on the necessity to understand the unique nature of each school.

Narrowing the Focus

Determining the content for professional learning directly results from identifying the learning needs of students and educators and the context that influences them. In *Barking Up the Wrong Tree: The Surprising Science Behind Why Everything You Know About Success Is (Mostly) Wrong*, author Eric Barker (2017) reminds educators, "You can do anything once you stop trying to do everything" (p. 99). Bryk (2020) notes while "staff may generate lots of plausible explanations for problems and possible targets for changing (*flaring* conversations), looking at data can inform improvers as they home in on the best places to start addressing them (*focus* conversations)" (p. 54). When the analysis of various forms and sources of data indicate students' level of thinking, content, and skill in particular strands are not yet meeting expectations, then teachers' learning follows to focus on how they are approaching those areas in their content and pedagogical decisions.

In the case of the biology team, the teachers might explore how to adapt student work or learning tasks to create more critical-thinking experiences, design different ways for students to express their learning, and extend or refine tasks students experience related to the content strands they are not yet proficient in. Teachers might explore the content together as students of the discipline to check for their own accuracy and consistency in each strand.

The teachers might want to extend their approaches to student expression of learning to integrate higher-order tasks or examine how to extend academic vocabulary for English learners. Coaches will then prepare to engage teachers in trials and data gathering to investigate how these changes affect student learning, deepen teachers' content and pedagogical practice, and surface and address assumptions that might create barriers in their practice.

Finally, principals will prepare to engage more actively in classroom visits and conversations with teachers using formative data to assess the shifts and monitor the implementation of what teachers are learning. These school leaders also commit to learning how to hold these conversations in nonthreatening ways to facilitate teacher growth and reflection on practice.

Narrowing the focus takes time and deliberation. Focusing on surface topics that appear easy or more enjoyable will do little to create opportunities for deep change. Educators might benefit from a discussion with a knowledgeable colleague who can guide them in making the best decision about narrowing the focus.

For example, a coach might facilitate a conversation with a team of teachers about the members' instructional design in the identified areas of need using an instructional framework to guide their assessment. Or a district science curriculum specialist might facilitate a conversation with the team to help members examine the learning progression on key concepts or student misconceptions that may interfere with student success.

Teachers may decide to divide the focus area among smaller groups for study and share what they are learning across the groups. To narrow their focus, instructional staff might answer these questions.

- ▶ In what areas do student results indicate opportunities for our ongoing professional learning?
- ▶ Which specific student groups do we address in our instruction?
- ▶ Which areas, once we address them, will likely have the greatest overall impact on student performance?
- ▶ What are our immediate priority areas, and what can we address later?
- ▶ What do we need as a group and as individuals?

Leaders answer these questions to narrow the focus of their learning.

- ▶ Given the area of focus for instructional staff, what will I learn to support, extend, monitor, and advocate their success?
- ▶ How will I know if the staff are successful?
- ▶ How will I convey to the staff the significance of their learning in meeting students' needs?
- ▶ How will I communicate with the larger community what the staff are learning, why they are learning, and the results?
- ▶ How will I celebrate staff success and intervene when necessary?
- ▶ How will we, as a school, collectively measure our progress and results?

The biology team from the earlier example decides the most significant area of focus is twofold: (1) increasing the rigor and level of thinking overall in their instruction, and (2) learning tasks for all students and varying the ways students express their learning. The team members also want to integrate a more intentional focus on developing academic vocabulary associated with the discipline and types of thinking they expect students to engage in. The teachers believe these actions will help all students meet the demands of increased rigor.

The key to narrowing the focus is to ensure a tight fit of the learning needs among students, teachers, and administrators, and nestle that focus within the school context. The focus for professional learning may be schoolwide, by team, by individual, or across several levels. When all classroom teachers decide to focus on differentiating instruction, the leadership team might establish goals and plan professional learning for the whole staff. Then teachers in course, grade-level, and department teams (or all members of a PLC) extend their learning within the specific content area or students' developmental level. For example, they can deepen their understanding and application of differentiation in mathematics versus literacy or physical education.

Occasionally, individual teachers might expand their learning because of their unique professional-growth goals and integrate that learning into team-planning conversations. Administrators can join in the learning by expanding their capacity about how to observe and supervise differentiation in classroom instruction; engage school leaders in conversations about how to monitor and assess progress and effects of their effort in differentiation; maintain a schoolwide focus on continuous improvement; and sustain support for implementation and refinement of differentiation in daily instruction.

Conclusion

Planning educator and student learning begins with understanding where the educators and students are currently. This is the purpose of data analysis. Every action related to professional learning begins with understanding where students are succeeding and where they are not yet meeting expectations. This understanding, drawn from examining multiple forms and sources of student data, informs decisions about what educators need to learn to address gaps in student learning. In making decisions about their own learning, educators also determine how the structural and psychological factors contribute to their willingness to engage in learning. Simultaneously examining data about students, educators, and school context increases the likelihood that subsequent professional learning is a pathway to excellence for students *and* staff.

Effective data-analysis systems have three parts, according to Bryk (2020). They include responsive and dynamic data tools; strategic routines to review and use the data in decision making; and differentiated supports for individual students. These systems also provide the same for educators primarily responsible for student success.

In his work with the charter school network New Visions, Bryk (2020) summarizes three reasons data analysis is so powerful. First, data analysis builds understanding of the actual problems; second, it guides the interventions designed to address the identified problems; and third, it leads to constructive actions resulting from a process of deep conversations about reality and leads to transforming mindsets of staff and their psychological safety and trust in their school.

Leadership Tips

When analyzing data to design school-based learning, it's crucial to maintain safety, understand how to select and analyze data, and narrow the focus on the highest-priority data. The following tips will help you get started.

- ▶ Increase the structural and psychological supports for data analysis and professional learning in the school.

- ▶ Meet with teams of teachers and individual teachers to inquire about how they are using student data to inform their professional learning decisions.

- ▶ Explain how you use student, staff, and school-context data to influence your professional learning goals and progress on those goals.

- ▶ Increase access to and use of data in all schoolwide decisions to model the expectation for data-informed decision making.

- ▶ Create multiple opportunities for staff to engage in data analysis in a judgment-free zone and identify and trial ways to address problems they identify.

Reflection Questions

1. What student, educator, and school-context data do educators use most often to determine their learning needs? How can those data sets be extended to include more varied forms of student, educator, and school-context data?

2. How are you developing staff capacity to analyze student, staff, and school-context data for professional learning decision making?

3. How are you using student, educator, and school data to shape your professional learning goals and assess progress toward those goals?

4. What structural and psychological factors in the school support professional learning and which hinder it?

5. How will you develop schoolwide and team plans to address the factors that hinder professional learning? How will you know when these factors are ameliorated?

Data-Driven Dialogue Note-Catcher

This tool guides teams to engage in data analysis and subsequent planning to address identified needs.

PURPOSE To engage in a process for analyzing data in a respectful, thoughtful manner that creates shared meaning of the data

To analyze data and student work according to a protocol that leads to effective and focused action

PRODUCT Visual, colorful, easy-to-interpret representations of the data to use during dialogue focused on the data, reduce defensiveness, and help teams make sense of the information

PARTICIPANTS School leadership team, grade-level or department teams, curriculum teams, or other district and school teams

MATERIALS Data-Driven Dialogue Note-Catcher

TIME Forty-five minutes to three hours, depending on the scope of the available data

PREPARATION Identify key questions, review available data, determine any needed data, and prepare data in a way that will help teams examine and interpret the information

PROCESS Before beginning the five-step process, do the following.

- Review relevant unit essentials, learning targets, success criteria, and assessment items.
- For frequently missed items or single open-response items, facilitate the data dialogue with the team, share solutions and strategies, and consider how students might have approached the task.
- Brainstorm what students need to know and be able to do to successfully complete the task.
- As you walk participants through the steps, record information on the Data-Driven Dialogue Note-Catcher (page 66).

Step 1: Predict
Make surface assumptions and predictions, and ask questions before looking at the data (for example, "I assume . . ." "I predict . . ." "I wonder if . . .").

Answer these guiding questions.

- What assumptions we have?
- What predictions are we making?
- What questions are we asking?
- What are the possibilities for learning here?

Step 2: Go Visual
Display large, vibrant, colorful, and easy-to-read displays of the data (for example, color-coded charts or graphs).

PROCESS (cont.)

Step 3: Observe

Examine the data for patterns or trends—just the facts, not interpretations or explanations (for example, "I am struck by . . .," "I notice . . .").

Answer these guiding questions.

- What important points stand out?
- What patterns or trends are emerging?
- What seems surprising or unexpected?
- What have we not yet explored?

Step 4: Infer or Question

Generate multiple possible explanations or hypotheses for what you observe (for example, "A possible explanation is . . .," "That may be because . . .," "A question I have now is . . .").

Answer these guiding questions.

- What explanations do we have for the patterns?
- What inferences can we draw?
- What tentative conclusions might we draw?
- How can we find out which of our hypotheses is correct?
- What questions do we have?
- What additional data might we explore to verify our explanations?

Step 5: Identify a Priority Problem or Goal and Next Steps

- Identify a focus for improvement, including who needs to improve what.
- Identify next steps, including what additional data you might need.

Data-Driven Dialogue Note-Catcher

Predictions

Observations	Inferences or Questions

Student Learning Problem or Goal

Next Steps

References

Research for Better Teaching. (2019). Coaching High-Impact Teacher Teams. *Acton, MA: Research for Better Teaching.*

Love, N., Stiles, K. E., Mundry, S., & DiRanna, K. (2008). The data coach's guide to improving learning for all students: Unleashing the power of collaborative inquiry. *Thousand Oaks, CA: Corwin Press.*

Wellman, B., & Lipton, L. (2017). Data-driven dialogue: A facilitator's guide to collaborative inquiry *(2nd ed.). Burlington, VT: Miravia.*

Survey for Assessing School Culture

Leadership teams can use this tool to gather data to assess school culture.

PURPOSE To assess school culture to identify and discuss areas for improvement

PRODUCT Summary of the qualitative survey data

PARTICIPANTS A faculty or school team, which reviews the survey data summary to learn more about staff members' perspectives (Teams can also survey parents, students, community members, and others.)

MATERIALS Survey for Assessing School Culture

TIME Two hours to prepare the survey, analyze the results, and prepare a report to share

PREPARATION Edit the survey and ensure the questions focus on issues most important to your staff. Distribute the survey to all faculty members.

PROCESS **Step 1**
Tell participants to rate how they think the school is doing using the 1–5 scale.

Step 2
After compiling the scores, discuss areas of strength (where the scores are high) and areas of weakness (where scores are low or where there are discrepancies), and explore ways to address the weak areas.

Survey for Assessing School Culture

Rate each item 1–5:

1 = Almost never; 2 = Less often than not; 3 = About half the time; 4 = More often than not; 5 = Almost always

Collegiality

1. We talk in concrete and precise terms about things we're trying in our teaching.　　1 2 3 4 5

2. We have productive observations of one another.　　1 2 3 4 5

3. We plan lessons and make materials together.　　1 2 3 4 5

4. We teach one another things we know about teaching.　　1 2 3 4 5

5. We all recognize teaching is inherently difficult and ask for and give assistance for problems with students and teaching issues. And we know we'll get assistance without judgment.　　1 2 3 4 5

Experimentation

6. Teachers and administrators encourage me and back me up when I try new things.　　1 2 3 4 5

Reaching Out to Knowledge Base

7. This is a curious school. We are always searching for new and improved ways to teach.　　1 2 3 4 5

Appreciation and Recognition

8. There is a close relationship between job performance and recognition of that performance in this school.   1 2 3 4 5

Caring, Celebration, and Humor

9. We enjoy being with one another. We offer comfort and help when needed and celebration together.   1 2 3 4 5

Traditions

10. We have events and ceremonies we look forward to each year.   1 2 3 4 5

High Expectations

11. Everyone takes good teaching seriously here. This shows up in the serious attention our leaders give to teacher evaluation and let me know clearly how I stand in relation to district expectations. I get prompt and useful feedback.   1 2 3 4 5

Protecting What's Important

12. Our leaders protect us from unreasonable demands on our time and energy that can interfere with student contact time and instructional planning.   1 2 3 4 5

13. Meetings are worthwhile and productive.   1 2 3 4 5

Tangible Support

14. Priorities for money and time use show me staff development is a top priority.   1 2 3 4 5

Professional Respect

15. I feel others trust and encourage me to make instructional decisions on my own, and my boss backs me up when I do.   1 2 3 4 5

Decision Making

16. I feel our decision-making processes are fair and legitimate.   1 2 3 4 5

17. I feel I am consulted and listened to about decisions in this school and can influence policy.   1 2 3 4 5

Honest, Open Communication

18. People speak honestly and respectfully to one another. We are not afraid to disagree and can do so without jeopardizing our relationships.   1 2 3 4 5

19. Conflicts between individuals are resolved quickly and intelligently.   1 2 3 4 5

20. The information flow keeps me informed about what's going on in the school.   1 2 3 4 5

Initiative

21. Staff members show initiative in developing new ideas for the school and seeing them come to life.   1 2 3 4 5

Source: Saphier, J. (1989). School culture survey. Acton, MA: Research for Better Teaching. Used with permission.

Here's What, So What, Now What?

This tool guides leadership teams to use data to plan actions or address identified needs.

PURPOSE To move data discussions into action-oriented plans

PRODUCT Action plan with an outline of the next steps based on team learning from the data

PARTICIPANTS
- Faculty reviews schoolwide data, needs-assessment data, demographic data, context data, survey data, and various other types of data.
- Grade-level or department teams analyze common assessments, benchmark data, writing samples, student projects, or other types of grade-level or department data.
- Individual teachers can also use this tool when assessing student work, assessments, or other data.

MATERIALS Teams begin with raw data or a data summary. (Note: It is essential to let the teams do the analysis to ensure everyone understands the information and can interpret the data.)

TIME One hour, although the task might take longer if the number of participants is large and the data extensive.

PREPARATION Determine what data will inform the decisions. Gather and prepare data sets for each participant.

PROCESS Apply this tool to a variety of situations. For example, use this tool to assess progress on a unit of study with analysis of student progress using student work. This tool helps group students who are above, at, or below grade level for one unit.

Step 1
Ask the team to review and analyze the data or student work.

Step 2
Discuss the findings and look for opportunities to understand what happened and why it happened.

Step 3
Determine the next steps and plan for all students to meet the standards.

Step 4
Adapt this tool for use with benchmark-assessment data, survey data, student work, and so on.

A Guide for Using Data to Plan Actions or Address Identified Needs

Unit _____   Date _____   Grade Level _____

Here's What!	So What?	Now What?

• What happened?
• What specific facts and data inform the decision?
• What stands out?
• What trends do we see?
• What are students in each group able to do?
• What do they know?
	• So, what does this mean?
	• Conclusions (be careful not to focus on test questions or format)?
	• Why do we think this happened?
	• What is the next level of learning for each group of students?
	• Students are . . .
	• Students are not . . .
		• What do we do now?
		• Implications?
		• What will we do to move students to the next level of learning?
		• What will be the focus of our lesson plans?
		  • Students need opportunities to . . .
		  • Students need to be exposed to . . .

Here's What . . .	**So What?**	**Now What?**

Clustering Students		
Here's What . . .	**So What?**	**Now What?**
Group one: Above expected level		
Group two: Meets expected level		
Group three: Below expected level		

Reference

Wellman, B., & Lipton, L. (2011). *Groups at Work: Strategies and Structures for Professional Learning.* Sherman, CT: MiraVia.

CHAPTER 4

Preparing to Design School-Based Professional Learning

If you don't know where you are going, any road will get you there.

—LEWIS CARROLL (CHESHIRE CAT TO ALICE IN *ALICE IN WONDERLAND*; PARAPHRASED)

To move forward, identify a destination and create a road map. Begin by analyzing data to identify current and emerging needs, which will trigger discussions about setting priorities, developing goals, and specifying how to achieve them. Next, identify desired changes in educator knowledge, attitudes, skills, aspirations, and behaviors (KASABs) to determine the actions that bring about those changes. Finally, develop a theory of change to provide a road map showing the actions that will generate the changes and their indicators of success. This chapter focuses on establishing priorities and goals to address identified needs, and introduces the theory of change as a tool for planning and organizing the work and engaging stakeholders.

Planning is an iterative process that may include two steps forward and one step backward, with an added sidestep. Planners need patience and persistence to succeed in this work. Planning begins with clarifying the foundational beliefs that drive decision making, setting goals and long- and short-term outcomes, planning the theory of change, identifying leading and lagging indicators to prepare for gathering progress data, and working simultaneously on creating the structures that support collaborative work. This work is a "big lift" that requires thoughtful and deliberate effort from many.

It is most effective to determine where you are going and then plan a way to get there. That means clarifying a school's vision, mission, and values first, creating goals based on those, and then developing specific outcomes that define the changes necessary to achieve the goals.

The language educators use in planning varies across schools and school systems, so the terms we use in this book may not be synonymous with the words you use in every situation. For example, just as some call schools *campuses*, sometimes they refer to *goals* as *key performance targets*. We offer definitions and some synonyms to facilitate the crossover. Although this book focuses on planning for professional learning, that planning is nested inside a school's improvement plan, which is often nested inside an annual district-improvement plan or a school-system strategic

plan. A school-improvement plan outlines the specific goals for a school and the actions educators plan to achieve them. It often serves to unify efforts of staff behind common schoolwide goals and is a way to assess the effectiveness of a school and its leadership team. Some school-improvement plans detail the focus for a single school year, while others might be multiyear if the goals require extended effort to achieve them. This chapter discusses clarifying a school's vision, mission, and values, setting goals, determining outcomes, and creating a theory of change.

Clarifying Vision, Mission, and Values

To start any initiative, particularly school-based professional learning planning, stakeholders need to join to review, revise, or write their foundational beliefs to guide their many decisions. A school's vision, mission, and values clarify its purpose, what problems it is trying to solve, and what beliefs govern how to solve them.

Before beginning work on a school's vision, mission, and values, consider ethnographer and inspirational speaker Simon Sinek's (2011) Golden Circle model, which emphasizes the power of starting with the *why*. The *Golden Circle* describes a value proposition about how leaders inspire change. Portrayed in three concentric circles, the Golden Circle places *why* at the heart, followed with *how*, then *what*. Sinek (2011) proposes leaders communicate the *why* because it engenders the passion that influences others to engage with the organization. Once the *why* is clear, people will want to know the *how*, or the actions to realize the purpose. The *what* is the achieved results or the outcome of the actions.

The stakeholders involved in reviewing, revising, or writing the vision, missions, and values may include the school's leadership team or a representative and diverse ad hoc team the school leadership explicitly creates for this purpose. The team may include representatives of the entire staff, community, students, and external partners. Wide representation has the advantage of infusing diverse perspectives and innovative ideation into the work. Including student voice brings an essential element to the work. Do this by including representative students, as age appropriate, or by meeting regularly to seek student perspectives and input as the work progresses.

Essentially, the team answers the following questions.

- ▶ What is the mission of our school?
- ▶ What is our vision of excellence in learning?
- ▶ What foundational values, propositions, or beliefs guide our decision making?

To check whether the vision, mission, and values are living in the school, we query staff and students for examples. Many schools already have vision, mission, and values or belief statements. However, often these documents exist only on paper rather than as living, breathing documents that inspire and inform decision making.

Many stakeholders refer to the school's vision, mission, and values only for student learning rather than for *all* learners, adults and students. Taking time periodically to review and update these documents is one way to keep them alive. Another important task is determining whether the documents incorporate continuous learning for adults and students in a school. The next sections will cover how to develop vision, mission, and values statements.

Developing the Vision Statement

Vision statements are lofty ideals the school aspires to. The following are vision statements for Port Morris schools and Summit Hill School District 161:

> P.S./M.S. 5 Port Morris School of Community Leadership (2021): Our vision is to prepare our students for a rapidly changing world by instilling in them critical thinking skills, a global perspective, and a respect for core values of honesty, loyalty, perseverance, and compassion.

> Summit Hill School District 161 (n.d.) ELL Vision Statement: Our vision is to ensure that our English Language Learners have meaningful access to rigorous instruction, materials, and academic choices. We will ensure equity for English learners while maintaining their cultural and linguistic identity.

Weston Public Schools (n.d.) offers a more elaborate statement but similarly focuses on student learners:

> Weston Public Schools and the wider school community are committed to multiple pathways toward excellence and achievement for all students.

> Students will imagine, reflect, and innovate within a safe, equitable, and responsive learning environment that develops their academic, social, and emotional growth and holistic well-being.

> Students will develop the critical thinking, creative problem solving, technological and media literacy, communication, and collaboration skills necessary for civic engagement and lifelong learning.

By replacing *students* with *learners* in the Weston Public Schools' vision statement, it will encompass student and adult learners in a school. This shift signals that learning is not something done to young people but is instead a responsibility and expectation of all community members. Visions about continuous learning and discovery cement the notion that learning is a lifelong journey.

Answer the following questions.

▸ How does the vision statement of our school include all learners regardless of their age?

▸ How does the vision statement create a lifelong aspiration for learning?

See the reproducible "Developing Vision, Mission, and Values Statements" (page 81).

Developing the Mission Statement

A *mission statement* expresses what the school does, defines its primary function or purpose, and identifies its responsibilities. For example, when analyzing skills employers seek in employees, educators and researchers Joseph A. Rios, Guangming Ling, Robert Pugh, David Becker, and Adam Bacall (2020) identify written and oral communication, problem-solving skills, and collaboration as the primary skills employers list in job advertisements.

Here are some sample mission statements:

We, the faculty and staff of Braddock Middle School, believe that all students can achieve. We are dedicated to providing an academic environment that will ensure student success. To this end, we will provide:

- A safe and orderly campus for all students
- Curricula that aligns with the Maryland Content Standards/Core Curriculum
- Daily instruction meeting individual student needs
- Programs and activities that enhance academic achievement, as well as each student's social and emotional growth. (Braddock Middle School, n.d.)

Sometimes, a mission statement can be succinct, like the one for Horseheads Central School District (2020): "Explore, Empower, Excel."

Other times, mission statements can have broad strategies that connect to the community:

The mission of the Three Village Central School District, in concert with its families and community, is to provide an educational environment which will enable each student to achieve a high level of academic proficiency and to become a well-rounded individual who is an involved, responsible citizen. (Three Village Central School District, 2022)

Many school mission statements only address students. For example, the mission statement, *Preparing young people for life after high school*, does not address the learning of adults in a school. However, an adaptation of that statement, *Preparing learners to succeed in life and work*, recognizes continuous life- and career-long learning for students *and* adults. Review your mission statement and answer the following questions.

▸ What is the primary purpose of our school, and how does that purpose apply to all in the school?

▸ What is our school's mission in relationship to learning for adults?

▸ What percent of the staff and student body can state the school's mission?

See the reproducible "Developing Vision, Mission, and Values Statements" (page 81).

Developing the Values Statement

Values are the beliefs that drive your practices. They express the foundational propositions on which educators make decisions and act. The following are sample values statements that use the term *learners* rather than *students* and express what all engaged in the learning process value in the school:

Respect: We believe in creating a safe, secure learning environment where respect, honesty, and appreciation of individual differences are fostered.

Collaboration: We believe cultivating and maintaining partnerships is essential.

High Expectations: We believe maintaining rigorous standards and high expectations for all learners are key to academic excellence and lifelong learning.

Responsibility: We believe that motivating learners to become independent learners leads to taking responsibility for their own learning.

Equity: We believe in providing all learners with a balanced curriculum aligned with quality instruction.

Pride: We believe in instilling a sense of pride in our schools and community (Norton Public Schools, n.d.)

Other examples describe the values for school staff and students:

We are committed to recognizing the importance of communication and to encouraging dialogue among all constituencies; to promoting intellectual and social growth and development within the school community; to providing a safe, supportive setting so that students have the opportunity to explore and to clarify their own beliefs and values, to take risks, and to think and speak for themselves; and to recognizing and responding to individual and institutional prejudices, both overt and subtle, based on gender, race, religion, ethnicity, sexual orientation, socio-economic status, age, and physical and mental ability. (Drew, 2022)

See the reproducible "Developing Vision, Mission, and Values Statements" (page 81).

Setting Goals

Goals act as guideposts for the journey, helping educators determine if they are on course. The primary goal continues to be increased success for staff and students. Test scores often measure the success of schools, yet these scores represent only a portion of what learners need to be successful. In addition to academic content knowledge and skills, students require competence in the following areas.

- How to adapt to changing environments
- How to communicate
- How to cooperate
- How to make decisions
- How to solve problems
- How to be responsible
- How to be critical thinkers
- How to be creative thinkers

Goals define the desired state schools seek to achieve. They are often lofty statements such as *Produce responsible citizens.* Specific, measurable, achievable, relevant, and time-bound (SMART) goals can make goals precise (Conzemius & O'Neill, 2014). Regardless of how schools and school systems delineate their end points, the stakeholders want clarity about where to be effective and efficient in their actions to achieve goals and maximize resources and effort along the way.

Educators extrapolate goals from vision statements. For example, at the P.S./M.S. 5 Port Morris School of Community Leadership (2021) vision statement (see page 73) may establish the following goal for students: *Increase learners' capacity to apply critical-thinking skills in independent and collaborative decision making and problem solving.*

For a student goal about the ability to apply critical thinking, the concomitant professional learning goal for educators reflects what educators need to achieve to meet the student goal. The sample educator goal that aligns with the previous student goal is: *Increase educators' integration of critical-thinking skills as specified in the critical-thinking learning progression into classroom instruction and learning tasks.*

Neither goal is measurable yet. Goals become measurable by identifying the specific indicators of success you use to measure each goal. While goals tend to be aspirational with lofty outcomes (we will discuss in more detail later), educators transform the lofty goals into specific, measurable outcomes. In addition to being specific and measurable, what makes a goal SMART is making it achievable and relevant to the particular situation by basing it on data analysis and determining the time frame for achieving the goal (Conzemius & O'Neill, 2014).

Determining Outcomes

Outcomes are descriptions of the specific, measurable changes necessary to achieve the goal. These changes emerge from data analysis, research, evidence about what works, and hypotheses about what will make a difference. What do students need to become more effective critical thinkers? Because this book focuses on professional learning, we'll concentrate our attention there; however, there are systemic elements necessary to achieve the goal in addition to staff competencies. They include the following.

- ▸ A delineation of critical-thinking skills

- ▸ A critical-thinking learning progression that specifies which critical-thinking skills are developmentally appropriate and the sequence of how to address those skills throughout the preK–12 curriculum

- ▸ Instructional materials that integrate critical-thinking skills

- ▸ A critical-thinking skills curriculum

- ▸ Assessments for critical-thinking skills

The KASAB framework is useful for specifying outcomes for educator professional learning (Killion, 2018). The *KASAB framework* delineates the full range of changes educators need to achieve the established goal. Because learning is so often reduced to transferring information, the framework helps professional learning designers and learners themselves clarify all the changes they need in the multiple elements of learning to achieve the goals. By delineating outcomes for each element of learning, professional learning designers can address how to achieve each outcome. For example, you can specify the outcomes for educator professional learning using the framework and the previous goal about critical thinking.

- ▸ **K = knowledge:** What does the instructional staff need to know to integrate critical-thinking skills into instruction and classroom tasks?

  - • *Example*—Ninety percent of the instructional staff define the six critical-thinking skills embedded in the critical-thinking learning progression.

- ▸ **A = attitudes:** What does the instructional staff need to believe when integrating critical-thinking skills into instruction and classroom tasks?

- *Example*—Ninety percent of the instructional staff express in interviews and focus groups the belief that teaching critical-thinking skills is a core component of the preK–12 curriculum and essential for success in school and beyond.

▶ **S = skills:** What does the instructional staff need to be able to do to integrate critical-thinking skills into instruction and classroom tasks?

- *Example*—Ninety percent of the instructional staff develop a unit of study that integrates developmentally appropriate critical-thinking skills from the critical-thinking skills learning progression and explains how the skills support the unit's learning intentions.

▶ **A = aspirations:** What does the instructional staff need to want to do to integrate critical-thinking skills into instruction and classroom tasks?

- *Example*—Ninety percent of the instructional staff express (in interviews and focus groups) the motivation to integrate critical-thinking skills into classroom instruction and learning tasks.

▶ **B = behaviors:** What does the instructional staff need to do to integrate critical-thinking skills into instruction and classroom tasks?

- *Example*—Ninety percent of the instructional staff integrate explicit instruction on critical-thinking skills into classroom instruction and learning tasks at least once per week.

- *Example*—Ninety percent of the instructional staff integrate critical-thinking skills from the critical-thinking skills learning progression into classroom instruction and learning tasks at least three times per week.

We contend the overarching purpose of professional learning in education is to improve student success. Because teachers and administrators' actions influence student success, professional learning seeks to refine, extend, and strengthen educators' competencies so their actions impact student learning. Unfortunately, most professional learning fails to address all five essential elements of KASAB and, therefore, limits the opportunity for deep change in educators.

For example, when teachers learn about a new instructional method, the professional learning often addresses their knowledge and skill level. Then, adding coaching to supplement these outcomes addresses their behavior or use of the knowledge and skill. Yet, professional learning rarely focuses on developing both their attitudes and aspirations sufficiently to sustain the change beyond the initial trial and occasional use. Deep, sustained change requires attention to all five KASAB elements in the learning process. When educators delineate KASAB outcomes, it is possible to plan how to achieve them. See the reproducible "Writing KASABs" (page 84).

> Deep, sustained change requires attention to all five KASAB elements in the learning process.

Creating the Theory of Change

A *theory of change* uses outcomes to map how change will occur. It contains three fundamental components: (1) the actions needed to reach the outcomes, (2) the sequence of these actions, and (3) the assumptions on which the actions and assumptions rest (Killion, 2018). A theory of change provides a picture of the desired result and how schools will achieve it. Those involved in any aspect of learning also have a record of what works and doesn't work when they pause to update and review their theory of change throughout the learning process.

Applying the theory of change to the critical-thinking goal might look like figure 4.1 (page 78). The assumptions embedded in the critical-thinking theory of change include the following.

▸ Developing the reason *why* is a crucial first step in any change initiative (step 1).

▸ Participating in multiple learning experiences leads to change (steps 2, 3, and 6).

▸ Engaging learners builds motivation and buy-in (steps 2, 3, 6, and 8).

▸ Emphasizing revision and adaptation lessens the effort associated with change (steps 4, 5, and 7).

▸ Coaching facilitates the implementation of new learning (step 7).

▸ Building clarity of expectations facilitates implementation (steps 4 and 9).

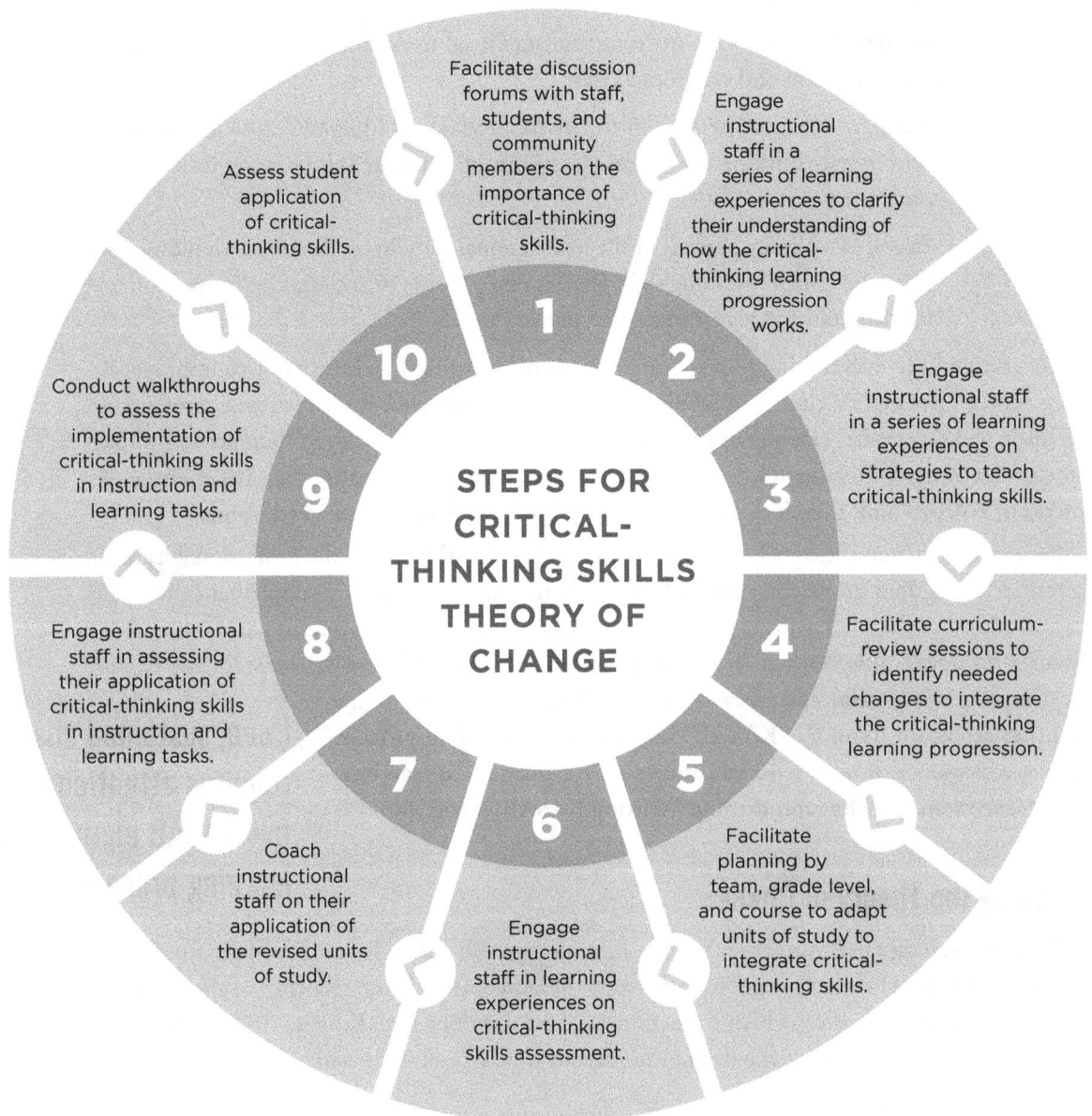

FIGURE 4.1: Steps for critical-thinking skills theory of change.

Educators can draw assumptions from research or practice. For example, researchers Bruce R. Joyce and Beverly Showers (2002) and Matthew A. Kraft and David L. Blazar (2017) report coaching positively impacts teacher effectiveness and student achievement. Therefore, building on this research, the professional learning leadership team integrates coaching into the theory of change because it is a research-based practice that accelerates the transfer of learning to practice.

Educators best develop theories of change collaboratively with stakeholders responsible for contributing to and reaching the outcomes. Those stakeholders might be an existing team (such as a grade-level, course, department, or school leadership team) or an ad hoc team. The process is recursive, with multiple opportunities to revisit and revise as you develop a theory of change. The thought processes various stakeholders use will vary. Some are linear and lockstep in their thinking, while others are random. The beautiful marriage of both types of thinking (and everything in between) contributes to a solid theory of change.

A theory of change also documents what professional learning and other concomitant system supports are necessary to achieve outcomes and goals. The completed theory of change maps out the intentions and how each component supports the others, giving leaders and those responsible for change implementation a plan to follow. It is also flexible, so educators can adjust it as needed.

A school leadership team can add helpful notes to the theory of change about adjustments made to the plan for unexpected successes or challenges. The team can use these notes to establish and monitor the professional learning efforts and interim benchmarks of success. The theory of change becomes a guiding document for a professional learning program and subsequent professional learning planning. A theory of change is a core tool for planning, monitoring, and evaluating professional learning. See the reproducible "Developing the Theory of Change" (page 87) for guidance on best practices for developing a theory of change. Chapter 7 (page 151) provides more about monitoring and evaluating professional learning.

Conclusion

Clarity about the desired results serves as the foundation for designing and implementing school-based professional learning. Without that clarity, any work might be wasted. Because resources, especially time and effort, are limited in schools, it's crucial to ensure professional learning is effective and efficient.

Aligning a school's vision, mission, and values, delineating goals and outcomes, and creating a theory of change will increase the efficiency and effectiveness of a school's improvement work and the success and satisfaction of contributors.

Leadership Tips

For leaders to successfully prepare for designing school-based professional learning, it is essential to determine the schools vision, mission, and values. The following tips will help you get started.

- ▸ Consider a past successful change in the school that required extensive learning from staff. Identify what made this change a success. Next, identify any challenges and how educators addressed them. Finally, list the conclusions you can draw from that experience.

▶ Examine the current vision, mission, and values to determine how the school addresses learning for educators and students.

▶ Engage the school leaders or professional learning team in writing value statements for professional learning in the school.

▶ Examine theories of change for past improvement initiatives to learn what contributed to the success.

▶ Develop a theory of change for the current or emerging professional learning initiative.

Reflection Questions

1. What is the role of a school's vision, mission, and values in professional learning?

2. How does professional learning align with the school's strategic priorities or goals?

3. Of the five KASABs, which do educators most frequently include as professional learning outcomes? What contributes to this inclusion? How can educators re-engineer professional learning to address all five elements?

4. What is the theory of change about the current professional learning in the school? How did educators develop the theory of change, and how did they use it to guide the work?

5. What assumptions does the current professional learning make? How did educators determine those assumptions?

Developing Vision, Mission, and Values Statements

Leadership teams use this tool to develop, review, or revise the school's vision, mission, and values statements.

PURPOSE To develop vision, mission, and values statements to guide the work of each team, encompassing all faculty and staff

PRODUCT Adopted vision, mission, and values statements

PARTICIPANTS Sometimes the school leadership team drafts the vision, mission, and values, and then engages staff in providing input to the process and a review of the drafts. Other times, the full staff is involved in the process.

MATERIALS Chart paper, sticky notes, markers

TIME Three to six hours, depending on whether participants are revising the current vision, mission, and values or developing a new one

PREPARATION Prepare directions for each of the protocols the team or staff will use to develop the vision, mission, and values statements.

PROCESS **Developing the Vision Statement**

Vision statements inspire and inform. They describe what an organization (or individual) aspires to, what drives it, and what gives it purpose. In his book, *The Vision-Driven Leader* (2020), leadership, productivity, and goal-setting expert and author Michael Hyatt describes the power of a vision to create a clear and compelling picture of the intended future. This vision guides decisions and actions to achieve that future.

Step 1

Discuss powerful visions. Some examples follow.

- Convention on the Rights of the Child (United Nations, 1989)
- Declaration of Rights of the Women of the United States (Anthony, Gage, & Stanton, 1876)
- Martin Luther King Jr.'s "I Have a Dream" Speech in Its Entirety (King, 1963)
- President John F. Kennedy's Inaugural Address (Kennedy, 1961)
- Our Vision Statement (World Vision, 2022)
- Who We Are (Save the Children, n.d.)

Step 2

Invite participants to name other visions that have a powerful influence on your country or schools.

Step 3

Share a few sample vision statements. Find several in the section, Developing the Vision Statement (page 73), and many others online.

Step 4

Project five or more years into the future and describe your vision of that future. Write visions in the present tense. So don't say, "We *will* be . . .;" say, "We *are*. . ."

Step 5

One protocol you can use to guide the vision process is the *affinity process*. To use this protocol, follow these directions.

- Write one idea on each sticky note, large enough for people to read.
- When you have run out of ideas, post your ideas on a shared wall. Use the ideas on the wall to trigger more ideas, and keep writing.
- Group posts and looks for themes on the shared wall.
- If you are aligning a school vision with a district vision, look for ideas that connect the responsibilities.
- Cluster the sticky notes and label the emerging themes.
- Break into small theme groups and ask members to write a narrative (one or two sentences) for that theme.
- Write the narrative on chart paper, and then share and edit it using a carousel process.
- Put themes together into one vision statement.
- Review first draft of ideas and use a group editing process to finalize the vision statement.
- Assign an editor or small group of editors to review the statement and revise it.
- Bring the vision statement back to the group for adoption.

PROCESS **Developing a Mission Statement**

A *mission statement* starts with determining what is unique about a school, what it cares most about, and what it does (Alegre, Berbegal-Mirabent, Guerrero, & Mas-Machuca, 2018). It is what gives meaning to a school which, according to organizational experts Ana Mendy, Mary Lass Stewart, and Kate VanAtkin (2020) "can be found in a deeper, more collective sense of purpose or mission" (p. 31). A mission statement captures the *essence of the vision* a community has for the future. It represents a commitment, a promise, an agenda, and a guide against which educators decide actions. It is a shared snapshot of the ultimate purpose of the organization all members share. It is generally short and easy to remember, and it does not include goals or specific objectives.

Step 1

Discuss powerful missions statements. Find several examples in the section, Developing the Mission Statement (page 73) and many others online.

Step 2

Invite participants to name other missions that have a powerful influence on an organization.

Step 3

Share a few sample mission statements. (To find examples online, we looked up humanities missions when working with a group of humanities teachers, CTE missions when working with a group of CTE teachers, and missions for large urban schools when working with the faculty of a large urban school.)

Step 4

One protocol you can use to guide the mission process is the *pyramid process*. To use this protocol, follow these directions.

- Each person writes a mission statement for the organization that aligns with the system mission.
- Two individuals pair up, put their best ideas together, and write one mission statement using the best of their individual ideas.
- Then, those two people pair up with two others, creating a team of four, and again putting their best ideas together to write one mission statement.
- Keep pairing up with others until everyone is building one or two statements. If there are two, ask each group to write their mission statement on a piece of chart paper. Look for commonalities and build a single mission statement.

PROCESS **Developing the Values Statement**

Values statements are the *beliefs* that guide the work of adults, students, and community members. They support and advance the vision and the mission, focus on driving learning for all, are written in the present tense, are specific, and speak to who you are (as a school) and what is important to the school.

One protocol you can use to guide the beliefs process is the *beginning-with-a-sample process*. To use this protocol, follow these directions.

Step 1

Divide the group into teams of three or four.

Step 2

Review a few powerful values statements. (Begin by looking at state, district, or other school beliefs, which are easy to find online.) Look for values statements of schools similar to yours—rural, urban, diverse, suburban, and so on). Find several in the section, Developing the Values Statement (page 74) and many others online.

Step 3

Look for ideas that resonate with your beliefs.

Step 4

Begin drafting four values statements on chart paper. Prepare to share these statements with the large group.

Step 5

Look for overlaps and similarities. Revise statements.

Step 6

Give each person ten (or fewer) dots and ask each person to choose the most powerful values statements. Use the dots to set priorities.

Step 7

Determine how many statements you want. (Most groups choose ten or fewer.)

Step 8

Assign an editor or small group of editors to review the statements and revise them.

Step 9

Bring the values statements back to the group for adoption.

Writing KASABs

This tool helps leadership teams determine the specific changes necessary for educators to achieve the results they desire. It can also serve as the framework for the professional learning content.

PURPOSE To guide district and school stakeholders as they develop lists of the knowledge, attitudes, skills, aspirations, and behaviors (KASABs) for professional learning

PRODUCT A chart to guide the design and planning of professional learning

PARTICIPANTS Some groups choose to ask the school leadership team, professional learning team, or professional learning facilitators to draft the KASABs

MATERIALS Chart paper, sticky notes, markers, training materials, references, and the following table

TIME Time for this task depends on the number of outcomes (Participants need twenty to forty-five minutes to delineate the KASABs for each goal and outcome)

PREPARATION A copy of vision and goals, preferably posted on large chart paper to use as reference

PROCESS **Step 1**
Define the learning outcomes for each professional learning program you want to plan.

Step 2
Make a list of what KASABs participants need to learn during the professional learning to achieve the desired goals. Answer these questions.

- **Knowledge:** What do educators need to know?
- **Attitudes:** What do educators need to believe?
- **Skills:** What skills do educators need?
- **Aspirations:** What aspirations, internal motivation, and clarity of purpose do educators need to inspire them to sustain application of new learning?
- **Behaviors and practices:** What do educators need to do routinely to achieve the goals?

Step 3
Discuss and agree about the level of learning participants need to achieve to be successful.

Step 4
Determine how participants will demonstrate acquisition of the learning outcomes.

Step 5
Share a draft of outcomes, KASABs, and levels of learning, and ask for feedback from a trusted team of colleagues (teacher leaders, school and central administrators, and others).

Ask the trusted team to give you their perspective about the following.

- Clarity and specificity
- Outcomes versus activities
- Application of learning

page 1 of 3

KASAB	Description	**Define Your Learning Outcomes** 1. What KASABs do participants need to learn? 2. What is the level of learning they need to achieve to be successful? 3. How will *you* know they have acquired the learning?
Knowledge	Conceptual understanding of information, theories, principles, and research	What do educators need to know and understand to be successful in implementing the new learning? The following questions help define the knowledge outcomes for a critical-thinking program. 1. What is critical thinking? 2. What critical-thinking skills will students learn? 3. What is the learning progression for critical-thinking skills for students? 4. What critical-thinking skills do we expect of students?
Attitudes	Beliefs about the value of particular information or strategies	What dispositions, attitudes, or beliefs will support educators in using and sustaining their learning? 1. What are the foundational beliefs that support educators' use of critical-thinking skills as a core part of their interactions with students and colleagues? 2. What are the values we share about students becoming critical thinkers?
Skills	Strategies and processes to apply knowledge	What skills or competencies do educators need to succeed with the new learning? 1. What do educators need to do to teach critical-thinking skills to students? 2. What do educators need to be able to do to integrate critical thinking into the curriculum? 3. What do educators need to do to assess critical thinking? 4. What do educators need to do to use critical-thinking skills in their interactions with one another? 5. What do educators need to do to encourage students' use of critical-thinking skills? 6. What do educators need to do to communicate to parents, families, and community members about the importance of students becoming critical thinkers?
Aspirations	Desires, dispositions, or internal motivation to engage in a particular practice	What motivates or inspires educators to apply their learning? 1. What are the internal drivers that encourage educators to persist with teaching and using critical-thinking skills? 2. What do educators aspire to that relates to the use of critical-thinking skills in their own work and with students? 3. When educators are frustrated with their own efforts or students' to use critical-thinking skills, what messages will inspire them to continue?

Elevate School-Based Professional Learning © 2023 Solution Tree Press • SolutionTree.com
Visit **go.SolutionTree.com/leadership** to download this free reproducible.

KASAB	Description	**Define Your Learning Outcomes** 1. What KASABs do participants need to learn? 2. What is the level of learning they need to achieve to be successful? 3. How will *you* know they have acquired the learning?
Behaviors	Consistent application of knowledge and skills the attitudes and aspirations drive	What do educators need to do to achieve the results they want? 1. What are the expected behaviors in- and outside classrooms that demonstrate educators integration of critical-thinking skills? 2. What do educators do to teach and engage students in applying critical-thinking skills? 3. What will educators do in meetings when applying critical-thinking skills? 4. What will educators do in classroom instruction, lesson and unit planning, student assessment, and learning task design and assessment that demonstrate integration of critical thinking?

Reference

Killion, J. (2018). Assessing impact: Evaluating professional learning (3rd ed.), p. 50. Thousand Oaks, CA: Corwin Press.

Developing the Theory of Change

This tool guides district and school stakeholders as they develop actions and assumptions to achieve professional learning goals.

PURPOSE To work together to determine the steps that teams can take to achieve the goals, the rationale for the actions, and the action assumptions

PRODUCT Theory of change

PARTICIPANTS Some groups choose to ask the school leadership team or the professional learning team to draft the theory of change.

MATERIALS Chart paper, sticky notes, and markers, or online tools including Google Jamboard (https://jamboard.google.com), XMind (https://xmind.app), or Mural (https://mural.co)

TIME Two hours to draft, review, and revise the theory of change

PREPARATION Copies of the vision, goals, and outcomes for reference

PROCESS **Step 1**
Clarify the goals, outcomes, and time frame for each. Remember, you can change them in the process of writing the theory of change.

Step 2
Generate assumptions or beliefs that drive or guide the work. Make a list of assumptions without seeking agreement at this point.

Step 3
Invite stakeholders to use sticky notes or online brainstorming or mind-mapping tools (such as Google Jamboard, XMind, or Mural) to generate what they believe must happen to reach the outcomes. Encourage generative thinking in no particular order.

Step 4
Ask multiple times what else stakeholders might not be considering. Probe them with questions such as the following: Who are we not thinking about including here and what might they want? Who else are we leaving out? What might they want? Who else can we support in this process? What does that support look like? Who else will need to be brought in to support this work? How do we engage them? Remember, additions to the notes will continue to surface as the process continues, so be sure to capture them.

Step 5
Clarify understanding of the proposed actions and cluster them. Eliminate direct overlaps and leave those that are different—they may provide insight into another needed action.

Step 6
Sequence the actions. Work on a whiteboard or blank canvas to arrange the proposed actions according to a time sequence. If there are many ideas, it might be helpful to cluster them first into early actions, midpoint actions, and later actions. These sequence can occur in layers for each stakeholder group or as one whole sequence. For example, when there are actions specific for administrators, parents, teachers, or others, sequence them separately or weave them into the whole.

page 1 of 2

PROCESS
(cont.)

Step 7

Revisit the time sequence and look for intersections among the various layers if used. For example, if principals are engaged in training on how to monitor classrooms for daily formative assessments, when does that action fall in relation to when teachers are participating in learning daily formative assessments, working with their teams to design the assessments, and when coaches are supporting teachers to use data from daily formative assessments to adjust instruction?

Step 8

Align the assumptions and actions, add other actions not reflected in the assumptions, and adjust assumptions as needed. During this step, seek to reach consensus on the assumptions that explain the rationale for the actions and their sequence.

CHAPTER 5

Planning School-Based Professional Learning

Tell me and I forget, teach me and I may remember, involve me and I learn.

—CHINESE PROVERB

Once school leadership or professional learning teams are clear about where they are going and have developed a theory of change as the road map for getting there, they decide what actions will lead them toward their goals. This chapter explores how to design, sustain, and share learning, and use collaborative teams to extend and refine learning. It discusses the factors to consider when selecting designs and examines various possible learning designs for individuals, teams, and the entire faculty. In addition, it guides team leaders to consider multiple protocols and processes for designing learning and facilitating rapid cycles of improvement in teams across the school. Finally, it incorporates processes for lateral learning across teams in the school.

A common mistake in planning and implementing professional learning is to decide the *how* before deciding the *what*. For example, you might hear, "Let's have a workshop" or "Let's go to the statewide literacy conference." *How* decisions are based on multiple factors that include understanding the intended results, who the learners are, what research recommends, and ways to integrate the learning into practice beyond initial learning experiences. Darling-Hammond and colleagues (2017) note that effective professional learning designs lean on research:

> Although research on the effectiveness of PD [professional development] has been mixed, positive findings have stimulated a general consensus about typical components of high-quality professional learning for teachers . . .
>
> 1. Is content focused
> 2. Incorporates **active learning** utilizing adult learning theory
> 3. Supports collaboration, typically in job-embedded contexts
> 4. Uses **models and modeling** of effective practice
> 5. Provides coaching and expert support
> 6. Offers opportunities for **feedback and reflection**
> 7. Is of sustained duration
>
> Successful PD models generally feature a number of these components simultaneously. (p. 4)

The default choice for professional learning is almost always some form of training. However, *training* is a broad term with layers of meanings for different people. Training, at its best, builds knowledge and skills, two of the five outcomes that lead to deep change (knowledge, attitudes, skills, aspirations, and behaviors or KASAB, page 76). However, training does little to address the remaining three outcomes of KASAB: attitudes, aspirations, and behaviors. So, training alone is insufficient for deep learning. Training without practice, feedback, coaching, and ongoing study lead to little transfer of learning to practice. Too often, professional learning plans and change leaders undersell the importance of comprehensive, detailed, and sufficient learning that integrates multiple forms of learning at every stage of a change effort. This chapter discusses learning design, the factors influencing the design, transferring the learning to practice, the research on learning design, and preparing the learning design.

> **Training without practice, feedback, coaching, and ongoing study lead to little transfer of learning to practice.**

Exploring Learning Design

According to the Australian Institute for Teaching and School Leadership (2014), *design* means "the process undertaken where choices are made toward developing new professional learning or reviewing existing professional learning" (p. 5). Essentially, leaders are answering the question: What are different ways to structure individual, team, and schoolwide learning for the most significant impact? The answer depends on the players, resources, and commitment to achieving the goals and outcomes. Without follow-up, sometimes called *coaching* or *extended study*, results will be moderate at best. Just as instruction for students involves art and science, the same is true in designing professional learning for educators. The *art* involves aligning learning with the learner, content, and context; the *science* involves applying research-based practices for adult learning.

In an extensive exploration of the elements of professional learning in *Designing Professional Learning*, the Australian Institute for Teaching and School Leadership (2014) summarizes the process of designing professional learning in the *learning design anatomy* (see figure 5.1, page 91), which "defines the elements of Learning Design which should inform those 'design choices'" (p. 5). Each element guides the series of decisions learning designers make to increase the likelihood that learning moves from knowing about a concept to implementing it in routine practice.

The learning design anatomy is based on the premise that professional learning responds to the context in which it occurs, such as the ecosystem of policies at the federal and local levels as well as student and educator needs. When the professional learning responds, it engages educators in learning experiences that will change their KASABs, which will change students' learning experiences in a positive direction (Australian Institute for Teaching and School Leadership, 2014; Killion, 2019). The next sections outline how each component of the learning design anatomy contributes to the success of professional learning.

Environment

In the first component, *environment*, decisions address the level of engagement, proximity to authentic practice, and the sense of safety for risk taking in implementing new learning. When the environment for learning fosters a culture of continuous improvement, learners understand the rationale for learning, have access to the necessary supports, and feel safe moving through the stages of new practice, from novice to accomplished, without threat or sanction.

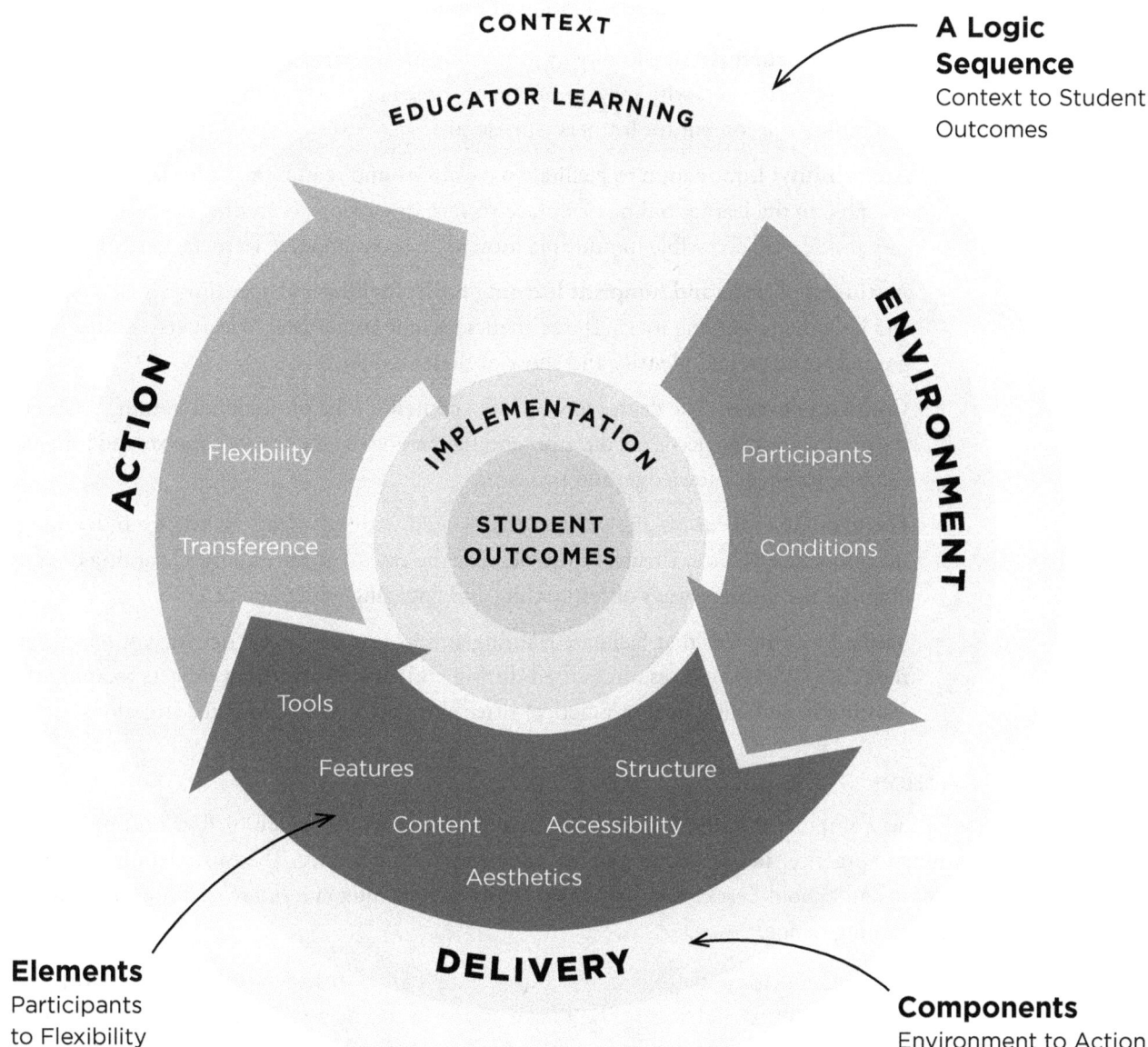

Source: © 2014 Australian Institute for Teaching and School Leadership Limited, Designing Professional Learning Report, AITSL, Melbourne, Australia. ISBN 978-0-9803323-3-9. First published: 2014.

FIGURE 5.1: Learning design anatomy.

Learning Process

The next component is the *learning process*. While the Australian Institute for Teaching and School Leadership (2014) uses the term *delivery*, we believe educators facilitate learning, rather than deliver learning. Of the many studies about effective professional learning, collaborative active participation (or engagement) is one of the core attributes historically consistent across multiple research studies (Darling-Hammond et al., 2017). Educators construct (rather than receive) learning through processes that require active engagement, experimentation, exploration, and examination (Killion, 2019). As Joyce and Showers (2002) determine, learning processes (such as presentation or demonstration) result in little transfer of learning to practice.

Areas for decisions related to the facilitation of professional learning include the following.

- ▶ **Degree of structure:** The fluidity or scaffolding of the learning progression that enhances flexibility for learners who may already have some familiarity with the content while also scaffolding the content for learners who do not

- ▶ **Accessibility:** Information to facilitate navigability and requirements for learning readily available to the learner online or in face-to-face discussions (Learning is uncomplicated, easy to use, and accessible in multiple formats to accommodate learners' needs.)

- ▶ **Aesthetics of print and nonprint learning tools:** Inviting and appealing visual, auditory, and kinesthetic learning tools (The aesthetics include connecting to learners' culture, background, context, and identity and those of their students.)

- ▶ **Content relevance:** The degree to which the content of the professional learning relates to the unique learning needs of educators and their students, the school context, and learners' prior experience, knowledge, and practice

- ▶ **Features:** The on- or off-site practices associated with how learners engage in learning, including face-to-face, virtual, or hybrid, and the ease of access and use (Learning designs consider the learners' ways of responding and engaging with content.)

- ▶ **Tools:** Learning aids that facilitate learning and its transfer to practice such as templates, models, scaffolds, and resources used during and after the learning process to apply the learning in authentic (real or practice) situations, rather than simulated situations

Action

The last component in the learning design anatomy is *action*, which focuses on transferring learning to practice. Taking action requires attention to transference. The Australian Institute for Teaching and School Leadership (2014) describes how to integrate *transference* into the professional learning design:

> Transference may be expressly supported through tailored materials and resources embedded within the learning, designed as scaffolds for use in context, such as templates, guides, or outlines. Alternately, transference may occur through the combination of elements within the learning design, for example: a series of learning experiences encouraging participants to reflect on implications of a new concept as part of a broader inquiry; examination of student data to determine needs and approach; receiving feedback from observation, linking this to theory. (p. 18)

The learning design anatomy (see figure 5.1, page 91) requires support and commitment to practice with opportunities for reflection and coaching. Implementation scientists note the importance of coaching and other forms of support, such as leadership advocacy and resources to increase efficacy, confidence, and certainty with the new practice (Fixsen, Aijaz, Fixsen, Burks, & Schultes, 2021; Fixsen, Blase, Naoom, & Duda, 2015).

In addition to transference, action acknowledges the need to address flexibility in transferring learning. The situations in which educators apply their learning vary. Facilitating understanding of how to adjust and adapt learning to various different situations prepares and supports educators to act on their new learning. Australian Institute for Teaching and School Leadership (2014) explains:

Flexible learning designs accommodate variability in application, support participants to reflect, review and reassess, and encourage a sustained, ongoing view of learning. Flexible learning designs consider how the learning may be applied and address the diversity of such applications. (p. 18)

Understanding Factors Influencing Learning Design Choices

To make sound decisions about learning design, leaders consider multiple factors, including the expected results, learner attributes, learning configurations, the learning culture, and learning supports and resources. The first four of these factors are discussed in this chapter. Explore learning supports and resources for implementing learning in chapter 6 (page 119). Additional information about a learning culture appears in chapters 3 (page 53) and 9 (page 179).

Expected Results

The intended results influence the level, rigor, and duration of learning. If the intended result is to transmit information, an hour-long webinar or a letter or email notification might suffice. If the expected result is implementation and routine use, provide opportunities for demonstrations, practice with reflection, continued refinement, and coaching.

In seminal research, Stanford University emeritus professor of education Robert N. Bush (1984), Joyce and Showers (2002), Showers (1982, 1987), and Showers, Joyce, and Barrie Bennett (1987) examined the outcomes of training for various learning-design components. Table 5.1 (page 93) summarizes the findings of these various studies.

TABLE 5.1: Effect Sizes for Training Outcomes by Training Components

	Knowledge and Information Gained	Skills Acquired	Transfer of Training to Practice
Information	0.63	0.35	0.00
Presentation of Theory	0.15	0.50	0.00
Demonstration	1.65	0.26	0.00
Theory + Demonstration	0.66	0.86	0.00
Theory + Demonstration + Practice	1.15	0.72	0.00
Theory + Demonstration + Practice + Feedback	1.31	1.18	0.39
Theory + Demonstration + Practice + Feedback + Coaching	2.71	1.25	1.68

Source: Killion & Harrison, 2017, p. 15. Used with permission of Learning Forward, www.learningforward.org. All rights reserved.

As educator and researcher Saul McLeod (2019) explains, "Effect size is a quantitative measure of the magnitude of the experimental effect. The larger the effect size the stronger the relationship between two variables." An effect size over 0.5 is considered a strong relationship. Studies find when educator learning includes information alone (as in a lecture format), participants were likely to remember what they heard, yet less likely to know how to use the information or apply the learning in their practice (as cited in Killion & Harrison, 2017). When learning includes a combination of underlying theory, demonstration of the learning, opportunities to practice, engagement in feedback processes, and participation in coaching, participants were far more likely to know the information, show what it looks like in practice, and use the learning in their practice to address problems (as cited in Killion & Harrison, 2017).

If *learning* means to change behavior and thinking, then the traditional forms of pedagogy trainers use in professional learning, often called *sit and gets*, will not generate those results. This is because these traditional forms of learning, as psychologists Steven Katz and Lisa Ain Dack (2013) describe, assume "the mind is devoid of ideas that need to be transferred from the expert to the learner. This is the idea of 'mind as a container' where the goal is to fill it with knowledge that is missing" (p. 27). Following this assumption, learning is a process of transmitting information from a knowledgeable other to the learner.

Katz and Dack (2013) further acknowledge this assumption falls short of the research on learning, noting, "True learning happens when the learner is an active participant in constructing knowledge and in constantly thinking about how new knowledge confirms or challenges previously existing beliefs and ideas" (p. 27). This assumption about what constitutes learning is consistent with the research-based attributes of effective professional learning and *Standards for Professional Learning* (Darling-Hammond et al., 2017; Learning Forward, 2022).

Knowing the intended goals and outcomes guide the scope and design of professional learning. However, not all professional learning has the same results. Imagine a school focused on increasing equity in classroom instructional experiences. This school has multiple options for how to design learning. Table 5.2 (page 95) looks at KASAB outcomes, learning designs for each, and how educators can scaffold both the KASABs and learning designs to build a comprehensive professional learning program. (See more information on KASABs in chapter 4, page 76.)

Learner Attributes

Learners learn differently, exhibit different readiness levels for learning, and have varying ability levels for learning experiences. They have different learning preferences regarding how they receive and process information. In addition, they require different levels of support and opportunities for practice, sometimes based on their current knowledge and practice related to the expected outcomes. Some learn best by trial and error or discovery; others by careful, detailed guidance and intensive support; some individually; and some in teams. Some respond more immediately to a request for change, while others are slower to respond and need mandates. Their levels of commitment and willingness to engage in learning vary as well.

Figure 5.2 (page 97) depicts a helpful model for examining learner attributes. It guides a school's professional learning or leadership team to consider the differences among learners as they plan learning designs.

The adapted model in figure 5.2 (page 97) offers guidance on when to use in-school or external expertise. While some might perceive it as prescriptive, this adaptation intends to be a way to meet each learner's unique needs. As the saying goes, "Prescription without diagnosis is malpractice." When teams use data and consider learners as individuals, their work in choosing learning designs will be responsive rather than prescriptive.

TABLE 5.2: KASAB-Based Learning Designs

If the Outcome (KASAB) Is . . .	A Sample Outcome Might Be . . .	A Possible Learning Design to Achieve This Outcome Might Be . . .
Knowledge	Increase teachers' understanding of how students in different populations experience school.	An efficient learning design for this outcome is a lecture, series of webinars, TED Talks, presentations, or book studies on how different ethnic and racial groups value and engage with the education system. Participants build understanding, but they likely will not change their practice to alter classroom experiences for students.
Attitudes	Cultivate a belief that all students deserve a fair and equitable learning experience every day and teacher decisions make a difference in creating these learning experiences.	To achieve this outcome, in a series of four sixty-minute sessions, educators analyze student data to construct an understanding of differences among student groups in academic performance, attendance, engagement in extra- and cocurricular activities, perception of safety, and other factors.\n\nNext, educators shadow students to observe how they experience learning. They also interview students or engage students in focus groups. They meet with parents and listen to their expectations of the school. After educators analyze the data, they use their findings to formulate a set of schoolwide beliefs to guide teaching and learning.\n\nFinally, educators reflect privately or with a colleague, coach, mentor, or supervisor on how the schoolwide beliefs align with their personal beliefs about equity in student-learning experiences and what their role as a member of the staff is in contributing to equity across the school and in their classrooms. At the end of these experiences, educators increase their appreciation of how they contribute to equity in student-learning experiences; however, they are unlikely to know how to build greater equity in their classrooms for their diverse students.
Skills	Acquire the ability to select instructional resources responsive to and respectful of students' backgrounds and identities.	To achieve this outcome, educators read a research article on the criteria for aligning instructional resources with student backgrounds, examine criteria from multiple sources for selecting instructional materials, and develop their own criteria for selecting culturally responsive instructional resources.\n\nNext, educators use the criteria to examine various resources in use across the school and in their classrooms for alignment. Finally, they might determine if there is a need to alter, eliminate, or introduce instructional materials so those in use more closely align with their students' backgrounds and identities.

continued ➡

If the Outcome (KASAB) Is . . .	A Sample Outcome Might Be . . .	A Possible Learning Design to Achieve This Outcome Might Be . . .
		When finished with this series of experiences, educators will know how to identify instructional materials that meet the identified criteria; however, they will not necessarily know how to use those resources in their current classroom curriculum.
Aspirations	Commit to engage each student every day in positive interaction to foster safe and productive relationships.	To support building commitment to increasing equity in their classroom learning experiences, educators discuss what they aspire to do, set a plan of action to address their aspiration, establish criteria for their success, determine how to gather ongoing evidence of their commitment, and build a learning team of colleagues to support one another and with whom they can reflect on their growth. All these actions will demonstrate educators' intent to act on their commitment; however, it is not yet evidence of acting on that commitment. Intent is the first step, yet it is insufficient alone.
Behaviors	Integrate instructional resources responsive to and respectful of students' backgrounds and identities.	A behavior outcome often is an accumulation of the previous outcomes. When a learner gains knowledge, shifts or clarifies attitudes or beliefs, gains skills, and commits, behaviors are far more likely to change. When their behavior changes, educators can affect student-learning experiences. Educators are more likely to change when they feel confident, have clarity, know how to make changes, and have support in applying their learning. To achieve the behavior outcome, educators meet in content or grade-level teams to plan the changes they will make in their units or courses of study, work together to make those changes, visit one another's classrooms to observe the implementation of the changes, and examine student work to reflect on the effects of their changes. Collaborative settings with nonsupervisory colleagues (such as peers, mentors, or coaches) create safe places for educators to ask questions, clarify their understanding, acknowledge when they feel challenged or unsure, engage in a feedback process to assess their progress, and benefit from the collective wisdom of their learning partners. Behavior changes over time become routines that facilitate practice and create the opportunity to re-examine their work and engage in continuous improvement.

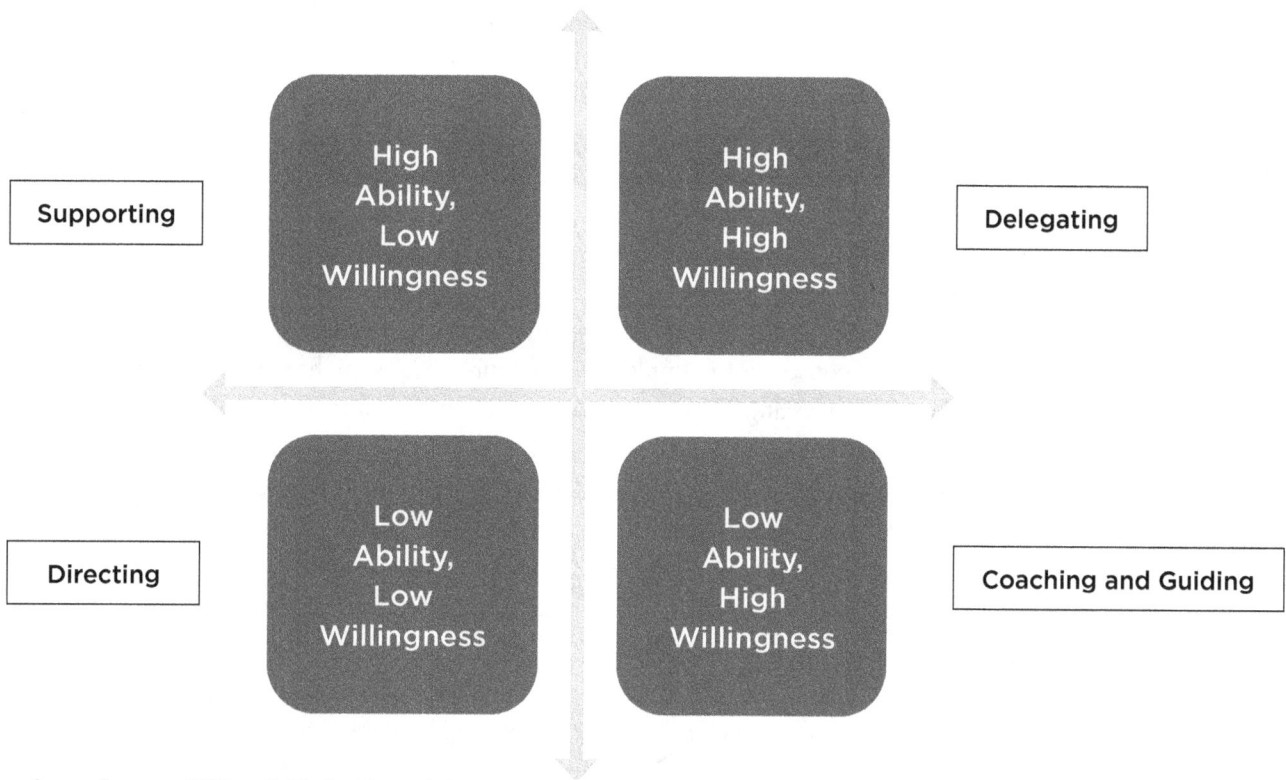

Source: Sommers, 2021, p. 3. Used with permission.

FIGURE 5.2: An adapted model of situational leadership with leadership styles.

Using collected data about educators (see chapter 4, page 75), teams consider learner ability and willingness, and use the information to choose learning designs that will meet the intended learning outcomes. The lower-right quadrant of figure 5.2 (page 97) includes people who are willing to learn and work together. For example, consider a fifth-grade team that has strong congeniality. Team members bring home-baked goodies to their meetings, often share personal stories of their children, commiserate when one member is struggling with a personal issue, and care deeply for one another as friends. However, their commitment to extending their learning and changing their professional practice is limited (low ability).

They may be comfortable with their work because it requires little effort—effort they redirect to their social interactions. With these attributes in mind, the leadership team plans to meet the fifth-grade team and individual members where they are. The leadership team minimizes training because it is unlikely to be effective. Instead, it increases coaching, mentoring, model teaching, micro-modeling, or lesson study to move the fifth-grade team to explore new approaches and celebrate their success.

The lower-left quadrant includes people who are low in their willingness and ability (see figure 5.2, page 97). They struggle with their practice and often mask their struggle with defensive and blaming behaviors. Others may perceive them as negative and uncooperative, yet the masking behaviors they exhibit are responsible for the negative perceptions. Learners in this quadrant may feel overwhelmed and believe they will never be able to meet the expected standards or live up to the expectations or the performance of those they perceive to be more competent and confident. The leadership team might choose more didactic learning designs, such as training with embedded public performance, frequent opportunities for individual feedback, coaching from an expert, and supervision.

The upper-left quadrant includes those who are high ability but tend to be unwilling to collaborate (see figure 5.2, page 97). Learners in this quadrant are high performers yet unwilling to change. They are proud of their success and worry that exhibiting a willingness to learn raises questions about their expertise. People in this quadrant benefit from support, opportunities to showcase their success, and opportunities to experience protocols such as the collaborative assessment conference, success analysis, or descriptive review process. Each protocol is a facilitated process for a group of teachers to work in a structured way to examine student or teacher work, looking for what worked and what didn't, and to extract information the learner can apply in other situations. These protocols for looking at student or teacher work products minimize corrective responses in favor of descriptive or constructive responses. For example, coaching interactions might emphasize noticing and wondering rather than correcting. See the reproducible "Deep Dive Into Student Work" (page 109).

The *collaborative assessment conference* focuses on a piece of student work for its "potential to reveal not only the student's mastery of the curriculum's goals, but also a wealth of information about the student: his/her intellectual interests, strengths, and struggles" (School Reform Initiative, 2021). The *success analysis protocol* guides individuals and teams to examine an out-of-the-ordinary experience for what makes it so successful (National School Reform Faculty, n.d.b).

The *descriptive review process* is another facilitated protocol for examining student or teacher work. It occurs in various forms and focuses on naming what the leadership team observes in a classroom or in student or teacher work samples, exploring how those observed practices impact learning, and reflecting on what is learned from the observations (Killion & Harrison, 2017).

The upper-right quadrant (see figure 5.2, page 97) includes learning omnivores consumed with learning and growing. People in this quadrant are eager learners and consumers of new knowledge, skills, and practices. They like to reflect on their practice and want to grow. These learners need little incentive to learn and are comfortable with any learning design, but benefit from designs that allow them to engage in inquiry cycles that include trialing multiple strategies, collaborating with colleagues, examining student effects, and adapting and adjusting in a continuous flow of their work.

Some designs that work well for learners in this quadrant are lesson study, the PLC process, action research, the *tuning protocol* (National School Reform Faculty, 2015), instructional rounds, peer visits, peer coaching, engagement in curriculum development, collaborative assessment and planning, serving as mentors or coaches, and opportunities to facilitate or lead teams. The Leadership Tips at the end of this chapter (page 108) include resources using these protocols.

Learning Designs to Transfer Learning to Practice

Transferring learning to routine practice and generating results for students, the ultimate goals of professional learning, require specific actions. Coaching and the practices within the PLC process are two essential learning designs for closing the knowing-doing gap and building the capacity to transfer learning to routine and accomplished practice. These designs also build a culture of continuous improvement and provide the support necessary to address hurdles and challenges associated with changing professional practice.

Learning Configurations

Learners are likely to learn in a variety of configurations. They may learn together with the whole school staff, in teams of staff, with colleagues from across schools, or individually. When selecting learning designs, it is helpful to explore which approaches work best for the learner and the intended results. Substantial research on professional learning confirms the importance of collaborative learning experiences (Darling-Hammond et al., 2017; Garet et al., 2001; Goddard, Hoy, & Hoy, 2000; Hattie, 2015; Wei et al., 2009). *Collaborative learning* (learning in partnership with others) is powerful, but some learners may occasionally benefit from learning alone.

The learning designs in this section are adaptable for large groups, small groups, or an individual. For example, a team might engage in action research, or individuals might conduct their action research project and share their results with colleagues in and across schools (see the reproducible "Action Research Design," page 112). Small groups of three might use the reproducible "Consulting Trio Protocol" (page 114). Sometimes, an individual or group might use text-response protocols to respond to professional texts (see the resources in the Leadership Tips section later in this chapter, page 108). Depending on their experience or performance level, some learners might seek individualized learning in addition to the professional learning available to others in the school.

For example, a teacher new to a school who is unfamiliar with specific instructional practices the school faculty uses will benefit from individual professional learning to acquire confidence and expertise in the practices. A teacher struggling with managing the classroom environment might engage in a coaching cycle focused on implementing classroom routines. This teacher may visit other teachers' classrooms to observe their routines in place.

All adult learners benefit from opportunities to have a voice and choice in their professional learning. Combine individual, team, and whole-staff learning experiences in a way that creates balance between individual educator learning needs and the learning needs of the entire school faculty.

To make the most of various learning configurations, sharing learning among colleagues extends the learning to others. For example, teams of teachers in a school system who teach a specific language might gather to participate in a workshop from an expert in the field of world language. They might share the language-learning strategies with teachers who teach other languages in their school. In this way, learning exponentially grows, as does the potential for impact on students.

Coaching

Coaching is a powerful learning design and an essential support for transferring learning to practice. Coaching facilitates personalized learning and specifically emphasizes transferring new learning to practice by engaging one professional (coach) with another professional client (partner teacher) to facilitate growth by inspiring the client to achieve the client's personal and professional potential (International Coach Federation, 2021). Coaching can be formal or informal. Killion (2012a) differentiates the two:

> In informal coaching, teachers volunteer to support one another in a collegial way . . . to promote shared learning. Formal coaching, often with a person designated as a coach who is a specialist or knowledgeable other and who has had some formal preparation to serve in the capacity, focuses on developing a specific body of knowledge or pedagogy. (p. 275)

Frequently, coaches who work in schools have many responsibilities other than coaching. However, coaches have a full-time position that, by its very nature, requires them to be in classrooms working with teachers. When they are working with small groups of students, decorating the main hall bulletin board, organizing trade books for literacy lessons, and so on, they are not fulfilling their responsibilities as a coach. School leadership teams, professional learning teams, and supervisors must monitor how coaching supports the implementation of the professional learning associated with schoolwide or team professional learning teacher and student outcomes. A core responsibility of school leaders is to ensure coaches are coaching. A parallel responsibility for coaches is to commit to *coaching heavy* rather than *coaching light* (Killion & Harrison, 2017; Killion & Roy, 2009).

Coaching heavy emphasizes student growth and uses it to measure the success of coaching. Coaches hold themselves accountable for deep and intensive work with teachers to shift their practice so student learning opportunities increase and eventually students succeed.

In *coaching light*, coaches use teacher satisfaction as a measure of success. They seek to increase teachers' comfort and confidence, often without regard to what is occurring to students. In coaching light, building relationships with teachers is the most important role of a coach. However, the focus on relationship building often does not shift to a focus on student success after establishing the relationships. Furthermore, spending years on relationship building may mean that years of opportunities for increased student learning are lost.

Professional Learning Communities

Another common design for professional learning in schools is the PLC process (DuFour et al., 2016). The research supporting the value of PLCs is long standing (Hord, 1997a; Little, 1982, 2003; McLaughlin & Talbert, 2001; Wenger, 1998). PLC at Work experts Richard DuFour and Robert Eaker (1998), DuFour and colleagues (2016), Austin Buffum, Mike Mattos, and Janet Malone (2017), and Rebecca DuFour, DuFour, Eaker, Mattos, and Anthony Muhammad (2021) shape how educators use this learning design. Research and practice in improvement science adapted PLCs as inquiry cycles (Regional Educational Laboratory West, n.d.) and network-improvement communities (Bryk et al., 2015).

A PLC is made up of teams of educators who come together to address issues related to their practice. The concept evolved and was adapted over the years and means many different things to different people. In many schools, nearly any gathering of people is labeled a PLC. The multiple variations of PLC contribute to a continuum of *PLC lite to PLC right* (DuFour & Reeves, 2016; Many & Butler, 2018). DuFour and Douglas Reeves (2016) indicated that *PLC lite* occurs:

> When educators rename their traditional faculty or department meetings as PLC meetings, engage in book studies that result in no action, or devote collaborative time to topics that have no effect on student achievement—all in the name of the PLC process. (p. 69)

When a PLC is implemented correctly (PLC right), educators gather purposefully to use a specified process to strengthen their practice to increase student success.

DuFour and colleagues (2016) note:

> It has been interesting to observe the growing popularity of the term *professional learning community*. In fact, the term has become so commonplace and has been used so ambiguously to describe virtually any loose coupling of individuals who share a common interest in education that it is in danger of losing all meaning. (pp. 9–10)

Collaborative team work in a PLC parallels the professional learning planning process presented in this book. It includes the following steps.

1. Analyze student data to determine what areas require improvement and which students specifically need differentiated opportunities for learning.

2. Identify learning outcomes for students and teachers and their measures that align with the schoolwide goals.

3. Clarify what teachers need to learn to adapt their practice to meet the students' needs.

4. Engage in learning.

5. Plan to integrate the learning.

6. Integrate the learning into practice.

7. Reflect using evidence on the success of the integration of practice, noting successes and additional opportunities for student and teacher learning.

8. Repeat the cycle.

Some collaborative teams fail to complete the cycle fully and emphasize only a portion of this process. For example, teams may focus on planning, analyzing data, or identifying student learning outcomes and measures without considering what learning the team needs or engaging in that learning. Missing some steps of the process makes it incomplete and will likely diminish the overall effectiveness of the investment in schoolwide or districtwide PLCs.

One strategy to increase the overall effectiveness and impact of the entire PLC process is to ensure adequate time for collaborative teams to meet, preferably several times a week, which keeps their work and learning closely tied to student learning and classroom practice. Another strategy is to ensure team leaders are well prepared and skillfully facilitate the process and team members. The last strategy for success is to invest in training team members on how to function as part of a collaborative team.

Studying the Research

Studying the research or evidence on how other districts or schools successfully address student learning needs is essential. The following are four foundational approaches schools can use to address gaps in student learning.

1. Allocate resources such as time devoted to learning, length of the school day, or supplemental support for students.

2. Increase the quality of instructional materials, including the curriculum, instructional learning guides (such as learning progressions), and student learning resources.

3. Expand teacher content and pedagogical knowledge and the expertise of others who indirectly influence student success.

4. Extend supports for teaching quality such as sound hiring, induction and mentoring, career-long talent-development systems, supervision and evaluation, and a culture of continuous improvement.

Professional learning is the vehicle to address two of these areas: staff expertise and increased supports. Formal and informal professional learning expands educators' content and pedagogical knowledge, skills, and practice. Incorporate implementation supports into professional learning to provide personalized assistance to encourage and facilitate transferring new learning to routine practice. Actively working to enhance the school culture and allocating sufficient resources, both responsibilities of the leadership or professional learning team, address the concomitant elements of successful professional learning.

The following questions can guide the review of research about other professional learning programs with successful results.

- ▸ What are the program goals?
- ▸ How similar are the goals to the goals we established for our school?
- ▸ What successes did the program generate?
  - Improved teaching practices
  - Improved student achievement
  - Other student successes
  - Other teaching successes
- ▸ What is the evidence of the successes?
- ▸ What actions led to the successes?
- ▸ How did the successful program design the professional learning?
- ▸ How did the successful program support professional learning?
- ▸ What is the time period of the successful program from beginning to end?
- ▸ What is the context of the successful program? Geographic? Demographic? Culture?
- ▸ Who were the participants? How did they engage in the successful program? Mandatory? Voluntary?
- ▸ What were the costs of the successful program?
- ▸ What types of staff associated with the successful program? Who served as the program facilitators, managers, coaches, and so on?
- ▸ What else is notable about the successful program?
- ▸ What is the same or different about our school and those in the successful program?

Preparing the Professional Learning Plan

Deliberate planning leads to success and opportunities to adapt and revise as needed. Whether as a part of a comprehensive school-improvement plan or as a separate document, the school's professional learning plan delineates what actions staff will take to achieve the identified goals and outcomes. A logic model format is a useful tool for planning professional learning because it builds on the theory of change and specifies the actions and benchmarks of success to monitor progress.

According to Killion (2018):

> A *logic model* uses the theory of change to depict the operation of a program by delineating several components of an action or operational plan, including
>
> 1. the program resources or inputs;
> 2. the actions or strategies program designers plan to use to produce the results (theory of change);

3. the outputs each action produces, if any;

4. the outcomes of the actions, both short and long term;

5. the goal of the program; and

6. the context of the program. (pp. 60–61)

To make the logic model template more specific for professional learning, teams might identify the persons responsible and the specific begin and end dates for each action.

Mason Elementary School's Professional Learning Plan

Mason Elementary School (a fictional example) experienced rapid growth in underperforming students because of boundary changes in the school system. Teachers were understandably concerned about meeting the needs of new students while maintaining their record of high performance. As a result, the school leadership team worked to create a schoolwide professional learning plan to prepare all teachers for their new students.

The leadership team's plan for professional learning, integrating the PLC process, included a multilayer approach throughout the school year to achieve the established goals. The school integrated the plan into a logic-model format, as figure 5.3 (page 104) shows.

Look at how Mason Elementary School's professional learning plan uses a logic-model format, beginning with the goals.

1. Create a school and classroom learning environment where all students are respected, included, and safe.

2. Increase student performance of all students by 5 percent and of underperforming student groups by 10 percent.

3. Increase teachers' use of differentiation strategies in Tier 1 (or core) instruction to meet the needs of all students.

When planners and implementers specify initial and intermediate outcomes, it helps them know where they are on the journey toward success. They also keep the focus on the outcomes rather than actions. Too often, they see checking off an action as completed as the action's measure of success. However, achieving the outcomes is the only measure of success, and knowing how to measure an outcome's success is crucial to the effectiveness of professional learning. Chapter 7 (page 151) addresses strategies for assessing and evaluating progress and results.

Use the following questions to reflect on the fictional Mason Elementary School case study.

▸ What design elements did the school leadership team include in its plan? How did those elements contribute to the plan's integrity?

▸ How did the plan include flexibility to meet the unique needs of educators and students?

▸ How did the plan address ongoing assessment of progress and adaptation based on data?

▸ How well does the plan respect educators as professionals?

▸ What are the strengths of, and possible upgrades to, this plan?

AUGUST

Inputs and Resources	Learning Designs and Actions	
• Professional learning day • Workshop facilitator and materials • Grade-level meetings • Student spring data • Unit planner	• Coaches facilitate schoolwide workshop on a review of six differentiation strategies (content, instructional process, assessment, product, learning environment, and group configuration). • Team leader facilitates analysis of student learning needs and plans to integrate at least one differentiation strategy for student groups into the grade level. • Teams identify various student groups in their classrooms, determine their unique learning needs, and integrate differentiation.	
Outputs	**Initial Outcomes**	**Intermediate Outcomes**
• Agenda • Participant list • Workshop materials • Student-data analysis and summary sheet • Completed unit plan	• Develop teacher understanding of how to differentiate instruction to meet the needs of students. • Identify students who need differentiation and explain how teachers will differentiate to meet their needs.	• Demonstrate capacity to implement differentiation strategies in Tier 1 instruction in regular education classrooms for all students. • Apply differentiation to planning instruction to meet the needs of students.

AUGUST THROUGH SEPTEMBER

Inputs and Resources	Learning Designs and Actions	

• Collaborative team time
• Student common assessments
• Student work samples
• Team leader
• Coach
• Time for teachers and coaches to meet
• Team collaboration time
• Resources on differentiation (video models, books, sample units, and so on)
	• Team leaders facilitate weekly team meetings using the following four PLC questions to guide their planning, implementation of their plans, review of student evidence, and reflection on student results.
	
	   1. What do we want students to know and be able to do?
	
	   2. How will we know when they achieve these outcomes?
	
	   3. What will we do if they do not?
	
	   4. What will we do if they succeed? (DuFour et al., 2016)
	
	• Teachers plan lessons and units to include differentiation strategies in Tier 1 instruction.
	• Coaches engage teachers in five-day coaching cycles focused on implementing differentiation strategies. Teams continue to meet every week.	

Outputs	**Initial Outcomes**	**Intermediate Outcomes**
• Meeting agenda and notes • Responses to the four critical questions • Units that integrate the application of differentiation • Teacher instructional unit and lesson plans • Coaching notes	• Understand how to integrate differentiation into unit planning. • Apply differentiation in a unit. • Apply at least two differentiation strategies in daily Tier 1 instruction.	• Increase student performance, particularly students with the greatest opportunity for growth, by 10 percent on unit common assessments. • Increase student engagement in classroom interactions by 15 percent, and performance in classroom daily formative assessments by 10 percent.

MID-OCTOBER THROUGH NOVEMBER

Inputs and Resources	Learning Designs and Actions	
• Principal walkthroughs • Coaching • Team collaboration time • Time for teachers and coaches to meet	• After reviewing student work samples from the unit and analyzing data from the Common Core assessments, teams determine the necessary adjustments to address gaps and successes. Teams continue to meet every week • Principal walkthroughs use evidence of differentiation via a checklist. • Coaches facilitate coaching cycles with individual teachers. • Teams of teachers engage in collaborative processes.	
Outputs	**Initial Outcomes**	**Intermediate Outcomes**
• Student-work analysis and data-analysis protocol • Student-data analysis • Walkthrough checklist summary	• Integrate two additional differentiation strategies for identified student groups into daily Tier 1 instruction.	• Increase student performance on schoolwide fall common assessments in English language arts and mathematics by 15 percent over last year's performance.

MID-JANUARY

Inputs and Resources	Learning Designs and Actions	
• Staff survey on classroom environment • Student survey on classroom environment • Data from surveys, student common assessments, and walkthroughs • Principal • Coach • School leadership team • Midyear common assessment data • Data from walkthrough	• Analyze data from surveys, student common assessments, and classroom walkthroughs to assess progress on implementing differentiation. • Analyze student data to assess the impact of differentiation on Tier 1 instruction. • Identify adjustments in the professional learning plan for remainder of the school year. Collaborative teams review their progress to date, adjust their meeting norms, format, and process, and continue their work. • Coaches continue coaching cycles with individual teachers. • Teams of teachers continue to engage in collaborative processes.	
Outputs	**Initial Outcomes**	**Intermediate Outcomes**
• Midyear report to staff about progress on goals and recommendation for the remainder of the year	• Increase teacher use of differentiation as measured by the walkthrough data. • Increase student performance on spring common unit assessments by 15 percent over fall common unit assessments.	• Increase student performance on common assessments and schoolwide fall common assessment by 15 percent.

FIGURE 5.3: A professional learning plan in a logic-model format.

continued ➡

LATE JANUARY THROUGH EARLY MAY

Inputs and Resources	Learning Designs and Actions	
• Coaching cycles • Principal walkthroughs • School leadership team member release time	• Repeat September–January processes. • Add peer visits, video capture, and coach-facilitated review in small groups. The school leadership team facilitates the classroom applications of differentiation by volunteer teachers and instructional rounds of volunteer teachers. • Principal walkthroughs use evidence of differentiation via a checklist. • Coaches facilitate biweekly voluntary extended learning and problem-solving sessions. • Coaches continue coaching cycles with individual teachers. • Teams of teachers continue to engage in collaborative processes.	
Outputs	**Initial Outcomes**	**Intermediate Outcomes**
• Report to staff on midyear progress and recommendation • Instructional rounds notes • Report summary on instructional rounds and walkthroughs • Materials teams share in biweekly sessions	• Increase teacher understanding and implementation of varied differentiation strategies appropriate for individual student learning needs in Tier 1 instruction.	• Increase student performance on common assessments and schoolwide fall common assessment by 15 percent.

MID-MAY

Inputs and Resources	Learning Designs and Actions	
• Student and teacher classroom environment surveys • Team collaboration time • Time for teachers and coaches to meet • Release time to participate in instructional rounds and peer visits • Video capturing equipment • Coaching cycles	• Teachers assess their overall use of differentiation and identify successes and opportunities for continued growth. • Students complete state assessments. • Students take classroom-environment survey. • Teachers take classroom-environment survey. • Conduct trend analysis on the use of differentiation strategies across the four PLC questions. Collaborative teams continue to meet.	
Outputs	**Initial Outcomes**	**Intermediate Outcomes**
• Data summary from teachers' self-assessment of their use of differentiation and their identified successes and opportunities for continued growth • Data summary from the classroom-environment surveys	• Increase schoolwide implementation of differentiation in Tier 1 instruction.	• Increase student achievement on English language arts and mathematics common assessments by 15 percent for students underperforming at the beginning of the school year and 10 percent for all other students.

EARLY JUNE

Inputs and Resources	Learning Designs and Actions	
• Time for showcase (see next column) • Location for showcase • Funds for refreshments and invitations	• Conduct a showcase in which each grade-level team shares its journey throughout the year, including examples of the team's differentiation strategies with video, teacher work, and student work, plus a summary of student performance in mathematics and English language arts common assessments. Collaborative teams synthesize their learning, successes, and challenges, throughout the year and their commitments for next school year, and prepare to share them with the school leadership team. • The school leadership team summarizes the showcases and writes an analysis of goal attainment based on the evidence each team presents.	
Outputs	**Initial Outcomes**	**Intermediate Outcomes**
• Success-analysis protocol • Summary of overall changes and goals attainment	• Increase implementation of differentiation in Tier 1 instruction schoolwide based on the classroom-environment surveys and walkthrough data. • Increase student achievement on English language arts and mathematics common assessments by 10 percent for students underperforming at the beginning of the school year, and 5 percent for all other students.	• Increase student achievement on English language arts and mathematics common assessments by 15 percent for students underperforming at the beginning of the school year and 10 percent for all other students. • Increase student performance on state assessments by 10 percent for all students.

Source: DuFour et al., 2016.

Conclusion

Designing professional learning is an art and a science. Understanding learner attributes, the intended outcomes, various learning designs, and the context in which learning occurs guides design decisions. The key to the success of professional learning is narrowing the focus to high-leverage areas. There is a saying, "Whoever chases two rabbits will catch none." Eric Abrahamson (2004), professor of management at the Columbia University School of Business, calls this *repetitive change syndrome*. Often, people initiate change by looking for a quick fix. However, when you complete the entire cycle of a well designed plan, you gain crucial data about what works under what conditions. *Change*, and its requisite companion *learning*, cannot be accidental; it results from efficiently, effectively, and intentionally designing learning that considers learners, the outcomes, and the context. A carefully articulated plan for professional learning includes thoughtfully selected learning designs as the basis for success. The next chapter (page 115) addresses how to sustain support and allocate resources for implementation.

Leadership Tips

When planning school-based professional learning, it is essential to explore learning designs, understand what influences those designs, and transfer the learning to practice. The following tips will help you get started.

- ▶ Expand professional learning planning to include the initial acquisition of knowledge and skills to integrate shifting attitudes, aspirations, and behaviors.

- ▶ Explore the learning preferences of teachers in the school and the most successful past designs.

- ▶ Analyze the culture of the adult-learning environment in the school.

- ▶ Review the current professional learning plan for its integration of learning designs to address all KASAB elements.

- ▶ Acquire resources to inform decisions about professional learning designs. See Sommers (2021); consultant, coach, and author Lois Brown Easton (2009, 2015); AllThingsPLC (n.d.); National School Reform Faculty (n.d.a); and School Reform Initiative (2021) for some examples.

Reflection Questions

1. What is the culture for learning in your school? What evidence supports your assessment?

2. What were key learnings from your review of research that relate to your school goals?

3. What successful learning designs did the school use in previous professional learning situations? Which have been less effective?

4. How will you address all five core elements of KASAB in professional learning to sustain change?

5. Who selects professional learning designs, and how are they deepening and expanding their understanding of learning designs?

Deep Dive Into Student Work

This tool offers a way for teams to learn collaboratively. It provides a protocol for teams to look at samples of their students' work together.

PURPOSE   To engage in analyzing student work to identify the effects of lesson design and instruction, and determine how to ensure all students succeed in achieving the intended learning outcomes

PRODUCT   Analysis of student success, errors, and performance and identification of next instructional practices to support student success

PARTICIPANTS   Team, department, or full faculty

MATERIALS   Copy of the protocol, sticky notes or additional paper, three samples of student work associated with a selected performance task, the rubric used to assess the work, and lesson plan or unit plan

TIME   Sixty minutes

PREPARATION   **Step 1**
Each teacher brings three samples of student work from the designated lesson or unit (one high performance, one mid-level, and one emerging). The work might be a writing sample, group work, a project, assessment task, quiz, end-of-unit assessment, and more.

Step 2
Teachers organize their student work into three groups: high, mid-level, and emerging performance.

Step 3
Teachers, working independently and quietly, analyze the student work samples in each group. Using the rubric, they make individual notes about student successes, misconceptions, errors, and challenges.

Step 4
Teachers collaborate to list all the successes and challenges they individually noted in a collective grid using the "Template for Summarizing Analysis" (page 111).

Step 5
Together, teachers determine what instruction and practice each student group needs to meet or reinforce the expected levels of performance.

Step 6
Teachers plan how to integrate the instruction and practice into the next series of lessons or unit.

PROCESS   The process consists of six steps that take participants through the process of analyzing student work, identifying successes and challenges, and defining next steps. The following chart (page 110) outlines this process.

Steps	Process	Person Responsible	Time
Step 1: Welcome.	Review the purpose of the process. Clarify the learning outcomes the student work sample measures.	Facilitator	Three minutes
Step 2: Sort student work samples.	Sort the student work samples into three groups: high; mid-level; emerging performance.	Teachers	Two minutes
Step 3: Analyze student work products.	Analyze each group of student work products in sequence. Each teacher independently and quietly examines each student work product using the rubric. Note the successes and challenges the student work represents on individual sticky notes or note paper attached to each work sample.	Team	Twenty minutes
Step 4: Summarize analysis.	Summarize the analysis on the template (see "Template for Summarizing Analysis"). Identify areas where teachers are not in agreement or want additional information. Discuss the areas needing consensus.	Team	Ten minutes
Step 5: Identify next steps.	Determine instruction and practice needed for each group of students. Determine when to integrate the instruction and practice into the next series of lessons or unit. Identify who will take what responsibilities for preparing instructional or practice materials. Set a timeline for implementing the actions and to discuss the effects of the additional instruction and practice.	Facilitator, Team	Twenty minutes
Step 6: Debrief, Wrap Up, Decide Next Steps.	Debrief the process. Share insights, lessons learned, clarifications gained, and so on. Schedule the next deep dive into student work.	Facilitator	Five minutes
		TOTAL	Sixty minutes

Template for Summarizing Analysis

Areas (as defined in rubric)	High Performance	Mid-Level Performance	Emerging Performance
Successes			
Challenges			

Action Research Design

Action research is a learning design individuals, small groups, or a whole faculty can use to study problems of practice in their work.

PURPOSE To guide educators to engage in *action research*, a "continual disciplined inquiry conducted to inform and improve our practice as educators" (Calhoun, 2002, p. 18)

PRODUCT Share results of the inquiry, with the intention to use the findings to direct next steps.

PARTICIPANTS Any small group, grade-level team or department, or full faculty can identify a question to guide the action research.

MATERIALS Protocol and *lots* of data

TIME Conducting action research can vary from several weeks to a multiyear period (The length depends on the scope of the research question or questions, the availability of data, and the expected time to see results from the interventions).

PREPARATION This protocol is dependent on the development of a research question or questions and the collection of sufficient data.

PROCESS The process involves six phases. The following chart includes key actions to implement action research and the steps necessary to carry out the key actions.

Phase	Key Actions	Process Steps
Phase 1	Faculty, leadership team, study group, or teacher identifies an area of interest and prepares the guiding question or questions to focus the work.	1. Identify the area of interest or concern. 2. Use open-ended questions to help narrow the focus. 3. Look to other members of your research group to give you feedback. 4. Ask teachers outside your group the following: "What do you think of this issue? Is this a worthwhile issue to pursue? What suggestions can you offer to improve this issue?" 5. Refine if necessary.
Phase 2	Faculty, leadership team, study group, or teacher identifies data to collect.	1. Decide what kind of data sources you need (Data sources are the people, artifacts, resources, and so on, from which data are drawn. The data collection methods/tools determine what kinds of data, qualitative or quantitative, emerge from the collection.). 2. Collect data from at least three sources. 3. Keep a data log recording of when you collect all information, noting the collected data, time, and place. 4. Organize your data. Make the data presentable and understandable for a person unfamiliar with the project.
Phase 3	Faculty, leadership team, study group, or teacher collects data.	Collect data from multiple sources in multiple formats.
Phases 4–5	Faculty, leadership team, study group, or teacher organizes and interprets the data. Share the findings with partners. Compare results with desirable future outcomes.	1. Analyze data. 2. Compare current state with the desired state. 3. Report findings. 4. Interpret results. 5. Plan next actions.
Phase 6	Determine whether action is needed. If so, take short-term action immediately and plan long-term action.	Summarize results of the research, lessons learned for future practice, and ways to integrate the learning into future practice.

Reference

Caro-Bruce, C. (2000). *Action research facilitator's handbook.* Oxford, OH: National Staff Development Council.

Consulting Trio Protocol

This tool offers teams of three a learning design to share their expertise and perspectives with one another.

PURPOSE To provide a structure for small groups of three to share recommendations, questions, perspectives, and expertise with one another

PRODUCT List of ideas the participants in the consulting trio generate

PARTICIPANTS Any group of learners gather in triads to share ideas. This protocol works for teams who share a similar role (for example, three science teachers) or have quite different titles (principal, paraprofessional, and guidance counselor).

MATERIALS Copy of the protocol

TIME Forty-five minutes

PREPARATION Any group of three or more can do this protocol with little preparation.

PROCESS The process begins by forming triads. One person presents at a time and participants go through the procedure the following chart outlines. Repeat the procedure for each member of the triad.

Procedure	Time
• Form triads. • Decide who will present first, second, and third. • Jot down several issues you are facing and your thoughts on the issues.	Five minutes
• Describe the issue. • Provide background information to help your triad members understand the situation. • Explain what you have done so far. • Use role names instead of personal names as you describe the situation. • Use facts when talking about the issue and situation.	Three minutes
• Ask clarifying questions; presenter answers with facts.	Three minutes
• Presenter describes type of help desired.	One minute
• Offer the type of help the presenter (who remains silent) requests. • Identify and share as many different ideas as possible. Do not advocate one idea.	Six minutes
• Presenter shares what seems most helpful and possible next steps.	Two minutes
• Repeat for each triad member.	Fifteen minutes

CHAPTER 6

Implementing and Supporting the Plan

We may encounter many defeats, but we must not be defeated.

—MAYA ANGELOU

Learning is not like turning on a light switch. School leadership and professional learning teams implementing their plans will realize greater results over time. This chapter explores ways to provide ongoing, sustained support to achieve high levels of mastery with new learning. As Darling-Hammond and colleagues (2017) write:

> The quality of a PD initiative's implementation has implications for its overall effectiveness in enhancing teacher practice and improving student learning. Researchers have found that willing teachers are sometimes unable to implement professional development practices due to obstacles that are beyond their control [Buczynski, & Hansen, 2010]. Even the best-designed professional development may fail to produce desired outcomes if it is poorly implemented due to barriers such as:
>
> - inadequate resources, including necessary curriculum materials;
>
> - lack of a shared vision about what high-quality instruction entails;
>
> - lack of time for implementing new instructional approaches during the school day or year;
>
> - failure to align state and local policies toward a coherent set of instructional practices;
>
> - dysfunctional school cultures; and
>
> - inability to track and assess the quality of professional development [Tooley & Connally, 2016] (p. 8)

This chapter discusses how to support and implement the plan for school-based professional learning. First, it explores the two dimensions of implementation, then continues by explaining how to sustain change. Finally, this chapter moves on to the value of coaching in implementing the plan, and discusses the need for ongoing monitoring.

Understanding the Two Dimensions of Implementation

Implementing new practices requires attention to internal and external dimensions of change. In the first dimension, the learner is willing to persist through the change, even when it becomes uncomfortable and messy. Without this internal drive or aspiration to change, little external support will have an impact.

In the second dimension, external support surrounds the learner with tools, encouragement, feedback processes, extended learning, and ongoing assessment of progress, all designed to promote and encourage implementation. The leadership team champions the change with supports for the individual, team, and whole-school areas of need. Supporting implementation becomes a significant part of the professional learning process and a key responsibility of professional learning leaders.

The following sections more fully address both internal and external dimensions.

Internal Dimension

Learners who understand the reason for change are more likely to want to change. Some school staff are eager to learn and grow, and some are not. This variance occurs in every setting and does not necessarily represent resistance as much as it represents not being ready for change. Those who are not eager don't yet understand the relevance of the learning to them.

Sinek (2011) says, "There are only two ways to influence human behavior: you can manipulate it or you can inspire it" (p. 17). To build aspiration, leaders engage learners to share their perceptions about the rationale for the change, and the leaders share how the learning will contribute to educator and student success. You can adapt the following questions for a literacy professional learning initiative for other professional learning initiatives.

- ▶ How do you see this issue manifest in your classes?

- ▶ What do you notice your students doing when they are responding to inferential questions?

- ▶ If there were one change you'd want students to make in this area to meet your expectations, what would it be?

- ▶ How do you want to be involved in helping to improve students' reading performance?

- ▶ When you look at the data on student performance in reading, what are you discovering?

- ▶ What might be your role in addressing the needs the data identify?

- ▶ What is one thing you would like to be more effective in teaching, learning, or leading?

Engaging in a discussion focused on clarifying the purpose of professional learning is one way to address attitudes and aspirations, two elements of KASAB (see chapter 4, page 76) essential for building the internal motivation to sustain learning through the discomfort of early implementation. This discussion invites learners to participate, builds agency for the change, encourages the learner to reflect on the possible effects of the learning, and most importantly, gives the learner a voice in the process.

As a result, learners can connect with professional learning goals and outcomes and begin to understand the benefits. Too often in schools, leaders overlook conversations like this because many assume all educators are committed to continuous learning. Therefore, the first step is cultivating the *desire* to learn.

External Dimensions

External dimensions, the conditions that support change, are the primary focus of this chapter in tandem with the internal dimension. *External dimensions* are supports a leadership or professional learning team uses to move learners from merely knowing about the learning to using it in practice. No single element alone is sufficient; an artful tapestry of the many factors this chapter later describes create the conditions for success.

SUSTAINING CHANGE OVER TIME

Shirley M. Hord, an eminent researcher on change and PLCs, served as a mentor and trusted colleague to us, the authors of this book. We each had individual and collective exchanges with her about her work. In one of our last conversations, we asked her what question education leaders most commonly ask. She responded that they ask her how to sustain change over time. The solution is easy, she said. First, implement the change. Without implementation, sustaining change is impossible. After implementation, data and information can direct adjustments to accommodate new ways of learning and teaching (personal communication, July 12, 2018).

As Hord's previous response highlights, the often-ignored hard work of change requires deep implementation, the accurate and consistent application of new learning, and sustaining learning until it becomes routine practice. Going back to Hord's (1997a, 1997b, 2013) research on change and the complementary work of other scholars such as Fullan (1982, 2007, 2016), there is insufficient attention to deep implementation. For example, although educators exert significant attention and effort on initiating change, they often assume others will fully and accurately implement the change after launch.

> **Without implementation, sustaining change is impossible.**

Fullan (1982, 2007, 2016), Gene E. Hall and Hord (2015), and others note that initiating, implementing, and institutionalizing (sustaining) change are three distinct phases; frequently, schools insufficiently plan, resource, or execute them. Hall and Hord's (2015) extensive work on the concerns-based adoption model (they explain in detail in *Implementing Change: Patterns, Principles, and Potholes*) is a solid foundation for those who want to better predict the emotional and behavioral complexity of implementing change.

Implementing and Sustaining Change

Without deep implementation, there is no resulting change for leaders to sustain. The following actions are necessary for implementing and sustaining change.

- Fostering a culture for learning
- Clarifying what success looks like when accurately implementing the learning
- Allocating sufficient resources for the professional learning, sustained support, and evaluation of the effects
- Delineating lead indicators and commitments required to achieve them
- Ongoing assessment of practice

▶ Engaging in feedback processes to encourage reflection

▶ Coaching to refine and extend the practice

▶ Coaching and modeling

▶ Coaching and extending study

▶ Ongoing monitoring of implementation supports to ensure equitable and accessible distribution for all

The following sections address each of these requirements.

Fostering a Culture for Learning

The school culture matters when selecting a learning design because the culture supports or inhibits growth. In schools, culture influences teacher learning. Researchers V. Darleen Opfer and David Pedder (2011) studied the relationship among the factors that influence teacher learning, and Cruse (2021) depicts the relationship in figure 6.1 (page 118).

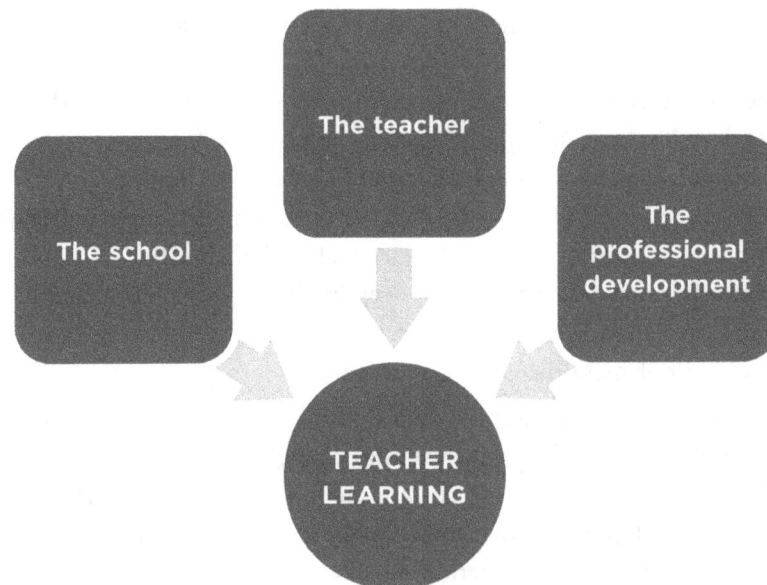

Source: Cruse, 2021, p. 108. Used with permission.

FIGURE 6.1: Subsystems of teacher learning.

Cruse's (2021) research on the relationship between teacher participation in professional learning and school culture finds, "Together, the six factors of school culture (collaborative leadership, teacher collaboration, professional development, unity of purpose, collegial support, and learning partnership) indicate a statistically significant effect . . . with 21.9% of the variance predicted by the six factors" (p. 97).

The culture of learning influences staff's openness and willingness to learn. It depends on the community members' commitment to collaboration, continuous improvement, and professionalism. In *Five Paths of Student Engagement*, coauthors and researchers Andy Hargreaves and Michael O'Connor (2018) propose ten factors of collaborative professionalism. Understanding the key features of a culture that supports adult learning designed to enhance student learning guides leadership and professional learning teams to consider the influence of the school's culture on learning staff experiences.

Notable in the features Hargreaves and O'Connor (2018) include are autonomy, collaborative inquiry, collective responsibility, joint work, and common purpose. These factors are some of the key features of a school in which teachers learn together to support student learning. *Autonomy* frees teachers from micromanagement and leaves decisions about student learning and teaching to those in classrooms with students. *Collaborative inquiry* is a commitment to work together to investigate what works and what doesn't, and to address issues in student learning that emerge from practice. *Collective responsibility* is the recognition that all students concern all staff; teachers are responsible and accountable for the success of *all* students in the school—not just those in their classroom.

Joint work emerged from early research of school reform expert Judith Warren Little (1996) on PLCs, which acknowledges when individuals create products and make decisions based on what everyone knows (rather than what one person knows), the team's work is stronger and more effective than the work of any one individual. *Common purpose* serves as the unifying factor that brings educators together. Team members commit to achieving results for students and place students' best interests over the team members' own individual interests.

In addition, author and researcher Jon Saphier (2015) identifies a set of observable features of a strong adult professional culture based on his decades of research and practice in school systems and schools. He organized these features into a survey format (see the reproducible "Survey for Assessing School Culture," page 67). The research- and practice-based features identify the perspectives of adults when they feel psychologically and emotionally safe, and engage productively in working and learning together.

When the culture fosters the practices Hargreaves and O'Connor (2018) and Saphier (2015) describe, the school leaders likely consider professional learning essential. A culture for learning supports risk taking, experimentation, and blame-free opportunities to explore and refine practice. It includes freedom from judgment to acknowledge strengths and gaps in practice. In addition, it includes support and expectations for ongoing learning. Finally, a culture of learning includes trust in leadership and transparency of practice. School leadership and professional learning teams can use these features to determine whether the culture in their school orients for learning, and if not, which features they need to address.

> **A culture for learning supports risk taking, experimentation, and blame-free opportunities to explore and refine practice.**

Sometimes, leaders delay professional learning to create the culture that supports it. This delay is a mistake. Professional learning can contribute to the development of the culture for learning while enhancing the culture and extending the impact of learning.

Clarifying Success

To minimize significant variance in implementation, define success and expectations early. In *Five Paths of Student Engagement: Blazing the Trail to Learning and Success*, educational change initiative consultants and coauthors Dennis Shirley and Andy Hargreaves (2021) note, "One of the greatest dangers to implementation of good ideas in education is not insufficient implementation, but poorly understood implementation of new practices even when they have been widely adopted" (p. 77). In their book, *Implementing Change: Patterns, Principles, and Potholes*, Hall and Hord (2015) note:

Pothole Warning

Do not assume that just because every staff member attended the two-hour session where the innovation was described that they all hold the same image of what it is—especially if it was described in general terms.

Pothole Repair

How to enable everyone to hold a common and authentic vision of the new practice is the challenge. Precision in describing what use looks like is the key, and the operable term. (p. 60)

In their work on implementing many change initiatives, Hall and Hord (2015) devise a tool they call an *innovation configuration map* to clarify the indicators for the successful implementation of learning. Hall and Hord (2015) posit that without specifically delineating to everyone what the ideal practice looks like in behavioral terms, there is too much room for variance, which may diminish fidelity of practice and dramatically reduce the impact of new behaviors.

The *innovation configuration map* defines the specific, observable behaviors associated with implementation of a new program or practice. The map helps staff understand what excellent implementation looks like, setting the standard for ideal implementation in a concrete way, rather than leaving it to individual interpretation. Finally, this map offers learners a way to self-assess their current behaviors and immediately see what they need to add to their practice to move closer to the ideal. Figure 6.2 (page 120) is an example of a section of an innovation configuration map on the responsibilities of a school leadership team to provide ongoing support. See the reproducible "Writing an Innovation Configuration Map" (page 141).

Level 1 Ideal Behavior	Provide continuous job-embedded coaching and other forms of support (for example, peer observation, instructional walk-throughs, demonstration lessons, and so on) to transfer educator learning to the classroom and schoolwide practice to increase student achievement.
Level 2	Provide periodic job-embedded coaching and other forms of classroom-based support (for example, peer observation, instructional walk-throughs, demonstration lessons, and so on) to transfer educator learning to the classroom and schoolwide practice to increase student achievement.
Level 3 Minimally Acceptable Behavior	Provide occasional job-embedded coaching and other forms of support (for example, peer observation, instructional walk-throughs, demonstration lessons, and so on) to transfer educator learning to the classroom and schoolwide practice to increase student achievement.
Level 4	Provide one opportunity for job-embedded coaching and other forms of support (for example, peer observation, instructional walk-throughs, demonstration lessons, and so on) to transfer educator learning to the classroom and schoolwide practice to increase student achievement.
Level 5 Unacceptable Behavior	Provide no job-embedded coaching and other forms of support (for example, peer observation, instructional walk-throughs, demonstration lessons, and so on) to transfer educator learning to the classroom and schoolwide practice to increase student achievement.

Source: Killion, 2018, p. 259. Used with permission.

FIGURE 6.2: Example of an innovation configuration map showing job-embedded support.

Allocating Sufficient Resources

The implementation, support, and evaluation of professional learning requires resources, including time, budget, staff, materials, technology, and policies or guidelines (Learning Forward, 2022). If sufficient resources are available to support learning and its transfer to practice, it is more likely learning will be successful. The success of professional learning depends on the learners' willingness to learn, transfer learning to practice, and sustain and refine practice over time, plus the quality of the learning design and the resources to support learning. When support structures are inadequate, the potential for professional learning to meet its goals diminishes. The next sections explore time, budget, staff, other resources, and policies, guidelines, or expectations as they relate to the allocation of sufficient resources.

Time

Time for educators is a precious commodity, and when leaders invest time, it signals value and importance. Providing time for learning, applying learning, and refining the learning for practice, signals to educators that learning directly associates with their work responsibilities and peers and supervisors value it. Some school systems arrange school-day schedules to accommodate shared planning and collaborative learning time weekly. However, occasional time for monthly learning or periodic days scattered throughout the school year are insufficient for deep and sustained learning. Killion and Hirsh (2012) recommend the investments of time that table 6.1 (page 122) depicts.

> **Time for educators is a precious commodity, and when leaders invest time, it signals value and importance.**

An ideal schedule includes time for planning and professional learning. For example, school-day schedules often set aside planning time for teachers to prepare for instruction, collaborate with peers, communicate with families, assess student work, and review and select instructional resources. However, those responsibilities rarely include time for teachers to learn from peers, reflect on their practice, participate in online learning, read professional journals, engage in professional reflection to extend and refine their content knowledge and pedagogical practices, and more. It is these latter tasks that professional learning encompasses.

School leadership teams have several ways to create time for professional learning within the school-day schedule. One way is to create schedules that include weekly time for staff to engage in individual and collaborative learning. Another is to create a schedule for early-release or late-start days that compress students' learning time. However, it is not always necessary to exclude students. Innovative scheduling and staffing can lead to common blocks of time for staff with similar student responsibilities. A substantial amount of professional learning can occur while teachers and students are in classrooms.

For example, coaching, peer visits, and co-teaching can occur while students are learning to avoid trading student-learning time for staff-learning time. Coaching, peer visits, shadowing students, and learning walks are some of the learning designs that work when students engage in learning. Learning walks are opportunities for a small team of three to five teachers to visit multiple classrooms for a brief time to observe for a designated learning behavior, such as student collaboration or engagement. The focus of learning walks relates to the school's improvement or professional learning goals. You can also use learning walks to see new practices in action to facilitate refinement of practice or to support implementation (Fisher & Frey, 2014; National Institute for Excellence in Teaching, 2021).

TABLE 6.1: Investments of Time for Professional Learning and Their Purposes

Investment	Purpose
Ten days embedded into educators' work year or expanding educators' work year	To extend individual, team, and school- and districtwide professional learning, teachers participate in university courses; enroll in expert- and peer-facilitated workshops; engage in blended, face-to-face, and online courses; attend local, state, or national conferences; interact virtually or in person with researchers and other experts
Adjust school-day schedules to provide three to four hours weekly for collaboration among teachers, between teachers and their principals, and among principals	To provide daily time for educators to transfer learning to practice, develop shared expertise, and refine practice through continuous improvement • Studying content standards and curriculum to plan units and lessons of curriculum, assessment, and instruction • Analyzing student learning progressions to identify and design interventions • Solving problems related to student learning • Calibrating student performance expectations • Supporting peer professional growth • Reflecting on and assessing practice

Source: Adapted from Killion & Hirsh, 2012b. Used with permission of Learning Forward, www.learningforward.org. All rights reserved.

When analyzing time for professional learning answer the following questions.

▸ How much time is available during the school day, workweek, and school-year calendar for collaborative and independent learning?

▸ How are you currently using the available time for professional learning?

▸ What available time can you repurpose to include professional learning?

▸ What is the school's goal related to time for professional learning for staff?

▸ What is a reasonable amount of time for initial learning, planning, and integrating the learning into practice, engaging in coaching to refine and extend the practice, and assessing professional learning?

Budget

Professional learning is often the first area leaders reduce or eliminate in times of fiscal tightening. As Killion and Hirsh (2012) write:

> The work ahead requires a long-term commitment to intensive professional learning for all educators and innovative, rich, and flexible classroom instructional resources that fill the gaps in learning for many of America's students. To undertake the efforts necessary so that every student leaves high school ready for college and careers, schools, districts, states, regional and national education agencies, and education vendors need to make thoughtful and deliberate decisions regarding resources, particularly resources for professional learning. (p. 5)

Continuous changes in curriculum, student learning needs, content, pedagogy, instructional materials, technology, and community needs mean educators must update their knowledge, skills, and practices, and reassess and rededicate their attitudes and aspirations to success. In *High-Quality Professional Development for All Teachers: Effectively Allocating Resources*, research and policy brief writers Sarah Archibald, Jane G. Coggshall, Andrew Croft, and Laura Goe (2011) emphasize, "Given the importance of teacher quality to student learning and the link between teacher quality and professional development, a greater investment is likely to lead to greater levels of student learning" (p. 13).

To adequately budget for professional learning, the school leadership or professional learning team considers the initial costs for training and resources as well as the cost for supporting the transfer of learning to practice and refining and sustaining the practice over time. Other costs include adequate resources to assess the effectiveness and impact of professional learning over multiple years so the school can make upgrades as needed. In one model of funding for professional learning, policy experts Allan R. Odden, Michel E. Goetz, and Lawrence O. Picus (2008) calculate the following allocations for professional learning.

- ▸ Instructional coaches (one per every two hundred students) to provide embedded follow-up

- ▸ Ten days of professional learning time in the summer for in-depth training

- ▸ One hundred dollars per pupil for other professional learning expenses, such as trainers, conferences, or travel

When analyzing the budget for professional learning, answer the following questions.

- ▸ What costs for professional learning does the professional learning budget include?

- ▸ What is the current budget dedicated to professional learning? What costs does it and does it not include?

- ▸ How does the school develop the budget for professional learning?

- ▸ What components of the professional learning costs do other areas of the budget include?

- ▸ How adequate is the professional learning budget to meet the learning needs of school staff?

- ▸ What amount of out-of-pocket expense does the district or school leadership team believe is fair for staff to invest in their professional learning that relates or does not relate to district and school initiatives?

Staff

Although not every school has staff positions dedicated to professional learning, some do. Whether these staff are called *coaches, instructional* or *building resource specialists*, or *instructional facilitators*, their role focuses on supporting the continuous learning of teachers. Other roles in the school, such as grade-level team or department leaders, devote a portion of their job description to professional learning.

A common mistake with professional learning is to assume learning will automatically transfer to practice. For example, if teachers attend a workshop on common formative assessment, the assumption is they will return to school ready and willing to implement common formative assessment in their classrooms the next day. Few consider the supports teachers need to redesign student assessments, develop a common assessment, understand the value of common assessments, or use the data from common assessments to modify instruction.

Coaches or others in the school-based professional learning roles facilitate the extension of the learning process to transfer learning to practice, support implementation, add extensions and reteaching as needed, maintain staff willingness to learn, offer ongoing opportunities for self- and peer assessment of practice, and solve problems related to implementing the new learning. The immediacy of an in-school person to reach out to when staff need assistance and the opportunity to work in the context of a teacher's classroom increases the likelihood of success of professional learning.

In addition to teachers on special assignment with responsibilities for professional learning, school administrators can assume some of those responsibilities. They might share in visiting classrooms to observe the implementation of new pedagogical practices, monitor and coach teachers when problems occur, locate and provide necessary resources to support implementation of new strategies, and facilitate increasing investments in time and budgetary resources to support professional learning. Consider the following scenario.

SUPPORTING STAFF

The English department chair at Manner Middle School had one release period per day for managing the business of the department and a second to support the implementation of the new literacy curriculum. In that role, she took the following actions.

- Facilitated lunch-and-learn sessions among teachers about the curriculum structure, its resources, and problems they were encountering
- Coordinated teachers' attendance at districtwide workshops focused on their respective grade-level curriculum
- Provided demonstrations in her classroom of some of the new instructional processes included in the curriculum
- Visited teachers' classrooms to observe how students were responding to various elements of the curriculum
- Integrated a glow-and-grow component into department meetings, during which teachers shared what was working and requested other supports to fill gaps they were experiencing
- Met with the assistant principal responsible for each grade level to request needed supports for specific teachers
- Contributed to the district's evaluation of the curriculum implementation
- Attended leadership workshops for curriculum leaders to extend her skills

In addition to the department chair's support, administrators conducted classroom walkthroughs with teacher teams to observe how students used the reading and writing strategies in other disciplines, and how the English teachers adhered to the curriculum. These supports increased teachers' capability, comfort, and confidence with the new curriculum and consistency in implementation; and contributed to student success with the curriculum.

When analyzing the staff allocation for professional learning, answer the following questions.

- ▸ Who in the school shares responsibilities for the management, coordination, facilitation, and evaluation of professional learning? What percent of this person's time is devoted to those responsibilities?

- ▸ Who provides direct support to staff to apply new learning in their work areas?

- ▸ How do teachers access support for implementing professional learning?

Other Resources

Access to other types of resources to support professional learning include professional journals and books, professional association memberships, curated collections of model units, assessments, anchor work from students, videos of exemplary instruction, and subscription services to other professional resources. Computers, tablets, connectivity, and other technology facilitate access to these professional resources. Ease and proximity of access to resources increase the likelihood of their use and provide staff with new information, diverse perspectives, and models to study and adapt that scaffold their learning process.

When analyzing school resources for professional learning, answer the following questions.

- ▸ What resources are available for staff for individual and collaborative professional learning?

- ▸ How accessible and equitable are the resources?

- ▸ Which resources do staff use most frequently and how do staff use them?

- ▸ Which resources do staff use less frequently and how can the school replace, update, repurpose, or eliminate these resources to increase their value or invest their cost in more productive ways?

- ▸ What resources do staff want available to them?

Policies, Guidelines, or Expectations

Most state departments and ministries of education establish regulations about ongoing learning for license or certification renewal. These regulations changed because of national and international studies between 2010 and 2020 that focused on increasing the quality of teaching, measuring the effectiveness of teaching, and elevating the teaching profession (Cantrell & Kane, 2013; Huguet, et al., 2020).

Some state regulations for professional learning have changed over the years. Michigan, for example, requires 150 hours of district-provided professional development or six university credits or a combination (one university credit equals twenty-five state continuing education clock hours) every five years (Michigan Department of Education, 2022). In 2022, Colorado requires ninety hours of professional learning for a teaching license renewal and (beginning with teaching licenses that expire after September 1, 2025), teachers with an elementary, English language arts, mathematics, science, social studies, or any middle-level endorsement must earn an English learner professional learning designation in one of several ways (Colorado Department of Education, n.d.). Louisiana requires 150 clock hours of professional learning for teachers who hold a Level 2 or Level 3 (nonprobationary) teaching license (Model Teaching, 2022). New York requires 100 hours of continuing education every five years to maintain teaching certification (New York State United Teachers, 2022).

However, policy analysts Melissa Tooley and Taylor White (2018), in an analysis of these requirements, question their effectiveness in supporting teacher professional learning:

> In fact, although relicensure is ostensibly intended to foster a culture of ongoing professional growth, this analysis of state teacher licensure renewal policies finds that the policies undergirding the licensure renewal system frequently conflict with what is known about best practices in adult learning and actually discourage more effective PD [professional development]. . . . These types of policies do nothing to encourage the sustained, targeted, and personalized learning opportunities that research shows are most likely to improve teachers' performance, favoring instead a one-size-fits all approach that offers convenience, often at the expense of quality. (p. 1)

Given these findings, it is essential for local schools and school systems to establish policies and expectations for professional learning aligned with research- and evidence-based practices. Recommendations for the renewal process from the Tooley and White (2018) study include aligning professional learning to demonstrated growth needs, investing in implementation capacity, reducing duplication, building coherence in the professional learning system, and exploring incentives for professional growth.

In addition, schools and school systems need policies and guidelines about the quality, equitable access, and effectiveness of professional learning. Districts, states, and ministries of education that adopt such policies or guidelines (for example, Learning Forward's [2022] *Standards for Professional Learning*) or create their own, take steps to ensure educators have access to professional learning that adheres to research- or evidence-based practices.

When analyzing school or district policies, guidelines, or expectations for professional learning, answer the following questions.

- ▶ What is the current requirement for professional learning for staff?
- ▶ How are staff meeting that requirement?
- ▶ How closely aligned are staff's individual and collaborative professional learning and the school's improvement goals?
- ▶ What policies or guidelines exist about the quality or effectiveness of professional learning?
- ▶ How does the school-based staff responsible for professional learning use those policies and guidelines?
- ▶ How do staff monitor the implementation of those policies or guidelines?

Delineating Lead Indicators and Commitments

To build momentum toward full implementation, set *lead indicators* (those necessary actions and results that contribute to the larger goal). Lead indicators provide benchmarks staff can divide into small segments, creating many opportunities to celebrate each small success toward achieving a goal.

In his best-selling book *Upstream: The Quest to Solve Problems Before They Happen*, author Dan Heath (2020) also stresses the importance of looking at the upstream causes of problems and addressing them. For example, if student performance is a problem, what issues are occurring associated with the poor performance staff can identify and address? When leadership and professional learning teams consider what is "upstream" contributing to the issues in a school, members can work backward to identify the lead indicators likely at the root of the problem and design a stream of small, tangible actions and indicators to undo the root causes. Nested together, the lead indicators create a chain reaction that moves the school's educators closer to achieving their goals for students.

Achieving a lead indicator moves the school closer to the goal. Determining the lead indicators (and commitments required from all the actors to reach them) will eventually generate success with the *lag indicator* (the goal). For example, if the goal is to improve differentiation in instruction to meet students' diverse learning needs and improve results for underperforming students, focusing on one step at a time might make the task seem less overwhelming. One lead indicator might be using one method of differentiation rather than three in a class. Once there is progress on one method, a teacher can introduce a second method. By focusing effort on a series of lead indicators together, teachers and students will see visible progress toward the goal of differentiating instruction.

The theory of change and logic model inform decisions about the lead indicators. Using the previously mentioned theory of change for critical thinking (page 77), one action is facilitating planning by team, grade level, and course to adapt a unit of study to integrate critical thinking. This action is a core benchmark in increasing students' critical thinking. The lead indicator of this action is revised units of study. Figure 6.3 (page 127) lists the commitments necessary to accomplish this lead indicator.

Lead indicator: Revise two units of study to integrate critical thinking into instruction and practice.

Duration: Four weeks

Completion date: October 15

School Administrators	Schedule time for teams to meet to revise units of study (September 9); minimize competing commitments (continuous); review revisions (October 1); meet with team facilitators to check on progress and provide resources and additional support as needed (September 15-October 15).
School Leadership Team	Coordinate with school administrators' scheduled time for revising units of study (September 9).
Team Facilitators or Chairs	Facilitate team meetings to revise two units of study to integrate critical thinking into instruction and practice (September 15—October 15).
Coaches	Support teams to select and integrate appropriate critical-thinking skills into units of study (September 15-October 15); provide support to teams as needed including additional instruction, resources, exemplars, and modeling (September 15-October 15); review revised units of study with administrators and team facilitators or chairs, and make recommendations for further revisions (September 15-October 15).
Teachers	Engage in team meetings to revise two units to integrate critical thinking into instruction and practice (September 15-October 15); make recommended adjustments (September 15-October 15); share work with whole faculty (September 15-October 15).

FIGURE 6.3: Sample commitments for accomplishing a lead indicator.

Visit go.SolutionTree.com/leadership for a free reproducible version of this figure.

School leaderships teams can map out lead indicators in advance and revise them often. Leader indicators are responsive to the progress, problems, and circumstances surrounding the work. For example, in the list of commitments in figure 6.3 (page 127), any interruptions can derail the intended plan to complete this portion of work by October 15. In this case, school leadership or professional learning teams working with school administrators review the lead indicator, commitments, and timeline, and adjust as needed to keep the work moving forward and respond to current circumstances. Focusing on the lead indicators provides data to inform adjustments.

Ongoing Assessment of Practice

Ongoing assessment keeps the leadership or professional learning team informed about where staff are in relation to their goals. The purpose of ongoing assessment of practice is to take a "temperature reading" of the current state to determine what the staff needs to meet the identified goals. When focused on the outcomes and goals, assessment provides information to make decisions about adjusting the professional learning or supports for implementation. It is not meant to punish anyone.

For example, in a middle school, all teacher teams commit to learn how to integrate more critical thinking into their units and revise the units to reflect critical-thinking skills their respective grade level emphasizes. However, a sixth-grade mathematics team was behind on revising the units of study it committed to in its professional learning plan. A midyear focus-group conversation with the school's mathematics coach and assistant principal to assess progress revealed the mathematics team needs additional support to better understand how to integrate hypothesis forming and concluding (two critical-thinking skills at the team's grade level) into the critical-thinking learning progression. Because minilessons with the coach, modeling, and reviewing exemplar units consumes a large portion of the team's available time for revising units, members also need an extension on their due date.

Without the assessments, the mathematics team may not get the support it needs nor gain an understanding about the cause of the delay. In addition, leaders may have expected members to achieve the next lead indictor without completing the previous one. This can create a snowball effect of falling further behind and getting more frustrated, which can eventually lead to abandoning the team's responsibility to help achieve the schoolwide vison, mission, values, and goals.

Self-Assessment

Self-assessment begins with individuals or teams reporting on the status of their commitments. Then, team facilitators summarize the individual and team statuses and report to the leadership or professional learning team. Together, the leadership team and administrators summarize the overall status of the commitments across the school, use this information to determine what supports teams need, and plan to make those supports available. Next, the leadership team communicates the summarized schoolwide status to the entire staff so everyone knows where they are in accomplishing the lead indicator. With data from across the school, individuals and teams can tap into those staff making more progress to learn how they are revising units and connecting their work for coherence across grade bands, courses, or departments. Finally, the leadership team provides supports where needed and adjusts the professional learning plan if necessary.

The frequency of self-assessment depends on the duration of the commitment for a lead indicator. For the previous example, weekly assessment is appropriate so the leadership team can identify and provide any additional supports teams need to meet the timeline. Sharing the summarized schoolwide status starts conversations among teachers, allowing them to identify what is working and what is not, and provides the opportunity for them to make requests to move forward. Starting with the individual reporting and expanding across teams and schoolwide fosters collective responsibility and enhances the possibility for professional learning success.

Publicly reporting assessment results builds transparency and announces practice. What might begin as a competitive spirit to finish first or have the best unit revisions can become an opportunity to learn from the work of others and increase the consistency and quality of the work schoolwide. The assessments provide the impetus for expanding the professional competence of all educators.

External Assessments

The previous example shows several external assessments. *External assessment* occurs when someone other than those who produce a product or engage in an action conduct a critique or analysis. For example, administrators and coaches review the units as they progress, using explicit criteria to offer commendations and recommendations to the teams to refine their work. External assessment identifies inaccurate practices to ensure coherence, articulation, and quality across the school.

Other forms of ongoing external assessment include classroom walkthroughs, coaching, peer classroom visits, showcases of teacher or student work, formative assessments, and examining teacher and student work. See the reproducible "Planning Peer Classroom Visits" (page 140). For example, teachers from all teams might use a collaborative assessment conference protocol to analyze a revised unit of study the science team completed. The benefit is the science team gets an objective review of its work, and others learn more about integrating critical thinking into instruction and practices in the science team's revisions. Teachers also can use the innovation configuration map to assess their collective practice and identify their successes and opportunities to share with their coach. See the reproducible "Writing an Innovation Configuration Map" (page 141).

Engaging in Feedback Processes for Reflection

The feedback process leads to constructing knowledge rather than transmitting information. As researchers John Hattie and Helen Timperley (2007) note, feedback is an instructional process with a high effect size. However, not all feedback is equally effective.

When feedback intentionally engages educators in analyzing evidence and forming their own conclusions, hypotheses, or generalizations about the evidence, educators can actively construct knowledge about their own work. This shift in constructing feedback, rather than receiving transmitted information, shifts responsibility for learning to the learner and generates more ownership, efficacy, and agency (Killion, 2019).

When feedback intentionally engages educators in analyzing evidence and forming their own conclusions, hypotheses, or generalizations about the evidence, educators can actively construct knowledge about their own work.

According to Killion (2019), the feedback process includes these steps:

1. Review the learning goal/outcome. Individuals or teams clarify the intended outcome of the learning and explain its purpose.

2. Specify indicators of success. Individuals or teams establish specific criteria for success that will be used to assess progress toward and achievement of the goal.

3. Determine data. Individuals or teams identify what and how they will collect data about the indicators for success to assess their efforts.

4. Collect data. Individuals, teams, or external partners collect the designated data to use in the next step.

5. Analyze data and evidence. Individuals or teams use a data-analysis protocol [such as the ones in chapter 3, page 53]. . . to formulate findings from the analyzed data.

6. Construct knowledge. Individuals or teams use the findings to identify lessons learned and to make those learnings explicit so it can be applied in other situations.

7. Deconstruct knowledge. Individuals and teams consider situations in which the newly constructed knowledge would not apply or would require some adaptation.

8. Determine next actions. Based on the newly constructed and deconstructed knowledge, individuals and teams plan their next steps for integrating their learning into practice.

9. Reflect on the feedback process. After completing the first eight steps, individuals or teams review their engagement in the feedback process, considering what they might alter next time, what didn't work as they had hoped, what contributed to their success.

10. Integrate knowledge. With the process complete, individuals or teams implement their newly constructed knowledge to enhance future practice (pp. 93–95).

Feedback contributes to ongoing practice refinement. When using the feedback process in a school, educators actively engage in their own learning, taking responsibility for their success. This shift from external accountability to internal responsibility builds commitment to success (Killion, 2019). In addition, it builds the capacity to engage in objective self-analysis, a critical skill for competent learners (Frey, Hattie, & Fisher, 2018; Killion, 2019). With this capacity, learners can continue to refine their practice both independently and collaboratively.

Coaching

Increasingly, research supports the benefits of coaching (Blazar & Kraft, 2017; Garet et al., 2016; Killion & Harrison, 2017; Kraft & Blazar, 2017; Kraft, Blazar, & Hogan, 2018; Quintero, 2019). Coaching for individuals and teams offers personalized support tailored to specific needs. When they interact with educators, coaches facilitate analysis, reflection, and discovery to realize potential. Coaching conversations are not didactic teaching episodes but rather, explorations of assumptions, beliefs, barriers, and possible actions to reach the desired outcomes. These conversations support continuous progress toward desired results and address barriers to change. Coaching builds confidence, competency, independence, and aspiration for success. The next sections explore coaching to refine and extend practice, coaching and modeling, and coaching and extending study.

Coaching to Refine and Extend Practice

An art teacher who serves on the fine arts team might struggle to productively contribute to her team's unit revisions because she does not understand how to connect her content standards with the grade level's critical-thinking skills. It isn't helpful to tell her everyone else understands and that she needs to understand too. What she needs are opportunities to clarify what she wants for her students, explore possibilities, receive encouragement to think from alternative perspectives, and identify initial steps. Dedicating time to coach her on these concepts signals that school leaders acknowledge and respect her concern, provides a forum for her to constructively raise the concern, gives her the support she needs to stay engaged and contribute, and meets her where she is. Without coaching, this art teacher may become resentful and disengage. In this situation, the coach serves in the role of a catalyst for change (Killion & Harrison, 2017).

Coaches need skillful preparation to facilitate conversations such as the one with the art teacher. They particularly must listen to understand, accept, and respect individual needs and concerns without judgment. Their mission is to facilitate self-discovery, inquiry, and reflection without striving to fix or solve others' problems, direct the work of others, or rescue others from the hard work associated with learning.

When working with teams, coaches facilitate the team processes rather than direct the work. They search for opportunities to help team members understand how they are working together, the roles they each play, and the nature of their interactions. By building healthy communication and productive processes in teams, coaches build team members' capacity to work efficiently and effectively, thereby facilitating success with their work.

Coaching and Modeling

Sometimes seeing the learning in practice clarifies and supports learning. Coaches may serve as classroom supporters and demonstrate a practice in a classroom with one or more teachers observing the model (Killion & Harrison, 2017). Modeling can also happen with video exemplars of the practices teachers can observe and critique, preferably in a facilitated and collaborative setting so what teachers notice and question align with the focus area.

Another way to provide modeling is to create demonstration classrooms where teachers commit to using the new learning and opening their doors to other teachers to observe their work. Modeling does not need to be perfect. Sometimes, seeing emerging practice, even if a teacher does not perfectly execute it, builds confidence and a willingness to try. In addition, modeling creates openness and transparency and provides authentic examples of the learning in action and encourages collaboration among teachers about their work.

Each modeling session requires three parts that occur before, during, and after (Killion & Harrison, 2017). First and *before* each session, discuss what will be modeled and how the modeling is planned, and provide guidance on how to take notes during the modeling. Second, actively observe and collect data or take notes *during* the modeling. Third, engage in a reflection conversation *after* the modeling. During the three parts of a modeling session, the observers and the person modeling the learning will understand more about the learning, criteria for success, and how modeling works. Without the conversations and data, the modeling session may not have the potential to promote deeper learning.

Coaching and Extending Study

Professional learning for educators fills a vital need, especially as nearly everything in the world changes—family structures, environment, economics, business systems, technology, and so on. These changes require changes in educational systems, and those changes mean teaching and learning are constantly evolving.

Some teachers might benefit from more opportunities to practice the critical-thinking skills they will be teaching. Others might want to explore critical-thinking skills not included in their learning progression to deepen their overall understanding. Some might want to read about how other teachers, schools, or scholars think about the role of critical thinking in the educational landscape. Some might want to explore the objections some educators occasionally raise regarding including critical thinking in the curriculum. Acting as learning facilitators, coaches design and facilitate these extensions to personalize and expand learning, deepen understanding, and explore beyond what the school routinely includes in professional learning (Killion & Harrison, 2017).

Extended studies respond to learners' needs and emerge from assessment and teacher requests. They are most often choices rather than mandatory experiences. In addition, extended studies can be collaborative or individual experiences. To maximize the benefits of extended studies, the leadership team can encourage sharing insights across the faculty and make opportunities for sharing part of routine meetings. In this way, all learners benefit from others' extended studies, and the practice may encourage some to seek out their own extended study experiences.

Ongoing Monitoring of Implementation

Oversight and monitoring of the implementation keep focus on the work and its effectiveness. If commitment to achieving a goal is genuine, then knowing what is being done and current results makes sense. Monitoring is the responsibility of the school leadership or professional learning team partnering with the school administrators. Team members review data and answer the following questions.

- ▶ What is working?
- ▶ How do we know?
- ▶ What isn't working?
- ▶ How do we know?
- ▶ What are we going to do based on these data?

Frequency matters because one-off conversations do not sustain change. Monthly monitoring in conjunction with ongoing assessment of practice gives leaders the necessary information to make adjustments. Leaders' monitoring focuses on ensuring actions taken are sufficient and equitable across the school. For example, if the world languages department hasn't started its unit revisions one week before the deadline, leaders could take many possible actions. There might be a supervisory intervention that reiterates expectations or a coaching response to discover any barriers to progress. Leaders might also provide additional resources, such as more time, exemplars, or extended study, to accomplish the tasks. Knowing in advance where the breakdowns and successes occur maintains forward movement and allows for quick response to meet emerging needs, surface unanticipated problems, and address those problems.

Monitoring also focuses on results in addition to the actions and commitments. If the results don't match the planned actions and commitments, it is vital to make quick adjustments. For example, if team leaders facilitate meetings to revise units of study, but the revised units don't meet leadership expectations for quality, the team may need intervention. Effort without results wastes time and energy. Focused effort with visible results creates momentum and opportunities to celebrate progress.

Communicating openly and honestly about discoveries and engaging all stakeholders in reviewing and reflecting on actions and results encourages collective responsibility for the success of the learning. Psychological safety is essential for this type of communication. Open, honest communication builds awareness, opens lines of communication for sharing challenges and ways to address them, and makes learning transparent. For example, suppose a health and physical education teacher finds a unique way to integrate a critical-thinking skill into a unit of study. All teachers can benefit from this teacher sharing the process that led to success.

Clarifying Leader Responsibilities in Implementation

Leaders have a weighty responsibility to support those implementing new learning into routine practice. *Leaders* include school administrators, the school leadership or professional learning team, and teacher leaders. While some leaders may not implement the changes themselves, they create and maintain a focus on the change; mitigate competing priorities that interfere with its success; communicate repeatedly to advocate success; and remove threats that inhibit psychological safety to maintain a culture of trust, support, and celebration to acknowledge effort and results. The leader responsibilities in the next sections target creating and maintaining a focus on change, mitigating competing priorities, communicating repeatedly, and removing threats to psychological safety.

Creating and Maintaining a Focus on Change

Learning takes effort, and moving learning to routine practice takes even more effort. This move requires assessing current practice, determining how to change the current practice to integrate new practice, adapting to new ways of thinking and acting, and contending with the cognitive dissonance between current and new desires and expectations. For some, this causes cognitive and emotional distress seemingly too difficult to handle. By keeping the main focus at the forefront, leaders send a message that affirms the focus and reminds implementers about the reasons and overall school vision, mission, values, and goals. In informal and formal conversations, leaders frequently inquire about the progress of new learning implementation. In addition, they listen to discover barriers teachers may encounter. Simple questions such as the following convey empathy and appreciation.

- ▸ What are you feeling good about now in terms of your work and students' learning?
- ▸ How did you make that happen?
- ▸ What support do you want?
- ▸ What's in your way?

Mitigating Competing Priorities

Schools are fraught with competing priorities that can instantaneously derail any initiative, particularly one focused on changing professional practice. Schools have so many moving parts, and any one part can set off a chain reaction that replaces one priority with another. For leaders, this creates the need for polarity management. Barry Johnson (1996, 2020), creator of *polarity mapping* (a visual framework to tackle problems), notes educators often view challenges as polarities rather than possibilities. Yet, Johnson (1996, 2020) notes that in nature, one's most basic functions exist as polarities and often cites inhaling and exhaling as prime examples.

Leveraging polarities examines competing priorities and finds positives in each. Leaders can facilitate moving from new-old– or right-wrong–thinking to understanding both opposites have value and can coexist in healthy ways. For example, some may apply new learning and value it, and some may not apply the new learning nor value it. *Polarity management* is a useful tool for leaders to encourage productive conversations about differences to find the best within each point of view. Leadership and coaching consultants and coauthors Jane A. G. Kise and Barbara K. Watterston (2019) offer the following tool (see figure 6.4) for helping leaders address polarities.

What opportunities do you see when teachers use their strengths individually?	What opportunities do you see when teachers collaborate?
• • •	• • •
What problems do you see if you focus too much on teachers' individual contributions?	What problems do you see if you focus too much on teacher collaboration?
• • •	• • •

Source: Kise & Watterston, 2019, p. 97.

FIGURE 6.4: Individual contribution and collaboration polarity tool.

Communicating Repeatedly

Patrick Lencioni (2000), the pioneer of the organizational health movement, writes of the importance to communicate, communicate, communicate in *Obsessions of an Extraordinary Executive*. Lencioni (2000) notes that people forget what they are told—they get busy, return to their routines, and lose track. Leaders, believing they have communicated, respond with frustration. However, frequent restating, elevating, and inquiring about the change is essential. Communicating in different formats, settings, and with different teams and individuals keeps leaders' commitment to change at the forefront. Repeated communication is how leaders convey their belief in the potential of the learning to make a difference in professional practice and student success. It also conveys leaders' belief in the capability of staff to implement the learning deeply to achieve the intended results. Finally, it conveys appreciation for and recognition of staff effort.

Removing Threats to Psychological Safety

Any change entails failures. How school leaders handle failure affects the psychological safety of individuals and teams. When people are threatened, they flee, fight, freeze, or appease. None of these options are healthy, and all can derail the transfer of learning to practice. Business professor and author George E. L. Barbee (2018) calls this the *yikes zone*:

> Moving into the yikes zone makes us uncomfortable, nervous, or downright scared. We worry we will fail and look bad in front of colleagues. Maybe our career will suffer. Often it is comfortable to retreat back into old habits, the ones that made us feel safe. Or to freeze and do nothing as opportunities to learn and grow pass us by.

Barbee (2018) encourages people to stretch themselves into the yikes zone and tackle what is causing the problem. This is easier to do when the environment champions making and learning from mistakes, and when people have a circle of support from which to draw courage. See the reproducible "Psychological Safety Survey" (page 138).

To maintain psychological safety, leaders must find ways to acknowledge and learn from setbacks, and use that learning in positive ways. The acronym *FAIL* (first attempt in learning) applies to learners of any age. Creating safe forums to discuss failures and encourage reflection can remove threats that may diminish the integrity or potential of any staff member. For example, one principal awarded a rubber chicken each week to a staff member who stepped forward in the faculty meeting to discuss a challenge the staff member faced, how she handled it, and what she learned. This process became an opportunity to alleviate stress and make the experience of facing challenges common. Staff came to value this recognition award.

The main idea of making challenges public is to help people understand that *everyone*, no matter how experienced, accomplished, or competent, faces setbacks. Organization psychologist Adam Grant (2021a) reminds educators, "No practice is ever perfect. The day you stop being open to improving is the day you start stagnating." An example of emerging practice can help others understand what initial or intermediate success looks like and scaffold the steps to achieve accomplished practice. How leaders handle challenges makes a difference in the overall sense of safety, trust, and willingness of others to persist in the face of these challenges. Remember, publicly addressing challenges is a healthy indicator that change is happening and people trust they are safe. When the challenges go underground, they can become destructive forces that build staff resentment, resistance, and retreat.

Maintaining Joy in the Work

The work of learning and transferring it to practice is rigorous, yet it can be joyful. Sheridan (2018) describes the importance of maintaining joy in the work and workplace. As a CEO, Sheridan (2018) acknowledges a good deal of the responsibility falls on his shoulders as a leader, and he advises leaders to be humble, authentic, transparent, and loving. He describes his dream for joy:

> We needed to replace the traditional model, which was marked by fear and bureaucracy, with one that allowed teams to bring their whole selves to work every day. This better model would support a collegial and productive environment, where innovation and imagination helped foster practical inventions that would serve and inspire customers. That creativity and innovation, in not just product but process, would also power the team's energy, creating a kind of human-perpetual motion machine. . . .
>
> What I was seeking was . . . . *joy at work*. . . . that's what I wanted above all else— joyful outcomes produced by people in a joyful place. (Sheridan, 2018, pp. 6–7)

The emphasis Sheridan (2018) places on joy rather than happiness, its fleeting distant relative, speaks to the deeper sense of satisfaction that emerges from a daunting and worthy challenge, meriting the sweat it takes to overcome it. Joy comes from within and without. Understanding the reason why makes a difference, as does seeing your place in the work and contribution to the whole. Joy comes from laughing at and learning from your mistakes, others loving you for acknowledging those mistakes as opportunities to learn, and your team valuing you as a team member. It also comes from recognizing and appreciating the hard work, effort, and personal investments that contribute to success. While happiness can wane, as Sheridan (2018) notes, joy does not. Instead, joy is like a flywheel that continues to move with little effort once it starts moving. See the reproducible "Remember the Joy" (page 144).

Conclusion

Learning plus implementation leads to results. Learning without implementation leaves results to chance. Therefore, to achieve success, school leadership teams commit to plan and invest in the two core dimensions of implementation (internal and external) by building an implementation system with diverse, sufficient, and continuous supports for individuals, teams, and the whole faculty. Each component contributing to success is a crucial piece of the puzzle.

Author Dolores Ambrose (1987) writes that complex change requires vision, skills, incentives, resources, action plan, and clear results. Without any one of these components, leaders are likely to come short of their expectations. In some respects, initial learning is the easier part of professional learning. Implementation through mastery is the more difficult part; it requires persistence, patience, and plentiful resources. Maintaining inspiration and joy throughout the complex journey of deep implementation also requires persistence, patience, and plentiful resources. Success for students and educators is the return on the investments.

Leadership Tips

To support and implement a school-based professional learning plan, leaders must understand how to implement and sustain change, clarify leader responsibilities, and maintain joy in the work. The following tips will help you get started.

- ▶ Coordinate implementation efforts and resources across the school, looping in different leaders in different ways to reach as many as possible with the desired support.

- ▶ Anticipate obstacles and address them before they occur or as quickly as possible.

- ▶ Create a problem-resolution process that encourages staff to surface emerging issues and invite multiple perspectives on how to address the issues.

- ▶ Communicate in multiple ways, at multiple times, and to multiple different audiences.

- ▶ Consider the message of symbolic behaviors—those that signal genuine commitment to the success of the professional learning.

Reflection Questions

1. Which components of the implementation process have we inadequately attended to in the past?

2. How will we maintain psychological safety, trust, and productive relationships in times of change?

3. What are some ways administrators, teacher leaders, coaches, and teams can keep the focus on results?

4. How do we identify the competing priorities—and thinking related to them—and manage to find a way for both?

5. How will we prepare leaders to assume their role in implementing the learning?

Psychological Safety Survey

This quick survey will help you gather information about perceptions during learning processes, which require changing one's practice.

PURPOSE To provide a check of perceptions about each individual's willingness to be open and honest when working collaboratively with others

PRODUCT Determining next steps by gathering the data, and sharing and discussing results from the survey ·

PARTICIPANTS All team members

MATERIALS Digital or paper copies of this reproducible "Psychological Safety Survey"

TIME Approximately ten minutes to complete the survey and approximately one hour to prepare, distribute, analyze, and prepare a report of the results

PREPARATION Send digital or paper copies of the survey to all team members

PROCESS **Step 1**

Prepare the survey to distribute to selected respondents. Note, there are two sections of the survey, each with its own score. Total the scores from each section to get a final score. Ask team members to assign a score of 1–5 for each question.

Step 2

Compile the scores from individual surveys into mean scores for the team. A higher score (35 possible points) indicates greater psychological safety.

Step 3

Share the survey results with team members and invite their comments about the results. Use questions such as the following.

- Where are we doing well?
- What do we want to strengthen?
- What might we consider that will strengthen individual members of the team?
- What are our individual responsibilities and collective responsibilities?

Step 4

Make commitments to improve each member's sense of safety. Set a date to review and revisit the effect of the commitments.

Psychological Safety Survey

Part One	Strongly Disagree 1	Somewhat Disagree 2	Neutral 3	Somewhat Agree 4	Strongly Agree 5
1. Members of this team can mention problems and tough issues.					
2. It is safe to take a risk on this team.					
3. No one on this team would deliberately act in a way that undermines my efforts.					
4. Members of this team value and utilize my unique skills and talents.					
Subtotals for part one					

Part Two	Strongly Disagree 5	Somewhat Disagree 4	Neutral 3	Somewhat Agree 2	Strongly Agree 1
1. People on this team sometimes reject others for being different.					
2. It is difficult to ask other members of this team for help.					
3. If you make a mistake on this team, members often hold it against you.					
Subtotals for part two					
Totals for parts one and two					

Reference

Edmondson, A. C. (2019). *The fearless organization: Creating psychological safety in the workplace for learning, innovation, and growth,* p. 20. Hoboken, NJ: John Wiley & Sons.

Planning Peer Classroom Visits

This tool offers a process for engaging teachers in peer visits to one another's classrooms and debriefing after the visits.

PURPOSE To create a safe process for teachers to visit one another's classroom and find ways to learn from one another

PRODUCT Peer support and key ideas for improving instruction and success for all students

PARTICIPANTS Peers

MATERIALS None

TIME Approximately ten to fifteen minutes to prepare for the visit; the duration of the visit (from ten to sixty minutes); and twenty minutes to debrief after the visit

PREPARATION To begin, ask your team to examine the definition of *peer coaching*. Next, ask your team to review possible definitions and discuss what the team can learn about the process. Then, ask the team to prepare an in-house definition of peer coaching and goals for the process. It might be helpful to consider how peer coaching is the same or different from instructional coaching.

PROCESS The following steps will help you create awareness, develop readiness, build commitment, and plan, implement, and maintain a peer coaching program in your school.

Step 1
Establish a small work group to explore ways teachers can learn from one another by visiting one another's classrooms. Develop a short, clear plan and begin to schedule visits.

Step 2
Discuss the current school culture by looking for supports for and challenges to classroom visits.

Step 3
Host small-group meetings to discuss how peer visits might work and what teachers might want to know more about. Identify needs and resources to support peer partners.

Step 4
Provide opportunities for teachers to choose their peer partners. Do not rush the process; it often emerges as partners share successes. Find ways to bring new and experienced teachers into the process.

Step 5
Discuss ways to schedule visits, including during prep periods or by asking for coverage from an administrator, coach, or other staff.

Writing an Innovation Configuration Map

Innovation configuration maps serve to guide the implementation of new practices and self-assess progress in the implementation.

PURPOSE To define and measure implementation of a new program or practice to ensure student success

PRODUCT Innovation configuration map

PARTICIPANTS Representative teacher team to complete the map for the full faculty (Getting input from the team is valuable to the process.)

MATERIALS Innovation Configuration Map Template (page 143), sample innovation configuration map from chapter 5 (page 93) and other examples from recommended resources listed in step 1 (page 141)

TIME One to multiple hours, depending on the complexity of the innovation

PREPARATION Choose an approach to describe levels of practice. Some begin with three levels and describe the levels (level 1: ideal or expert; level 2: acceptable or developing; and level 3: unacceptable or novice). Others may opt to begin with four, five, or six levels of performance rather than just three. In other words, they identify ideal, near ideal, acceptable, approaching acceptable, and unacceptable (or eliminate the unacceptable level). The decision depends on the complexity of the practice and how many components it involves. Write the best or highest level in the left column, and the lowest level in the right column of the chart (see page 143).

Choose *looks like*s and look-fors visible to an observer or implementer to use as the descriptors of the implementation levels.

PROCESS **Step 1**
Study the examples of an innovation configuration map in chapter 6, page 119. Next, review the following resources to develop a foundational understanding of the purpose and design of an innovation configuration map: *Implementing Change Through Learning: Concerns-Based Concepts, Tools, and Strategies for Guiding Change* (Hord & Roussin, 2013), and *Innovation Configurations | Concerns-Based Adoption Model* (American Institutes for Research, 2010).

Step 2
Determine the key components of the professional learning. Those key components may include the use of particular practices, frequency of use, accuracy of use, or some combination.

For example, if a new mathematics curriculum is the focus of the professional learning, implementing the ideal number of units is a core component. Additional core components of the new curriculum could be adhering to instructional practices that align with mathematical practices in the units, reteaching students (when necessary) in flexible groupings, and providing enrichment options. List core components in a chart (see page 143) in the left-hand column.

PROCESS
(cont.)

Step 3

Determine if there is a priority among the identified core components or if there is a natural sequence in the occurrence of the behaviors in practice. For example, teams consider adhering to the instructional practices aligned with mathematical practices more important than the number of units they implement. Position the components in the table according to priority or natural sequence order.

Step 4

Describe in specific terms the actual behaviors associated with the ideal or accomplished level of practice for each core component. List the ideal behaviors in the second column of the table under the agreed-on label. Some innovation configuration maps use a numerical designation for the variations; others may use terms such as *accomplished* or *ideal* practice to identify the first variation.

Step 5

Describe the variations from ideal practice. A *variation* is what teams consider a step down from the ideal. The number of variations for each core component varies depending on the potential variations.

For example, the number of units taught might include five variations, while the accuracy of using instructional practices aligned with mathematical practices may have just three variations. Each progressive variation from the ideal includes what is likely evident in practice as educators are extending, refining, and strengthening their practice over time. Furthermore, each progressive variation helps identify the current state of those teachers in various stages of practice before they reach the ideal stage. Place the subsequent variations in order in the same row as the ideal practice.

Step 6

Determine where acceptable behavior falls on the continuum of variations. For example, teachers may find it acceptable to implement 85 percent of the units of the new mathematics curriculum, even though that particular variation rests in the third variation. Use a dotted line to indicate the division between acceptable and unacceptable behavior.

Step 7

Introduce, explain, and discuss the map with participants to build their understanding and capacity to use the map for self-assessment. Innovation configuration maps encourage learners to determine their current state among the variations and identify what they need to do differently to move increasingly closer to the ideal or accomplished state. A well written map makes these changes explicit, so the tool becomes educative for learners.

Innovation Configuration Map Template

Innovation configuration maps come in a variety of forms. This template explicitly identifies the core components to facilitate the development of a new map. When fully developed, it may be unnecessary to label each core component and use different terms to describe levels of practice, yet this is helpful in the development phase.

Variations	Ideal or Accomplished Practice	Near Ideal or Accomplished Practice	Acceptable Practice	Early Stage or Emerging Practice	Unacceptable or Nonexistent Practice (Optional)
Core Component 1					
Core Component 2					
Core Component 3					
Core Component 4					
Core Component 5					

Remember the Joy

This tool is helpful to appreciate the joy of learning and its effects.

PURPOSE To pause, reflect, and remember the joy, creativity, delight in students' eyes, and fun of our work

PRODUCT A more joy-filled culture

PARTICIPANTS All team members

MATERIALS None

TIME Thirty to sixty minutes for each suggestion

PREPARATION While some activities may require preparation, it is the attitude that brings openness to the learning process.

PROCESS The following steps will help you bring joy to the workplace when staff are engaging in learning.

Step 1
Conduct action research and inquiry as part of your daily work.

Step 2
Use or adapt a new productivity tool.

Step 3
Keep a log to track the experiments you're running and reflect on what you're learning along the way.

Step 4
Let go of old habits that no longer serve you.

Step 5
Relearn resilience.

Step 6
Visit one another's classrooms and look for opportunities to learn from others.

Step 7
Set a goal of having one *curiosity coffee chat* each month, virtually or in person, with someone you haven't met. (This might be someone in a different department, grade level, or school, or someone in a vastly different profession who can help you view your classroom through a new lens.)

Step 8
Make learning a team activity.

PROCESS (cont.)

Step 9
Try a weekly or monthly skills swap, when educators share a skill they are happy to help others learn.

Step 10
Practice mindfulness.

Step 11
Maintain a *to-learn list* and dedicate time to your personal growth.

Step 12
Make learning part of your daily practice and teach your students the habit.

Reference

Tupper, H., & Ellis, S. (2021). Make learning a part of your daily routine. *Harvard Business Review.* Accessed at hbr.org /2021/11/make-learning -a-part-of-your-daily-routine on May 9, 2022.

CHAPTER 7

Monitoring and Measuring

Valuing is creating: hear it, ye creating ones! Valuation itself is the treasure and jewel of the valued things. Through valuation only is there value; and without valuation the nut of existence would be hollow. Hear it, ye creating ones!

—FRIEDRICH NIETZSCHE

Knowing the current state of any professional learning initiative provides crucial data to guide program managers, facilitators, and participants. As accountable, responsible leaders, they use evaluation to determine how to support professional learning and transfer it to practice, what problems need attention, and what successes to celebrate. Chapter 6 (page 119) explored assessment as a vital part of the implementation process. This chapter extends the examination of ongoing formative assessment of practice and unpacks professional evaluation. It includes a description of several formative assessment processes to check progress and summative evaluation to measure results and impact.

Leadership teams invest in assessment and evaluation to accelerate results, adjust learning designs, support teachers, and celebrate success. Every effort to produce change merits evaluation. Killion (2018) notes, "Evaluating a professional learning program begins with a commitment to continuous improvement and to impacting educator and student success. It is within this context that the evaluation of professional learning becomes necessary and beneficial" (p. 203).

Evaluation takes time and effort. The value of professional learning evaluation rests in building a reasonable and supportable argument that the learning adults experience and implement in their practice affects student learning. While leaders desire a positive effect, they might discover the effect is neutral or negative. Understanding if the effect occurred and the direction of the effect informs future professional learning.

Evaluation allows leaders to move from guessing based on opinion or perception to decision making based on data and evidence. In addition, evaluation produces information to share with stakeholders, including participants, about progress. It guides the leadership team to reflect on its overall planning and implementation to inform future professional learning efforts. Finally, evaluation generates information about the work's success to fuel team celebrations.

> The value of evaluation of professional learning rests in building a reasonable and supportable argument that the learning adults experience and implement in their practice affects student learning.

People tend to be averse to evaluation. They frequently view evaluation as a judgment of them rather than of the program. However, this is not how evaluation in school-based professional learning works. As Nietzsche (2019) writes, evaluation is a process for creating knowledge that currently does not exist. By examining the relationship between professional learning and student success, evaluation allows leadership teams to claim with evidence that educator learning influences student learning.

Leadership teams are well on their way to planning for assessment and evaluation once they clearly define goals and outcomes, select and apply learning designs, and put implementation supports in place. This chapter presents key terms, common mistakes in evaluation, user-focused evaluations, and how to implement a comprehensive evaluation process.

Learning Key Terms

The practice of assessment and evaluation of learning is routine in classrooms; however, applying those practices to initiatives such as improving professional learning is less common. Unfortunately, a significant amount of energy and effort goes into planning and implementing professional learning but not into measuring its results. Understanding some key terms before diving into details will facilitate the process.

- ▶ **Professional learning event:** A single or episodic professional learning experience disconnected from other experiences

- ▶ **Professional learning program:** A planned sequenced series of professional learning experiences that occur over time, coupled with implementation supports

- ▶ **Assessment:** Using data to determine the current state based on criteria to make decisions

- ▶ **Evaluation:** Using data to judge the merit, worth, and impact of professional learning

- ▶ **Formative:** Informal or formal interim assessment that occurs during the process provide data about progress toward the goals and attainment of lead indicators and may include recommendations for adjusting the current professional learning

- ▶ **Summative:** Informal or formal evaluation that occurs at key benchmark points or at the end of the program provides data about goal and outcome achievement and the effects of the professional learning and may include recommendations for adjustments in current and future professional learning

- ▶ **Activities:** Actions to produce results

- ▶ **Outcomes:** Results or changes that occur because of the activities

Understanding the key concepts involved in monitoring and measuring practice makes it easier to create a valid, reliable, and trustworthy system for monitoring and measuring the implementation and effects of professional learning. When people lack trust in an evaluation system or perceive that it is unfairly judging them, they tend to be less open and unwilling to contribute to the work. In addition, those developing an evaluation system need basic competencies on how to design monitoring and measuring tools that begin with understanding the fundamental concepts of evaluation. The ability to understand and distinguish among the terms is the beginning of gaining those competencies.

Understanding a Common Mistake in Evaluation

A frequent mistake in evaluation is assuming planned actions produce intended results. For example, the leadership team gathers teacher attendance data for a schoolwide workshop on early literacy. They might assume teacher attendance at the the workshop is sufficient to increase literacy results for students in grades preK–3. However, they find the results in student reading scores are unchanged at the end of the year. The top row of figure 7.1 shows an example of a *black-box evaluation*, where the input is teacher workshop attendance and the outcome is student achievement. However, the center through line is unexplained, and, as a result, any relationship the team perceives is faulty. Many possible explanations exist for the unchanged results.

SAMPLE BLACK-BOX EVALUATION

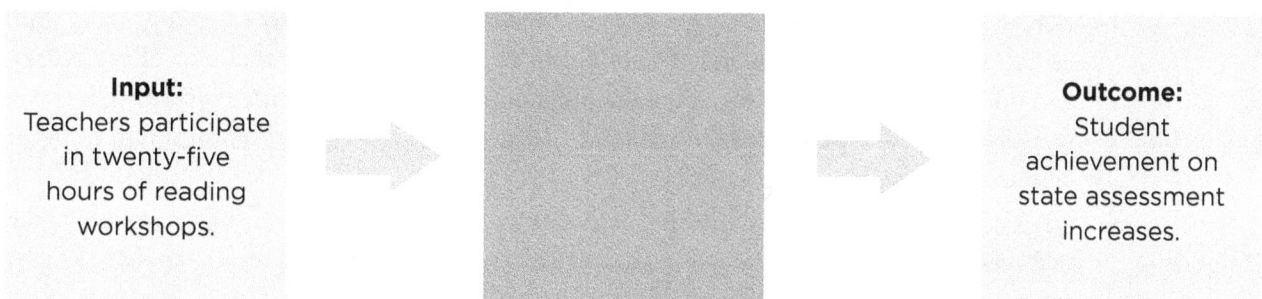

Input:
Teachers participate in twenty-five hours of reading workshops.

Outcome:
Student achievement on state assessment increases.

GLASS-BOX EVALUATION

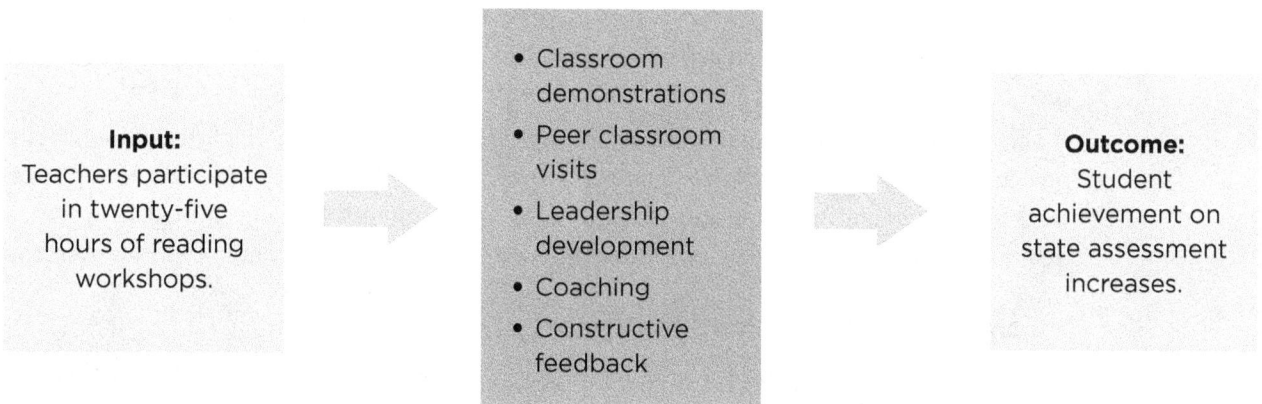

Input:
Teachers participate in twenty-five hours of reading workshops.

- Classroom demonstrations
- Peer classroom visits
- Leadership development
- Coaching
- Constructive feedback

Outcome:
Student achievement on state assessment increases.

Source: Killion, 2018, pp. 24, 32. Used with permission.

FIGURE 7.1: Black-box versus glass-box evaluation.

A black-box evaluation provides no information about what happens between the workshop and the final measurement of results for students. This leads to faulty conclusions about the program and provides no useful information about adjusting the program to strengthen results. Black-box evaluations attempt to make causal connections between variables that may not be causally connected. For example, attendance may relate to the results for students; however, it is certainly not a single cause of the result. Some teachers might achieve results for their students without attending the workshop.

As the bottom row of figure 7.1 shows, a leadership team gains more information throughout the program's duration when the "black box" transforms into a "glass box." Then, the team can use that additional information to make a series of adjustments during the program to strengthen its success. A *glass-box evaluation* uses a chain of effects from the data teams collect from the program's initiation at the workshop through various implementation points. In addition, it looks at the effects of various supports teams apply to the student results. These data points paint a picture of how change occurs throughout the process and provides interim points to adjust actions to respond to indicators at each benchmark.

Engaging in User-Focused Evaluation

Educators often perceive evaluation as something extraneous to any change-initiative process. Evaluation consultants and coauthors Michael Quinn Patton and Charmagne E. Campbell-Patton (2022) designed *utilization-focused evaluation* to encourage evaluators to engage practitioners in the process from the beginning. In *Utilization-Focused Evaluation*, Patton and Patton (2022) note, evaluation is intended be useful to its users—to increase the value of the process and inform future decisions regarding the program. *User-focused evaluation* incorporates stakeholder interests and needs into the evaluation design to keep those needs at the forefront of the evaluators' work.

A leadership or professional learning team begins the evaluation process by determining who takes responsibility for the evaluation. This person or people might be a team member, a smaller team, or an adjunct team made up of others (some or all of whom may not be members of the team) interested in evaluation or who want to contribute to its success. A single member or the evaluation team then commits to using ethical and responsible evaluation practices, being as objective as possible, and keeping the best interests of evaluation users at the forefront of decisions. Schools might rely on an external evaluator for high-stakes professional learning programs such as those an external organization funds or those requiring an external evaluation.

The remainder of this chapter unpacks two approaches to evaluation. The first is a more comprehensive approach that includes eight steps. The second is a rapid cycles of evaluation process for short-term initiatives within a more comprehensive professional learning effort. This approach examines results on small-scale interventions to contribute to a cycle of continuous improvement.

Comprehensive Evaluation Process

Evaluating professional learning includes the following eight steps, several of which leaders may have already completed if they planned the professional learning well (Killion, 2018).

1. Assess evaluability.

2. Formulate evaluation questions.

3. Construct the evaluation framework.

4. Collect data.

5. Organize, analyze, and display data.

6. Interpret data.

7. Report, disseminate, and use findings.

8. Evaluate the evaluation.

The following describes the steps of the comprehensive evaluation process, along with the key actions necessary to accomplish each step and the necessary evidence to have in hand. See the reproducible "Creating a Plan for Comprehensive or Rapid Cycles of Evaluation" (page 166).

Step 1: Assess Evaluability

Evaluability is a term to describe readiness for evaluation. In this case, it means leaders have sufficiently designed and resourced the professional learning so it is likely to produce the intended results (Killion, 2018). To accurately assess the evaluation process, you know the program goals, theory of change, outcomes, design, and the incorporated implementation supports. (Chapters 3–6 address these aspects of the plan for and design of professional learning.)

To complete the evaluability assessment, evaluators examine the professional learning plan critically to ensure the following components are clear, precise, and complete.

- ▸ Goals for the professional learning
- ▸ Theory of change that maps out the program's overarching design
- ▸ Outcomes (KASABs) for educators
- ▸ Learning designs delineated to accomplish each outcome
- ▸ Implementation supports planned

(Chapters 4–6 address planning and designing professional learning.)

Step 2: Formulate Evaluation Questions

The evaluation questions specify what the leadership team and stakeholders want to know about the program. Many evaluation attempts merely document who attends or participants' level of satisfaction, rather than focusing on whether the professional learning makes a difference. Primarily, evaluation questions inquire if the professional learning produces its intended results, but evaluators may also want to know if a particular learning design or support type had a differentiated effect on learners. For example, did more experienced teachers require less or more implementation support than teachers with less experience? Gathering data to answer this question can inform future professional learning planning, potentially increasing its effectiveness and efficiency.

The two types of evaluation questions are formative and summative, just as they are for evaluations of student learning. *Formative evaluation* questions are those about the initial and intermediate outcomes, the lead indicators that help determine if there is progress toward the goals and outcomes, the lag indicators. For example, formative evaluation questions may be about changes in educator practices and impact on students. *Summative evaluation questions* inquire about the overall effects of professional learning at significant points during the program's implementation. For example, a middle school makes a three-year commitment in its school-improvement plan to increase students' critical thinking. The end of the three-year period is the summative point for the schoolwide effort. However, the leadership team will want to examine annual progress, establishing year-one, year-two, and year-three summative evaluation questions.

A challenge with evaluation questions is focusing on those most useful to the leadership team and participants. Frequently, evaluations become too complicated and lack what Patton and Patton (2022) call *usability*. If there is no practical reason to collect data, then there is no reason to create the data burden that may occur with collecting extraneous data.

The following sample evaluation questions use the critical-thinking professional learning program example we described in chapter 4 (page 75). Summative evaluation questions mirror a program's goals, while formative evaluation questions mirror program outcomes or lead indicators.

Program goal: Increase learners' capacity to apply critical-thinking skills in independent and collaborative decision making and problem solving.

Summative evaluation question: Did learners' capacity to apply critical-thinking skills in independent and collaborative decision making and problem solving increase?

Program goal: Increase educators' integration of critical-thinking skills into classroom instruction and learning tasks.

Summative evaluation question: Did educators' integration of critical-thinking skills into classroom instruction and learning tasks increase?

Program outcome: Ninety percent of the instructional staff develop a unit of study that integrates developmentally appropriate critical-thinking skills from the critical-thinking skills learning progression and explains how the skills support the unit's learning intentions.

Formative evaluation question: Did 90 percent of instructional staff develop a unit of study that integrates developmentally appropriate critical-thinking skills and explains how the skills support the unit's learning intentions?

Program outcome: Ninety percent of the instructional staff integrate explicit instruction on critical-thinking skills into classroom instruction and learning tasks at least once per week.

Formative evaluation question: Did 90 percent of the instructional staff integrate explicit instruction on critical-thinking skills into classroom instruction and learning tasks at least once per week?

The previous evaluation questions indicate that pre- and post-professional learning data are necessary to measure the degree of change and whether an increase occurs. Compare baseline data to post-professional learning data to determine whether an increase occurred.

Leadership teams know if their evaluation questions are useful when they do the following.

- Align the questions with the goals and outcomes.
- Indicate what type of data the team will need to answer the questions.
- Align the questions with the interests and needs of evaluation users.
- Avoid extraneous data that might require unnecessary work for the contributors or evaluators (Killion, 2018).

Step 3: Construct the Evaluation Framework

The *evaluation framework* is the plan for the evaluation. It builds on the evaluation questions, delineates data the team needs to answer the questions, specifies the timeline for collecting the data, determines the data-analysis process, and indicates the person or people responsible for each part of the evaluation process. When evaluators develop the goals, outcomes, and evaluation questions well, a solid plan comes together quickly. The framework in figure 7.2 (page 153) helps organize decisions.

Evaluation Questions	Data Needed	Dates to Collect	Analysis Method	People Responsible	Date
Summative evaluation question: Did learners' capacity to apply critical-thinking skills in independent and collaborative decision making and problem solving increase?	Pre- and post-measures of students' critical-thinking applications in independent and collaborative situations requiring decision making and problem solving include teacher-designed assessments, student performance assessments, or student products.	Spring before the implementation of the critical-thinking initiative and at the end of each of the three years of the initiative	Scores teacher teams (which have calibrated their scoring using a predetermined scoring tool such as a rubric or checklist) compile and compare with baseline data	Evaluation team	May
Formative evaluation question: Did 90 percent of instructional staff develop a unit of study that integrates developmentally appropriate critical-thinking skills from the critical-thinking skills learning progression and explains how the skills support the unit's learning intentions?	Teacher-developed units	End of each marking period	Rubric applied to completed units	Evaluation team and team of volunteer teachers	August–October
Did 90 percent of the instructional staff integrate explicit instruction on critical-thinking skills into classroom instruction and learning tasks at least once per week?	Self-report via a survey on the frequency of integration of critical thinking into instruction and learning; principal walkthrough records, peer visits, and coaching logs using specified look-for visits and observations supplement the survey.	Data teachers enter monthly into logs by week; survey data teachers collect twice annually; walkthrough data principals collect in every classroom twice annually; peer visit data teachers collect once annually; and logs coaches collect monthly	Counts of responses indicating *yes* or *no* with trend analysis over time; trend analysis with walkthrough and coach and peer visit data	Evaluation team	October–May

FIGURE 7.2: Sample evaluation framework.

When possible, use available data rather than creating additional data needs. For example, rather than creating a separate walkthrough process, school administrators can add two or three additional items associated with integrating critical-thinking instruction into their routine walkthrough list.

Data from multiple sources and in multiple formats increase the reliability and validity of an evaluation. The following are some examples.

▶ Teachers reporting they are implementing critical-thinking instruction at least weekly

▶ Principals seeing the identified items during their walkthroughs

▶ Coaches adding their data to those of teachers and principals

These data points from different sources strengthen the confidence in the overall data set. When planning what data are necessary to collect during an evaluation, consider several different sources (people, artifacts, or documents) and different methods (survey, observation, or interviews). A variety of sources and methods can validate the accuracy and increase data reliability. For creating surveys, see the reproducible "Writing Surveys" (page 164).

> **A variety of sources and methods can validate the accuracy and increase data reliability.**

Table 7.1 (page 155) includes sample data sources for different types of outcomes.

Data-analysis decisions can occasionally generate trepidation in those who fear working with statistics. However, most data-analysis processes for school-based professional learning are descriptive rather than inferential. Descriptive-analyses processes include basic mathematical operations such as counting, addition, subtraction, and averaging. Inferential-analyses processes include more sophisticated operations such as correlations, hierarchical-linear modeling, and significant tests. If an evaluation question merits the application of an inferential-statistical analysis, school staff with less experience in statistics can reach out to more knowledgeable colleagues.

It is crucial to create solid timelines for data collection as part of the evaluation framework. Collecting data for the formal evaluation must not detract from the overall implementation efforts or occur so infrequently that teachers miss opportunities for interventions. Ongoing informal assessment as a routine part of the implementation process may generate data that contribute to the formal evaluation.

Step 4: Collect Data

The next step of the evaluation process is collecting data. This step requires evaluators be methodical and organized. During this step, one of the biggest challenges results from missing data, which are unavailable or uncollected data. Missing data can occur because someone didn't submit the required evidence or didn't complete a data-collection process (such as walkthroughs or logging the information).

During data-collection periods, it is helpful for evaluators to be precise about the necessary data, timelines, and processes for submitting the data. Review the data to see if they contribute to the overall knowledge the evaluation generates. Evaluators update participants on how they will use the data during data analysis. Those implementing and supporting the implementation of professional learning want to understand the role they play in the overall professional learning process and how their contributions to the evaluation process are adding value to the professional learning process and the evaluation.

TABLE 7.1: Sample Data Sources for Different Types of Outcomes

Type of Outcome	Sample Data Sources
Knowledge	Tests of knowledge Quizzes Teacher explanations Assessments (open ended, multiple choice, and so on) Visual representations Assessments (open ended, multiple choice, and so on) Student explanations Criterion-referenced tests Common assessments Daily formative assessments Concept maps
Attitudes	Preferred choice surveys about beliefs or behaviors Degrees of acceptance or favorableness
Skills	Simulated demonstrations Process maps Simulated performances Process explanations Work products (lesson plans, instructional tools, and so on)
Aspirations	Degree of willingness survey Preferred-choice survey Interview responses
Behaviors	Role play Simulations Observations of authentic practice Observation logs Reflection analyses of practice Work products Frequency logs Accuracy assessments using explicit criteria such as innovation configuration maps, rubrics, or look-fors

Another important consideration during data collection is maintaining promised participant anonymity and confidentiality. When participants collect data, each participant wants to know if evaluators will associate individual results or cluster them into a group of data. For example, the eighth-grade English teachers might want to know if evaluators will compare individual scores to other teachers' scores. If there are only three eighth-grade English teachers, their concerns might be higher than if there are seven teachers in the cluster. These decisions, made during evaluation framework construction, contribute to the overall integrity of the evaluation process. In addition, the decisions are the ethical responsibility of evaluators and can engender positive relationships between the evaluation team and those responsible for implementation.

Sometimes anonymous comparison among groups of teachers or students yields useful information. For example, the comparison might show the eighth-grade English curriculum needs upgrading to include more opportunities for independent application of critical thinking in student-learning tasks. When teachers are not integrating those opportunities, is not the teachers' fault but rather a failing curriculum.

Step 5: Organize, Analyze, and Display Data

To transform words and numbers into meaning, evaluators collect, organize, analyze, and display the data. This step of the evaluation process also requires precision and methodical practices. Evaluators determine what data are missing and seek to add them (if late additions to the data set will not contaminate it). For example, if a teacher forgets to submit a weekly log about his inclusion of critical-thinking practices, including that log later may not be a problem if the teacher's records are accurate. However, suppose the same teacher does not submit student work samples by the deadline, giving his students an extra week to complete the product. In that case, this late submission may contaminate the data.

When data are numerical, evaluators can calculate means, modes, percentages, and ranges. For example, in the critical-thinking example, determining the percentage of staff who report including critical-thinking instruction and learning tasks requires a numerical operation. These simple descriptive statistics are sufficient for most analyses. If the data are qualitative, perhaps resulting from interviews, focus groups, or student or teacher work samples, the analysis process is more time consuming and requires decisions about how to cluster and report the information.

Two processes typically suffice for handling qualitative data. One is *semantic analysis*, which involves looking for key terms and ideas in the data and reporting the frequency of those key terms and ideas. Usually, semantic analysis begins with reading the data set to identify the key terms and ideas, creating a legend of those key terms and ideas, and then clustering responses by those key terms and ideas. For example, suppose twelve teachers reported students were more likely to engage in critical thinking in the classroom with teacher guidance than in other situations. In this case, the *classroom teacher guidance* is the key term or idea.

Another way to handle qualitative data is to look for emerging patterns, trends, and outliers. Report frequent patterns and trends by the number of occurrences, location of the occurrences, or the content. This process may eliminate some infrequent information.

For example, suppose a single teacher reports his students are using critical thinking socially or outside the classroom, such as in hallways and commons areas. In that case, the information may not surface as a pattern. However, it may be useful to investigate how this positive deviance occurred, when it occurred, and if there are practices the teacher can extract and share with others to extend students' critical thinking outside the classroom.

Once you analyze the data, display the data to help identify findings and create summary statements. Using color, clear legends, and multiple displays of the same data are helpful for those who prefer visual representations. For example, a table or a graph can display the number of teachers who weekly report integrating critical-thinking instruction and learning tasks. Figure 7.3 (page 157) shows three ways to display data.

Weekly Application of Critical Thinking

Weekly Application of Critical Thinking

Weekly Application of Critical Thinking	Yes	No
Number of teachers	37	4
Percent of teachers	90 percent	10 percent

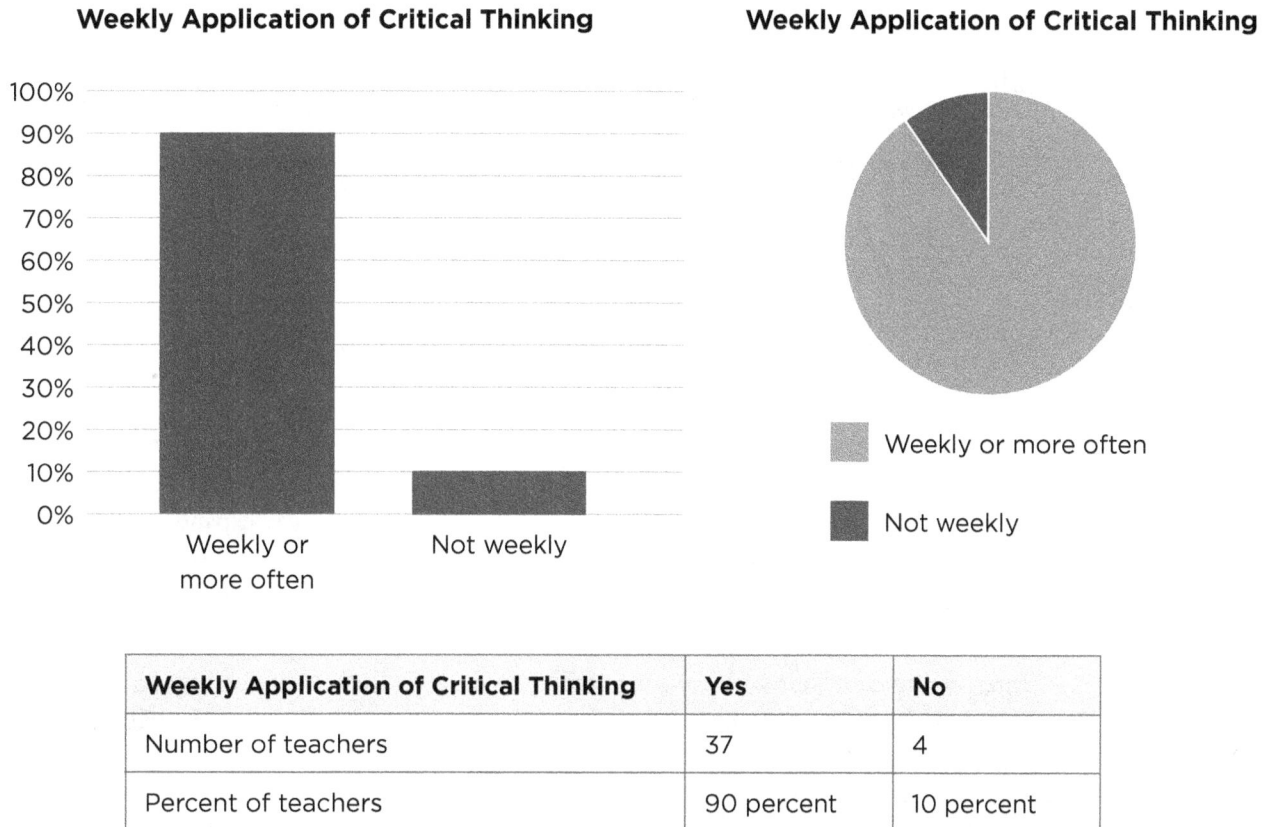

FIGURE 7.3: Three ways to display data.

The analysis process ends with noting the findings from the data. The findings are observations you draw directly from the data and summarize the data. "More teachers report . . .," "One-third of the students . . .," "Nearly half the students . . ."—each finding ties directly to some portion or the whole set of analyzed data. "One way to think about this process is grouping independent, isolated bits of information (data) into a more meaningful, yet broader, finding. . . . Findings summarize, describe, or make observations about the analyzed data" (Killion, 2018, pp. 153–154).

Data are unusable until the analysis and interpretation turn them into information. Engaging others in analyzing data is a healthy way to support their involvement and eventual use of the evaluation. Therefore, it is important to establish norms for using and discussing data to maintain safety and confidentiality. A series of data-analysis questions such as the following can support this process.

- ▸ What do you see in these data?
- ▸ What patterns exist?
- ▸ How would you describe the data?
- ▸ What is evident in these data?
- ▸ How can we summarize these data?
- ▸ What outliers exist?

See the reproducible "Setting Norms for Data-Analysis Meetings" (page 163).

Step 6: Interpret Data

The next step of the evaluation process is interpreting the analyzed data. In *Qualitative Research and Evaluation Methods*, author Michael Quinn Patton (2015) describes this process as:

> . . . going above and beyond the descriptive data. Interpretation means attaching significance to what was found, making sense of findings, offering explanations, drawing conclusions, extrapolating lessons, making inferences, considering meanings, and otherwise imposing order on an unruly but surely patterned world . . . . All of this is expected—and appropriate—as long as the researcher owns the interpretation and makes clear the differences between descriptions [findings] and interpretation. (p. 570)

Engaging implementers, facilitators, leadership team members, and other stakeholders in the interpretation process enriches the meanings of the findings. Varied perspectives can interject insights and explanations evaluators might not make. These perspectives expand and extend what evaluators know is useful for making decisions about next steps. As Patton (2015) notes, the key is distinguishing the findings from the interpretations so the evaluation does not devolve into a subjective process in which one person's perspective has more significance than others' perspectives.

Interpreting data ends with forming recommendations. These recommendations reflect the thinking of those who participate in the interpretation; recommendations offer ideas about how to improve future professional learning, and may also include suggestions for the particular (evaluated) professional learning.

The fundamental recommendations fall into three areas: (1) continue unchanged, (2) continue with modification, or (3) abandon. For example, the evaluation may show that more time or resources are necessary to realize the full benefits of the professional learning. It may be more classroom-focused coaching is necessary to transfer the learning to routine practice. Alternatively, it may be a poorly designed effort and educators might reconsider the entire effort before allocating additional effort or resources to it. Using the recommendations, educators can determine which actions to adjust.

Step 7: Report, Disseminate, and Use Findings

Evaluations are only worthwhile if evaluators report, disseminate, and use the knowledge gained. Therefore, the evaluation team is responsible for providing the results to those involved with professional learning at any level, engaging them in examining the results, and inviting them to contribute to using the results to strengthen both the specific work and future professional learning.

Reporting results in multiple formats for different audiences helps tailor the information to the audience's particular interests. For example, teachers may be interested in a more detailed report than parents or community members. To help evaluators prepare reports to meet the needs of various audience groups, consider the specific audiences' role in professional learning, their interest level, and the complexity of the information. For example, slides, one-page summaries, briefs, executive summaries, articles for newsletters or professional publications, and technical reports are several ways to package the evaluation reports.

The evaluation team is responsible for widely disseminating the results. The key to dissemination is *the more, the better*. For example, a neighboring school might benefit from reading an evaluation report about the school's professional learning to help design and implement its own professional learning. Another district might find value in studying the methodology a particular school uses. Sharing results in communities of practice in- and outside the school builds a collateral learning network that enriches the practice of all responsible for student success (Fullan, 2020; Hargreaves & Fullan, 2013).

Using the results is the last component of this step. Evaluations illuminate the overall work of professional learning within the specific context of the school and school community. In addition, results lead to discussions about what to include in planning, what to avoid, what was previously overlooked, and how to handle problems. Finally, results serve as a record of collective wisdom for future professional learning initiatives. Answering these three simple questions about past efforts extends the value of any evaluation into the future.

1. What do we want to continue doing?

2. What do we want to stop doing?

3. What do we want to change?

Step 8: Evaluate the Evaluation

The last step of the evaluation process is evaluating the evaluation. This meta-evaluation takes the focus off the professional learning results and turns to the evaluation process and the evaluators' skills and efforts. It is a process of reflection, external review, and learning about the evaluation process and the decisions and work of the evaluation team. Evaluation team members may conduct the process internally or (preferably) they can invite others to contribute. Contributors might include program participants or stakeholders and evaluation experts who can serve as critical friends during the meta-evaluation.

During this step, the evaluators answer questions such as these to examine their work.

▶ What are the strengths of the evaluation process? What contributed to those strengths?

▶ What were our challenges during the evaluation? How did we address those challenges?

▶ What changes would we make in the evaluation if we could redesign it? How would those changes contribute to improving the evaluation?

▶ What did we learn about our ability as evaluators? In what areas did we feel confident and competent? In what areas do we wish we had more expertise?

▶ How well did we distribute the available resources for the evaluation?

▶ How well did we tap the talents and interests of the team members?

▶ What do we want to remember to do in future evaluations?

▶ What lessons have we learned about evaluation?

Answering these questions can serve as a record to inform the design of future evaluations of professional learning or other school initiatives and serve as knowledge to share with colleagues at other schools interested in doing their own evaluations. Investing in an evaluation of the evaluation is "the hallmark of a reflective practitioner and allows evaluators to model evaluation behaviors as a routine part of their work and to engage in continual improvement" (Killion, 2018, p. 197).

Rapid Cycles of Evaluation

When leadership teams, collaborative teacher teams, or other collegial teams want to evaluate their efforts more rapidly or over shorter periods, they might embed rapid cycles of evaluation into the comprehensive approach to evaluation. Based on the practice of inquiry cycles for continuous improvement and action research, *rapid cycles of evaluation* generate knowledge to use immediately, often related to a time-limited series of actions. Use these rapid cycles as a formative assessment during a more comprehensive professional learning program or as a series of repetitive evaluations you then aggregate into one data source as a part of the comprehensive evaluation.

Consider a school seeking to integrate critical thinking across the curriculum to increase the rigor of student-learning experiences. Teachers have redesigned instructional units to integrate the specific critical-thinking skills students are learning and want to know quickly if their redesign efforts are resulting in students using critical-thinking skills. Although the comprehensive evaluation addresses this question, teachers want more immediate results so they can adjust their efforts or seek additional supports. They aren't willing to wait until the summative evaluation to know if their small steps are moving them closer to the intended results.

To conduct rapid cycles of evaluation, the team follows a similar process to the comprehensive evaluation. Team members can do the following.

- Clarify what they want in terms of goals or outcomes and their actions to achieve them.
- Write an evaluation question.
- Determine what data they will collect to answer that question.
- Determine how they will analyze the data.
- Set a timeline for the intervention and data collection.
- Implement their intervention.
- Gather data.
- Analyze data.
- Make decisions based on data.

Let's look at an example of how rapid cycles of evaluation work in practice.

RAPID CYCLES OF EVALUATION IN PRACTICE

The sixth-grade team members were finding inferential thinking challenging for their students. They read an article about how to help students use metaphor to infer about abstract ideas and want to apply the strategies in their lessons. They set a learning outcome: After the series of lessons, 90 percent of our students will meet or exceed the performance standard on the rubric. They wanted to answer this question: Did teaching the students how to use metaphor to infer about abstract ideas contribute to students' success?

They designed two common assessments, one using a passage about honesty and another about respect, selected both for their age-appropriate relevance and text-complexity level. They developed the rubric to reflect students' level of inferencing and use of metaphor. They planned three sequential lessons, taught those lessons, and had students complete the first common assessment during the same week. At the end of the second week, students completed the second common assessment.

Teachers collaboratively scored the students' work, with each teacher contributing to the students' scores. They compiled the data and analyzed the results. Their findings revealed students performed better on the second assessment than the first. Now, the teachers had the information to make another set of decisions about how to reach students who had not yet performed as the teachers expected and how to extend, reinforce, and sustain the learning of those who met the teachers' expectation.

The teachers discovered students with linguistic diversity scored lower overall; students who had been underperforming previously scored higher than teachers anticipated, yet not at the level desired. Only 79 percent of students scored at the expected level. They made decisions based on data from this rapid cycles of evaluation process, and shared them with other teams across the school for their insights and suggestions. Overall, teachers concluded that helping students use metaphor to make inferences about abstract ideas was helpful; it was just insufficient to cement inferential thinking for all students.

Some might look at the process of rapid cycles of evaluation as a traditional approach in PLCs, inquiry cycles, or other continuous-improvement processes. And while there are many similarities, the distinction comes in the thoroughness of the process, the careful planning about the outcomes and intervention, the questions to answer, the data to collect, and the analysis process. This process is done intentionally with a focus on evaluation and not planning alone. The overarching purpose of rapid cycles of evaluation is to learn the effects of the interventions and how to use that knowledge to adapt actions rather than change outcomes.

Conclusion

Evaluation is a core part of any professional learning effort. Investing in evaluation elevates the significance of a professional learning initiative; fosters commitment and buy-in to the learning; and engages those responsible for implementation in collaborating about their work using a defined, safe, and transparent process. Evaluation illuminates the value of the professional learning, encourages objective analysis of the effort, provides evidence of the effects, and informs future efforts. Making decisions about who will serve on the evaluation team, the scope and type of evaluation, and the level of effort to invest in the evaluation are decisions school leadership or professional learning teams make simultaneously as they plan professional learning. If professional learning is worth doing, it is also worth evaluating.

Leadership Tips

Evaluation is crucial for improving and maintaining school-based professional learning. Leaders need to engage staff in the evaluation process and ensure everyone understands the value of evaluation. The following tips will help you get started.

▸ Engage interested staff, those on the leadership or professional learning team, and others as members of the evaluation team.

- ▸ Reinforce the importance of evaluation that seeks to understand the effects on educators and students rather than mere satisfaction levels about professional learning.

- ▸ Serve as an advisor or a member of the evaluation team to model its importance to the success of professional learning.

- ▸ Provide multiple opportunities for the evaluation team to report on its work.

- ▸ Create multiple forums for the evaluation team to engage staff in analyzing data, interpreting findings, and using the evaluation results.

Reflection Questions

1. How have we evaluated past professional learning initiatives in the school? What knowledge did we gain from those evaluations?

2. What expertise do current leadership or professional learning team members have in evaluation? What do they need or want to know to conduct evaluation?

3. Who in the school or school system can support the evaluation team in its work?

4. Given the nature of professional learning in the school, which approach to evaluation (comprehensive or rapid cycle) might be the best starting point for initiating evaluation of professional learning?

5. How can leadership or professional learning team members help staff understand the importance of evaluating professional learning?

Setting Norms for Data-Analysis Meetings

The tool offers guidance on working with a team to develop agreements for data-analysis meetings.

PURPOSE To make agreements to ensure a safe environment for all participants (This tool can help team members maintain clarity about how to interact during data analysis to keep the process objective and safe for those who participate.)

PRODUCT Team norms for data-analysis meetings

PARTICIPANTS Leadership team, grade-level or department collaborative teams, and other school or district teams

MATERIALS None

TIME Thirty minutes

PREPARATION It's sometimes helpful to have some sample norms to help the team get started in this work. Step 3 of the Process section includes sample norms, and you can find others online.

PROCESS **Step 1**
Make agreements about how to use data well.

Step 2
Discuss how norms can guide the work of the data team.

Step 3
Share sample norms to get the conversation started.

Sample Norms
- Students are at the heart of our decision making and problem solving.
- We are committed to a culture of inquiry.
- We are committed to the use of data to guide decision making and problem solving.
- We believe in locally developed solutions.
- We will openly examine contradictory data.
- We will use multiple sources of data to ensure we have an accurate picture of our work.
- We are committed to building trust in one another and in our data so we can reduce suspicion and inaccuracy.
- We work hard together to develop our evaluation frameworks to ensure we have an action plan. We create a detailed framework that includes specific evaluation questions, data needed, dates to collect the data, analysis method, and the people responsible. (See page 167 for more details about the evaluation framework.)
- We communicate our story to staff, students, families, and school community members. We include our successes and challenges.
- We include all voices in the data process.

Step 4
Use the team norms for data-analysis meetings.

Writing Surveys

Teams can use this tool to write surveys to collect data from various audiences.

PURPOSE To write a survey that accurately collects opinions, experiences, and insights of people in a variety of roles

PRODUCT A survey

PARTICIPANTS The data team, with guidance from a university partner or other local survey expert

MATERIALS Sample surveys and opportunities to revise questions and write new questions to gather important data

TIME Time varies based on the scope of measured constructs and survey length, plus time for development, field-testing, administration, and analysis

PREPARATION Draft the survey. Some teams use an online tool such as SurveyMonkey (https://surveymonkey.com), Qualtrics (https://qualtrics.com/free-account), Blue from Explorance (https://explorance.com/products/blue), or GetFeedback (https://getfeedback.com) to help gather data with greater accuracy.

Ask a local data expert to review the draft survey to ensure the data from it will accurately gather the needed information.

PROCESS **Step 1**
Write a strong opening to help people understand what the survey is asking and why.

Step 2
Sequence the survey questions in a logical way. Page breaks, section themes, and instructions help respondents keep focused on the task.

Step 3
Use the same question in a series of surveys or use the same survey over time to build a baseline and measure changes in respondents' attitudes.

Step 4
Be brief. Respondents really don't like long surveys.

Step 5
Save personal or sensitive questions for the end of the survey—*if they're absolutely necessary.* Asking these questions at the beginning can create anxiety for respondents.

Step 6
Create survey questions that explore one idea at a time to ensure respondents understand what you are asking. Vague, general, multipart questions can be confusing and tough to answer.

Step 7
Be specific. Provide details about any question people could interpret in more than one way.

page 1 of 2

PROCESS (cont.)

Step 8

Keep it relevant. Create a survey that asks respondents questions that directly apply to them to keep the respondents focused.

Step 9

Avoid yes *or* no *questions.* These questions don't capture the answers of indecisive people or consider nuances of opinions.

Step 10

Use words when possible. When designing answer choices, use phrases such as *slightly likely* or *extremely likely*, not numbers to indicate degree of preference. However, if you are using a Likert scale, it's helpful to use an even number of options. Often people will choose a 3 (neutral) on a scale of 1–5. On a scale of 1–4, people choose agree, strongly agree, disagree, or strongly disagree.

Reference

SurveyMonkey. (n.d.a). *How to create surveys.* Accessed at surveymonkey.com/mp/how-to-create-surveys on June 23, 2022.

Creating a Plan for Comprehensive or Rapid Cycles of Evaluation

This tool offers a quick review of the evaluation process and how to thoroughly address each step.

PURPOSE To review the evaluation process and plan the professional learning evaluation

PRODUCT An evaluation plan

PARTICIPANTS Data team members who manage this evaluation plan

MATERIALS Directions for the process, quantitative and qualitative data, and formative and summative data

TIME A few hours or many more, depending on the complexity and scope of the evaluation

PREPARATION The data team studies the eight-step process detailed in the section Comprehensive Evaluation Process (page 167) for either a comprehensive or rapid cycles of evaluation. It is essential to identify the questions and determine the data to provide guidance on the decision-making process.

PROCESS **Process for Comprehensive Evaluation Process**
The comprehensive evaluation process has eight steps (see page 167). The checklist in the following chart provides a simple step-by-step list of tasks.

PROCESS **Process for the Rapid Cycles of Evaluation**
The rapid cycles of evaluation process is simpler than the comprehensive evaluation process. Teams follow these steps.

Step 1
Clarify what goals or outcomes team members want and their actions to achieve them.

Step 2
Write an evaluation question.

Step 3
Determine what data the team will collect to answer the evaluation question.

Step 4
Determine how the team will analyze the data.

Step 5
Set a timeline for the intervention and data collection.

Step 6
Implement the team's intervention.

Step 7
Gather data.

Step 8
Analyze the data.

Step 9
Make decisions based on data.

Comprehensive Evaluation Process

Steps	Brief Description	Date Completed
Assess evaluability (page 151).	Review the goals and outcomes, theory of change, design, and incorporated implementation supports for professional learning.	
Formulate evaluation questions (page 151).	Focus on the questions most useful in coordinating the professional learning and for participants in their application of the learning. Evaluation questions can be formative and summative.	
Construct the evaluation framework (page 152).	Design the evaluation framework based on the evaluation questions; delineate the data to gather to answer the questions; specify the timeline for collecting the data; determine the data-analysis process; and indicate the people responsible for each part of the evaluation process.	
Collect data (page 154).	Be organized and precise about the data-collection process and timelines and processes for submitting the data. Understand how the data contribute to the overall knowledge the evaluation generates.	
Organize, analyze, and display data (page 156).	Sort and organize the collected data for analysis; determine what data are missing and seek to add them if late additions to the data set will not contaminate it; formulate findings; and display analyzed data. The following series of data-analysis questions support this process. • What do you see in these data? • What patterns exist? • How would you describe the data? • What is evident in these data? • How can we summarize these data? • What outliers exist?	
Interpret data (page 158).	Use the analyzed data to generate meaning from the findings; generate recommendations based on the interpretations related to professional learning.	
Report, disseminate, and use findings (page 158).	Prepare reports about the evaluation results in multiple formats for diverse audiences; widely report results to audiences associated with professional learning and others who might learn from the experience; use the results to make decisions about future professional learning.	
Evaluate the evaluation (page 159).	Reflect on the evaluation process and the evaluators' competencies to strengthen future evaluation efforts.	

Reference

Killion, J. (2017) Assessing impact: Evaluating professional learning, *3rd edition. Thousand Oaks, CA: Corwin Press.*

CHAPTER 8

Reporting and Celebrating Success

People often resist change for reasons that make good sense to them, even if those reasons don't correspond to organizational goals. So it is crucial to recognize, reward, and celebrate accomplishments.

—ROSABETH MOSS KANTER

Recognizing and celebrating success and the efforts to achieve that success reinforces a culture of continuous improvement and is an integral part of professional learning. This chapter focuses on how to celebrate and communicate staff contributions to professional learning and its effects. It explains the rationale for recognition and celebration and recommends various ways to acknowledge success and effort. Recognizing and celebrating success contributes to building a culture for learning. Unfortunately, employees say that lack of recognition is one of the primary reasons they leave a job. Researchers Annamarie Mann and Nate Dvorak (2016) write:

> According to Gallup's analysis, only one in three workers in the U.S. strongly agree that they received recognition or praise for doing good work in the past seven days. At any given company, it's not uncommon for employees to feel that their best efforts are routinely ignored. Further, employees who do not feel adequately recognized are twice as likely to say they'll quit in the next year. . . .
>
> Beyond communicating appreciation and providing motivation to the recognized employee, the act of recognition also sends messages to other employees about what success looks like. In this way, recognition is both a tool for personal reward and an opportunity to reinforce the desired culture of the organization to other employees.

Leadership expert Judith E. Glaser (2015) offers another reason for celebration and recognition. "Creating a feeling of celebration helps meet people's needs for inclusion, innovation, appreciation, and collaboration." People are social beings who want to feel valued, acknowledged, and included. When leaders make celebration a part of what Glaser (2015) describes as their *conversational rituals*, people feel a part of the team, are more willing to take on ambitious goals, and gain the confidence to share their ideas with others. In her book *Positivity*, author Barbara Fredrickson (2009)

advises using a 3:1 ratio of positive to negative feedback to maintain constructive and productive relationships.

Celebrating success of your own or others is also a way to reinforce continuous improvement. In *One More Time: How do You Motivate Employees?*, management professor and psychologist Frederick Herzberg (2008) notes the importance of recognition as an intrinsic motivator. Recognition provides the opportunity to review progress, take stock, and recommit to goals. It leads to self-confidence and self-fulfillment. In addition, recognition is a reminder that the journey is as important as the result. Leaders reaffirm that progress matters by recognizing effort and the path toward the goal. *Endorphins* and *dopamine*, the chemicals that produce the feel-good sense in human bodies, are released when people feel satisfied or successful (Cleveland Clinic, 2022; Watson, 2021). As people recognize and celebrate success, the physical sensation of feeling good about accomplishments generates more desire to continue the work.

Sometimes, acknowledging and celebrating overcoming challenges help minimize their negative impact. For example, school leaders might consider recognizing the best failure of the week, how it was discovered and addressed, and the lesson learned. School leadership team members can be the first to model this practice by taking the risk to identify a challenge they experienced. Others might follow their lead. This degree of vulnerability and transparency among staff speaks to the school's culture and staff appreciation for the complexity of the work, and creates a space for people to be honest and open.

This chapter explores the many ways to recognize and celebrate success plus how to handle negative responses to the changes you are creating.

Creating Ways to Recognize and Celebrate Success

Frequent communication about the professional learning goals, processes, and interim steps toward achieving the goals help keep professional learning in stakeholders' frame of reference. The more staff and school community members hear about the goals and how professional learning affects student success, the more likely they are to appreciate the contribution of professional learning to the school's success. See the reproducible "Ideas for Rewards and Celebrations" (page 175).

Recognition can come from peers, yet the most appreciated and memorable recognition comes from a supervisor (Mann & Dvorak, 2016). As Mann and Dvorak (2016) report in a Gallup study of workplace conditions, employees cited the six types of recognition they most appreciate:

- public recognition or acknowledgment via an award, certificate or commendation
- private recognition from a boss, peer or customer
- receiving or obtaining a high level of achievement through evaluations or reviews
- promotion or increase in scope of work or responsibility to show trust
- monetary award such as a trip, prize or pay increase
- personal satisfaction or pride in work

When you consider recognition, you may think about remarkable accomplishments. However, it is also important to acknowledge small and sometimes simple accomplishments. Recognition also depends on the person you want to recognize. For some, small accomplishments are monumental, while others find them less meaningful. Therefore, personalizing recognition is an essential part of the process.

Leadership teams can find multiple pathways to broadcast celebrations. Most recognition involves some form of public announcement, but framing the recognition may matter most. The guidelines for communication are simple—make them personal, specific, and frequent.

People most appreciate personal, specific messages about success. These messages include three parts: (1) who is recognized, (2) what the person did (provide examples), and (3) the person's efforts to make an impact. Down-to-earth and specific language is preferable. Consider the following messages. Sample B is likely to be more effective in celebrating and recognizing the effort, promoting a culture of continuous improvement, and building motivation and commitment across the school.

- **Sample A:** "We recognize the first-grade team, both teachers and students, for their extra effort during fall assessment week. Hats off to you."

- **Sample B:** "The first-grade team stepped in several times during fall assessment week to assist students and teachers in other grades. The team sent encouraging notes and small tokens of appreciation to each teacher and a personal letter to each class about the importance of doing their best during assessments. In addition, the team celebrated the beginning of fall assessment week by having a team of first graders visit each class and cheer on the teacher and students. Taking time to celebrate matters to everyone, and the first-grade team did its part to make a stressful week more enjoyable. The first-grade team's recognition of colleagues and fellow students brought us all joy and made us more determined to do our best."

The frequency of communication also matters. The guidance for this is also simple: communicate in multiple ways as often as possible. The more frequently leaders and school leadership teams communicate, the more they remind others what is important. When leaders report about goals, outcomes, progress, and efforts, they keep the main things at the forefront. They acknowledge the staff's extra effort and hard work. Frequent communications about staff learning remind staff and the community that professional learning is purposeful and leads toward a greater goal.

The more widely leaders and school leadership teams share successes, learnings, challenges, and progress, the more appreciation they gain for their efforts. Audiences for sharing celebrations and recognitions include the following.

- Staff
- Families
- Students
- Community members, especially nonparents
- Central office leaders
- Business and government leaders
- Community-based service organizations
- Professional networks

Each audience is unique and may require a different form of communication. For example, families may not be as interested in technical information as central office staff. However, families will still want to know specifics about how staff learning is contributing to changes in students' classroom experiences. Business and government leaders will want to know more about how educators' professional learning contributes to building strong, successful schools in the community. Nearly all audiences will be interested in learning how the school makes decisions related to resources (including how the school allocates those resources) and time for professional learning, and how the school realizes the progress, efforts, and results.

The format for celebrating and recognizing the results of professional learning depends on the audience and the scope of the message. Before choosing a form for communication, consider the audience's needs and interests, and offer each audience multiple choices for receiving the communication. Some ways to communicate include the following.

- Staff and family newsletters (see the reproducible "Creating a Weekly Newsletter," page 176)
- School and social media websites
- Personal notes
- Texts
- Briefs
- Emails
- Automated messages
- Billboards or reader boards

- Community newspapers
- Community celebrations
- Technical reports
- Blogs
- Professional publications
- Video messages
- Invitational meetings
- Student-led conferences and presentations
- Informal conversations

Handling Negative Responses

When leaders and school leadership teams broadcast celebrations and recognitions, particularly about staff accomplishments and their professional learning, there might be pushback and derogatory comments. Staff members might make comments about others getting recognized. In some schools where the culture is competitive rather than collaborative, teachers might suffer from *tall poppy syndrome* (Ranosa, 2019). Journalist Rachel Ranosa (2019) notes, "In a society that values praise and recognition, being an achiever—ironically—has its downside. There is a tendency for some to criticise those who stand out. This phenomenon is called the 'tall poppy syndrome.'"

In other words, the less a teacher stands out, the better. This behavior contradicts those in a culture of continuous improvement and collective responsibility for student *and* peer success. Parents might doubt teachers' competence if they need another day of professional learning. Even school board members have shared that same reservation. During a school board meeting discussion about professional learning days, one of the authors of this book heard the board president ask if the school system was hiring ill-prepared teachers. In addition, community members might wonder about the reasons for professional learning, especially if it occurs when students are not in school. One way to minimize these complaints is to embed professional learning into the school day.

It is essential to establish a process for handling these less-than-positive comments so there is a cohesive and consistent way to respond. When possible, an internal process for handling negative comments helps head off any downward spirals. All staff have a responsibility to learn about and use this process, which might include the following guidelines.

- Invite community members to share their perspectives by speaking directly, openly, and honestly with school staff.

▶ Engage the appropriate people. Direct any communication about challenging or complex issues to the person responsible to avoid a "he said," "she said," or "they said" situation. Consider creating a ladder of responsibility for handling negative comments. For example, who among the staff is the first, second, third, and so on, person to respond?

▶ Invite a neutral facilitator to assist with interactions, particularly if one party is uncomfortable or unable to directly communicate.

▶ Determine the guidelines regarding confidentiality and anonymity, and monitor to ensure everyone follows them. Rumor mills can create havoc.

▶ Consider if it is necessary to prepare a public message to respond to negative comments, and if so, distribute it through available and appropriate channels.

▶ Weigh negative comments by their scope, severity, intent, and relevance. A response or action is not necessarily needed. Revisit your goals, processes, and progress before determining if adjustments are needed.

Consider offering the following guidance to staff as a framework for responding to negative comments.

▶ Check yourself. If you can't remain neutral and even appreciate the opportunity, request a break while you center yourself.

▶ Refrain from rationalizing, explaining, defending, or stating your views. This is not the conversation's purpose. The purpose is to understand the other's view.

▶ Listen more than you speak. Paraphrase to demonstrate you both hear and understand the message. Ask questions to clarify.

▶ Appreciate that the person is sharing the information with you. This person cares enough to take the time and effort to offer another perspective.

▶ Find common ground. Identify what you both care about.

▶ Refrain from asking for the solution. Solutions at this stage are inappropriate. Before you can talk about what to do, it is important to clarify the issue or problem and determine all parties' interests to formulate the criteria for a solution.

Using these tactics, and tools such as "Listening to Families" (page 177) reproducible, can facilitate communication between school staff and those who share information that might be undesirable, yet important to hear. By investing in and being open to hear perspectives that may be different, school leaders and leadership teams can open the door to constructive interactions and stronger relationships.

Conclusion

A vital part of professional learning is recognizing and celebrating success often and in appropriate and novel ways. This means continuous communication about the goals, processes, and progress that relate to professional learning, as well as sharing achievements and challenges. Sometimes, acknowledging success can generate negative comments. Having a clear process and preparing staff members to receive (rather than refute) negative comments allows for more open and honest interaction, and may minimize adverse effects.

Leadership Tips

It isn't enough to achieve success. Individuals and teams need leaders to take time to recognize and celebrate all the effort that went into the success. The following tips will help you get started.

▶ Communicate frequently (internally and externally) about the goals, processes, and progress of professional learning.

▶ Build a system to recognize and celebrate success, personalized to meet staff preferences.

▶ Create a process for handling negative comments.

▶ Prepare staff to handle negative comments in appropriate ways.

▶ Assess the school's culture to determine whether tall poppy syndrome (see page 172) exists and work to reverse its effects.

Reflection Questions

1. What is the school's current process for communicating (internally and externally) about the goals, processes, and progress of professional learning? How well is the process working to inform the various audiences?

2. How are staff members recognized and celebrated? What processes do the staff most appreciate? Which processes do the staff less value?

3. How do staff members respond to the recognition of peers? What implications might there be regarding the culture for continuous improvement and collective responsibility in the school?

4. What are some novel ways to recognize and celebrate professional learning the school might implement?

5. Consider the recommendations about addressing negative comments. What adjustments might the school make to strengthen its current process?

Ideas for Rewards and Celebrations

This tool guides leadership teams to consider making schoolwide, classroom, team, and individual celebrations part of their routine.

PURPOSE To ensure leaders and teams recognize and celebrate student and staff successes

PRODUCT A list of ideas for rewards and celebrations

PARTICIPANTS Students, principal, school leadership team, central office staff, board of education members, communications office staff

MATERIALS None

TIME A week or more to gather ideas and generate the list; implementing the ideas happens throughout the school year

PREPARATION Create a letter or other form of communication asking teachers and students their ideas for rewards and celebrations.

PROCESS **Step 1**

Distribute your letter or other form of communication asking teachers and students their ideas for rewards and celebrations.

Step 2

Make a list of all the ideas. Include additional ideas for staff and student recognitions not previously identified.

Step 3

Prioritize the ideas you want to implement.

Step 4

When you are ready to implement the prioritized ideas, ask parents or the parent-teacher association to help implement the celebrations. Invite staff members to volunteer to help implement celebrations for students and other staff members.

The following ideas will help you get started.

- Write a personal note of recognition and appreciation.
- Maintain a "gift library" for students, teachers, staff members, and teams. Consider gift cards for fast food, pizza, art, local restaurants, ice cream, bookstores, gas, groceries, and so on. Some groups look for VIP privileges, online resources, theater tickets, or special events like field trips, faculty versus student games, and field days, or schoolwide events like dances or movies. Invite local businesses to donate gifts if appropriate.
- Announce students' and staff members' names during morning announcements or add their photos and names to a special display in the building. Recognize students and staff for helping hands, empathy, leadership, kindness, and so on. Tie this recognition to a Student of the Month Award or Staff Member of the Month Award.
- Ask local businesses to "adopt" a classroom or student group and host a monthly celebration.
- Plan breakfasts or lunches with administrators or parents who do the student lunch prep, serving, and clean up.
- Reach out to the district communications office to share great news in the building.
- Make contact with local reporters to share celebrations, highlights, and good news.

Creating a Weekly Newsletter

This tool helps leaders communicate frequently and efficiently.

PURPOSE To frequently and efficiently communicate important information to staff in ways that reduce traditional meeting time, freeing up time for teachers' professional learning

PRODUCT An informative weekly newsletter that provides key information for the coming week

PARTICIPANTS All staff

MATERIALS None

TIME One to two hours to write and distribute the weekly newsletter

PREPARATION Ask for volunteers to gather highlights, news, schedules, and other important information to share in the weekly newsletter. You may want to designate the same people for each task every week or rotate the responsibilities periodically throughout the year.

PROCESS **Step 1**
Have designated staff members share information with you throughout the week.

Step 2
At the end of each week, compile the information and distribute a weekly newsletter containing the information you received from staff, as well as any other pertinent information staff need to know. Consider using an online platform all staff can access or whatever method works best for your school.

Staff might want to consider the following for the weekly newsletter.

- Cite something notable observed in a classroom, lunchroom, or hall.
- Share observed kindnesses.
- Share lesson ideas (instructional strategies, sentence starters, composition ideas, and other successful ideas).
- Praise students' or staff members' work or activities in appropriate media.
- Share district or union letters or news.
- Recognize experts in the building.
- Encourage teachers to visit other classrooms to see how their fellow teachers are creating "walls that talk," small-group learning spaces, and positive learning environments.
- Share directions for emergency or crisis preparedness.
- Discuss parts of the school's code of conduct, dress code, or other agreements.
- Encourage staff to keep the school looking good.
- Share ideas for rewards and incentives that provide opportunities for students to succeed.

Other ideas to share good news include the following.

- Invite local newscasters to visit the school. Establish a schedule and identify teacher and student escorts to guide visits to designated classrooms.
- Schedule daily time for the leadership team to connect to share good news, perhaps sharing morning coffee to plan for appreciating and recognizing staff and students throughout the day.

Listening to Families

This tool guides leadership teams in engaging with families to support student success.

PURPOSE To create opportunities to keep the lines of communication open, create a common language, improve communication between the school and families, and among families in the community, and to share ways to engage in joy-filled family- and student-centered learning

PRODUCT Open communication to ensure the success of every student

PARTICIPANTS Families, teachers, district and school administrators, and community members

TIME This ongoing simple and sometimes complex activity may include a five-minute call or an hour-long visit to celebrate a school win.

MATERIALS Phones, emails, regular mail, social media, local newspapers and reporters, and so on

PREPARATION Create a culture of inclusion and openness to ensure families feel welcome and included in the learning community. Some schools offer transportation, childcare, or both to support parent and family engagement. Remember to include translators when needed.

PROCESS **Step 1**
Begin early to make positive contact with every family each year. Open the school and classrooms. (Remember, some family members may not be at ease inside schools due to their past experiences.)

Step 2
Ask family members to share talents and ideas. Families can often share ideas about what might work with their children when a teacher or principal gets stuck.

Step 3
Listen carefully.

Step 4
Share ways parents can support learning at home: "You can help your child with her mathematics homework by asking her to explain how she got an answer," "Ask your child to make a prediction when reading together," or "Share something you learned today that surprised you."

Step 5
Invite families to participate in school activities and support their experiences.

Step 6
Schedule learning opportunities for the adults who support students. Offer programs such as "How to Talk So Kids Will Listen and Listen So Kids Will Talk," "Learning About Mathematics at Home," "Understanding Adolescents," and so on. Some schools with large English learner populations offer English, Spanish, or other language classes for adults and students.

PROCESS (cont.)

Step 7

Include students in parent-teacher conferences so they can participate in sharing learning stories.

Step 8

Some schools schedule home visits to open the door to more communication.

Step 9

Schedule student performances or fun events with food (ice cream socials, pizza parties, movie nights, and so on) that provide engaging activities for students and their families.

Step 10

Seek information about ensuring home access to the internet. Students and staff can share blogs or access an online document to have input into the process. Consider open or closed groups on social media. Twitter lets you share what's happening throughout the day, and live streaming may allow families to watch an assembly, read to a class, or share a cultural or holiday story.

CHAPTER 9

Reflecting on the Work

Without reflection, we go blindly on our way, creating more unintended consequences, and failing to achieve anything useful. It's amazing to me how much we do, but how little time we spend reflecting on what we just did.

—MARGARET WHEATLEY

The work of planning, implementing, and evaluating professional learning takes considerable time and effort, yet the work is incomplete until reflection occurs. Reflection is a core attribute of accomplished practitioners. This chapter offers a definition of reflection, a rationale for reflection, and protocols for engaging in reflection as an individual and team process.

What Is Reflection?

Reflection is a process of looking back, looking inward, and looking forward to construct learning from lived experiences. The esteemed Danish philosopher Søren Kierkegaard said, "Life must be understood backward; but it must be lived forwards" (as cited in Ratcliffe, 2017). Leaders plan for action, reflect on actions while performing tasks, and use past actions as sources of learning for future actions. They might integrate reflection into the evaluation of professional learning, yet when done separately (and with some distance from the work), there are opportunities to involve a broader, more diverse group of stakeholders and realize the gift of perspective separation from the work affords.

There are three types of reflection. In *Educating the Reflective Practitioner: Toward a New Design for Teaching and Learning in the Professions*, Donald A. Schön (1987), who developed the concept of reflective practice, describes two forms of reflection: *reflection-on-action* and *reflection-in-action*. Killion and coauthor Guy R. Todnem (1991) add a third form of reflection, *reflection-for-action*. According to Killion and Harrison (2017):

> Reflection-on-action is a process of looking back at an experience, analyzing it to understand what occurred and why, and drawing from the experience learning that will inform future actions. Reflection-in-action is a similar process, but it occurs alongside the experience. In a split-screen process, the reflector is simultaneously experiencing the event and reflecting about it to understand more deeply how his or her actions are affecting the event and vice versa. Reflection-for-action is analyzing an experience, forming conclusions or generalizations that can be drawn from the experience, and then using these learnings to inform future decisions or actions. (p. 120)

Schön (1987) adds that *reflection-on-action* is "thinking back on what we have done in order to discover how our knowing-in-action may have contributed to an unexpected outcome" (p. 26). He continues, "[When] one reflects-in-action, he becomes a researcher in the practice context. He is not dependent on the categories or established theory and technique, but constructs a new theory of the unique case" (Schön, 1987, p. 68).

As Schön (1987) notes, the process of reflection extends your understanding of your experiences. By taking the time to reflect, you turn *tacit knowledge* (or what you may not fully understand nor have the ability to overtly state) into explicit knowledge you can share with others to use. In addition, routine reflection can lead to more deliberate and thoughtful actions.

In his study of reflection as a practice for professional learning for student teachers, professor and author Muhammad Zafar Iqbal (2017), states, "Reflection-in-action refers to active evaluation of thoughts, actions and practices during action. It also refers to '*thinking on feet*' during the process of teaching (Schön, 1987). Reflection-in-action also means the exploration of professional beliefs, practices and experiences during teaching" (p. 66).

Killion and Todnem (1991) coined the term *reflection-for-action* in their review of personal theory building, calling it the desired outcome of the other two types of reflection. They state, "We undertake reflection, not so much to revisit the past or to become aware of the metacognitive process one is experiencing (both noble reasons in themselves), but to guide future actions (the more practical purpose)" (Killion & Todnem, 1991, p. 15). Reflection has become a core part of practice for educators who seek to refine and extend their understanding of their work, the effect of their decisions on their practice, and the effects of their actions on their work context. See the reproducible "After-Action Review" (page 186).

Why Is Reflection Important?

The reflection process aligns with professional practice standards, extends leaders' repertoire to address multiple situations, and supports future success. If practitioners become stuck in routine practices, they are unable to adapt to the new situations or circumstances that occur daily. Numerous variables affect educators' daily work, which some consider a combination of art and science. Sommers (2021) says when he facilitates workshops on reflection, "Reflection is the difference of having one year of experience twenty-five times and twenty-five years of experience honing our behaviors for better results."

There is a saying commonly associated with philosopher and theologian Thomas Aquinas that reminds educators to beware of the person who carries only one book. Reflection becomes a way to combine implicit and explicit knowledge to build deep understanding about education practice. While it is possible to absorb a great deal of explicit knowledge about professional learning theory and practice from research and texts, the real learning comes from the actual practice, analysis of the experiences, and lessons learned from unique experiences (York-Barr, Sommers, Ghere, & Montie, 2016).

Table 9.1 (page 181) summarizes the distinctions among the three types of knowledge and offers examples. *Explicit knowledge* is the easiest form of knowledge to access. It is known and transmittable to others. Reflection surfaces implicit knowledge, and potentially tacit knowledge. *Tacit knowledge* is less accessible because it cannot be expressed or transmitted. It is known, but the knower cannot yet express it with language, diagrams, or nonverbal representations. *Implicit knowledge*

TABLE 9.1: Explicit, tacit, and implicit knowledge.

	Explicit Knowledge	Tacit Knowledge	Implicit Knowledge
Definition	"Explicit knowledge, as the first word in the term implies, is knowledge that has been articulated and, more often than not, captured in the form of text, tables, diagrams, product specifications and so on." (Nickols, p. 3)	"Tacit knowledge is knowledge that cannot be articulated. As Michael Polanyi (1997), the chemist-turned-philosopher who coined the term put it, 'We know more than we can tell.'" (Nickols, p. 3)	"Knowledge that can be articulated but hasn't [yet] is implicit knowledge." (Nickols, p. 3)
Example	Knowledge about how to set up classroom routines; sharing the steps of the process, skills required to manage them, and ways to implement them	Inherent knowledge and skills to set up, implement, and adjust classroom routines, yet an inability exists to explain to others how to do so	Knowledge and skills about what works and what doesn't work in setting up, implementing, and managing classroom routines in different situations (types of classes, varied student groups, etc.) gained from multiple lived experiences with classroom routine

is acquired over time through experiences and practices. It emerges from engagement with specific situations in specific contexts. Implicit knowledge can eventually be articulated, yet extracting it requires examination and reflection.

Individually or collaboratively conducted with others, reflection processes facilitate learning from experiences in which conditions and context are situative, unique to each individual, and rich with opportunities to refine, deepen, and extend practice.

How Does Reflection Happen?

Reflection can occur at any point in the professional learning planning, implementation, or evaluation. It is most helpful at the end of a professional learning initiative, such as at the end of a year of implementing a professional learning plan. In addition, reflection can be a type of formative assessment at the end of each professional learning experience. As a collaborative experience, reflection has the potential to contribute to a community's understanding of the collective and individual experiences from multiple and potentially diverse perspectives.

At the core of the reflective practice is reviewing your actions, listening to others to gain additional perspectives, and making necessary modifications to your practice to accelerate learning and behavior changes. Reflection involves several steps. The first step involves gathering data and recalling what occurred. For some, reflection stops here. It is merely a matter of recalling the sequence of events. However, reflection is so much more. It moves from recall to analysis and lessons learned to new actions.

The second step of reflection is analysis. Analysis within reflection includes unpacking the contributing factors in the sequence of events and noticing how those events affect the people involved, their environment, their interactions, and the event's facilitator.

For example, in reflecting on the implementation of a professional learning plan, the school leadership team might explore which aspects of the plan had the greatest and least impact on learners. The team also could explore how learners responded to various forms of professional learning, how their level of engagement influenced their willingness to implement the learning, or how the level of available support contributed to their use of the learning. These subtle queries are usually qualitative and depend on the learner, school conditions, other participants, expectations for use of the learning, nature of the learning, and the learning facilitator.

Following analysis, the leadership team completes the third step, reflection. Team members draw conclusions or hypotheses that help them understand their experiences at a deeper level and generate tacit knowledge from the unique experiences and their context. Members must discover and construct this new knowledge. This level of analysis also allows the team to move that knowledge into the explicit realm.

The final step of reflection is to use the newly constructed knowledge. The school leadership team applies this new knowledge to plan for future professional learning experiences. By doing this, the team is more likely to streamline its work, avoid previous problems, and achieve results more effectively and efficiently. In other words, the team is smarter than it was previously.

Steps in Reflection for Implementing a Professional Learning Plan

When reflecting on the professional learning plan implementation, it is helpful to have the plan available and use the following four steps to take notes and conduct analysis to generate tacit knowledge for future professional learning planning and implementation. See the reproducibles "Individual, Team, or Staff Reflection" (page 188) and "Critical Events Analysis" (page 191).

Step 1: Review Actions

Take notes on what occurred during implementation of the professional learning plan. Particularly note challenges and unexpected situations, comments, questions, and ideas from participants or the professional learning team, plus changes made and other issues.

Construct a history of the professional learning experiences using notes from reflection-in-action and individual and collective recall. Note the sequence of events, people present, circumstances, context, environmental factors, time, actions, decisions, consequences, responses, and so on. In essence, this step paints a picture of what happened for use in step 2.

Step 2: Analyze the Actions

Use the following questions to analyze the actions and draw conclusions or formulate hypotheses, insights, new perspectives, or deeper understanding.

- ▶ What influenced the sequence of events, responses to those events, and results?

- ▶ Who significantly negatively or positively influenced the results of the professional learning? What circumstances made that influence significant?

- What contextual factors (such as the combination of people, environment, resources, supports, time of day, location, facilitators, content, or learning designs) negatively or positively played a role in the results of the professional learning? What circumstances made those factors significant?

- What were the notable negative or positive responses to the professional learning? What might have contributed to those responses?

- What were we expecting? How was what occurred different from what we expected?

- What surprised us in the professional learning experiences? What made those areas surprising?

Step 3: Formulate Lessons Learned

Articulate the newly constructed knowledge from the conclusions, insights, hypotheses, or perspectives. Then, explore how you might use that knowledge in planning, implementing, and evaluating future professional learning. Use the following questions to guide your efforts.

- What conclusions, insights, hypotheses, or perspectives are we drawing from these experiences? What are we basing them on?

- What lessons are we learning?

Step 4: Apply New Knowledge

Explore how you will use the newly constructed knowledge in planning, implementing, and evaluating future professional learning.

The core to undertaking reflection is trust. Trust in the team occurs when members feel safe, avoid judgment or blame, and accept diverse perspectives. Teams earn trust through integrity, follow-through, and disclosure. Reflection requires and increases trust. When team members engage in reflection, they are simultaneously modeling open and honest conversation, which contributes to trusting relationships and increases their level of trust with one another. Setting clear norms for team members engaging in community-based reflection builds a safety net for reflection.

In her research on trust in schools, Megan Tschannen-Moran (2004), a professor of educational policy, planning, and leadership at the College of William and Mary School of Education, identifies the following five dimensions of trust.

- **Benevolence:** The confidence that others have each person's best interests at heart and will protect those interests

- **Reliability:** The extent to which one person can depend on someone else to act consistently or follow through

- **Competence:** The belief in another person's ability to perform required tasks

- **Honesty:** The degree to which one person can count on others to represent situations fairly

- **Openness:** The degree to which one person freely shares information with others

Journalist Charles Duhigg (2016), in his study of teams at Google, reports organizations in which people work in teams are more flexible and better able to solve problems, find creative options, and avoid mistakes more quickly. Duhigg (2017) cites five factors common to effective teams: (1) psychological safety, (2) dependability, (3) structure and clarity, (4) meaning, and (5) impact. In addition, best-selling author Stephen M. R. Covey (2006) acknowledges that trust changes everything in terms of how positively and collaboratively people work together to advance the mission and vision of an organization.

Building trust with one another through reflection has several benefits. First, it models the value of reflection as a core professional practice. Second, reflection can influence the level of trust among the entire staff. Third, it creates psychological safety for people to be vulnerable:

> [T]o feel "psychologically safe," we must know that we can be free enough, sometimes, to share the things that scare us without fear of recriminations. We must be able to talk about what is messy or sad, to have hard conversations with colleagues who are driving us crazy" (Duhigg, 2016).

Coauthors Bryk and Barbara Schneider (2002) report a positive correlation between trust among the staff, staff and administrators, and the school and community, and student achievement. *Educational Leadership* magazine contributor Jane Modoono (2017) recognizes that trust leads to collaboration, noting, "After more than 30 years as a school leader, I have come to believe that trust is the most important factor in building a collaborative and positive school culture."

Finally, reflection provides a process to objectively examine practices, learn from each experience, and refine future practice. Bryk and Schneider (2002) conclude that "trust fosters a set of organizational conditions, some structural and others social-psychological, that make it more conducive for individuals to initiate and sustain the activities necessary to affect productivity improvements" (p. 116). There are four reasons for trust in schools.

1. Trust among educators lowers their sense of vulnerability as they engage in new learning and apply practices of which they are uncertain.

2. Trust opens up public problem solving in an organization.

3. Trust "undergirds the highly efficient system of social control found in a school-based professional community" (Bryk and Schneider, 2002, p. 117). Staff members understand their own and others' roles and obligations as members of the school community and need minimal supervision or external pressure to carry them out.

4. Trust "sustains an ethical imperative . . . to advance the best interests of children," and thus "constitutes a moral resource for school improvement" (Bryk and Schneider, 2002, p. 34).

Conclusion

Reflection is an essential component of planning, implementing, and evaluating professional learning. When school leadership or professional learning teams reflect in, on, and for action, they deepen their understanding of their experiences and increase their expertise. Without reflection, teams may repeat routine practices with diminished effectiveness. Reflection surfaces tacit knowledge and makes it explicit for strengthening and refining future professional learning planning, implementation, and evaluation. Reflection has the added benefits of modeling the value of reflection and increasing trust among the staff, which might promote more reflection schoolwide.

Leadership Tips

Reflection is a core attribute of accomplished leaders. In addition, the school-based professional learning cycle isn't complete until reflection occurs. The following tips will help you get started.

- ▸ Use the reflection process to build trust across the school.

- ▸ Teach team leaders how to facilitate reflection to support analysis of their work and build trust among team members.

- ▸ Engage in reflection on your practice and invite others to contribute to your analysis.

- ▸ Make time for reflection during leadership or professional learning team meetings, especially at the end of a school year.

- ▸ Create a process to encourage teams and individuals to share the tacit knowledge they construct in team meetings or through individual reflection.

Reflection Questions

1. How are staff members currently engaging in reflective practice?

2. Which types of reflection are most prevalent among staff members and teams?

3. Where are opportunities to extend the types of reflection in the school?

4. What are possible ways to expand the types of reflection and the frequency of reflection across school staff?

5. Who can be instrumental in supporting the expanded use of reflection as a vehicle for building trust among staff? How can they contribute? How will you prepare them to make these contributions?

After-Action Review

The after-action review guides teams to look back at their work to identify successes and opportunities for improvement.

PURPOSE To assess the process and progress of actions or initiatives

PRODUCT Completed after-action review template

PARTICIPANTS Any team

MATERIALS After-action review template and any available quantitative or qualitative data

TIME Thirty to sixty minutes, depending on the complexity of the action or initiative

PREPARATION Gather available quantitative and qualitative data about the action or initiative.

PROCESS **Step 1**
Review the purpose of completing the after-action review template.

Step 2
Use the questions in the template to guide discussion about various aspects of the work and use the template to record responses.

After-Action Review Template

Team Name: _____ Date of Review: _____

Participants: _____

Part 1: Successes

What went well? How do we know? What's the evidence? How did we achieve success?

Successes	How to Ensure Future Success

Part 2: Changes

What do we want to change? What can we improve? What didn't work well? How do we know? What's the evidence? What do we want to change? What do we want to do going forward?

Changes, Revisions, and Improvements	What Will We Do to Make These Changes?

Part 3: Next steps

Given what we have learned, what will be our next steps?

Next Steps	How Will We Monitor These Steps?

Individual, Team, or Staff Reflection

This tool guides the reflection process. Individuals, teams, or the whole staff can adapt this tool for various experiences.

PURPOSE To analyze actions, decisions, or processes used to achieve individual or collective goals

PRODUCT Future-focused action plans past experiences inform

PARTICIPANTS Individuals, teams, or whole staff

MATERIALS Guiding questions for the reflective processes

TIME Fifteen to sixty minutes

PREPARATION Determine if individuals, partners, teams, or the whole staff will conduct the reflection process. Prepare questions to guide the reflection process (see the following examples). Modify questions to align with the type of experience and timing of the reflection process.

PROCESS **Reflection Following a Visitation to Peer's Classroom**

Step 1
Review notes taken during the observation.

Step 2
Consider what happened and what influenced the actions.

Step 3
Discuss the following, preferably in collaboration with the peer.

- What were the highlights of the class? What made them highlights?
- What decisions did the teacher make? What impact did those decisions have on students' learning?
- What unexpected occurred? How did the teacher handle that situation?
- What was the most significant learning each partner took away from the visitation?
- How might that learning influence the observer's future actions?
- What was the most significant learning the teacher can take away from the visitation?
- How might that learning influence the teacher's future actions?

Reflect on Progress
- What accomplishment during this school year makes you most proud?
- What do you wish we had accomplished that we neither addressed nor completed?
- What accomplishments have given this school a solid base for the future? How will those accomplishments contribute to future success?
- What is currently happening in our school that needs development and expansion? How will addressing these areas benefit students and staff?
- What have we learned from this past year that will help us be stronger in the future?

Reflection-on-Action

- What can you tell me about a teaching or leadership event you want to think about more deeply?
- What aspect of this experience do you want to dig into?
- What happened?
- What explanation can you give for what happened?
- How did the context influence what happened?
- If you could replay the situation, how would it go?
- What contributed to those events or experiences? How did these things contribute? If you had known one thing going into those events or experiences, what do you wish it had been?
- What did you realize as you explored these events or experiences? What is clearer to you now as you look back?
- What can you take away from those events or experiences to apply to future ones?

Reflection-in-Action

Answer the following questions *during* the event or experience, and report the responses *after*.

- What is capturing my attention at this moment? What might be the reason for that?
- What am I noticing about myself in this moment? What am I noticing about others in this moment?
- Am I doing what I had planned? What's the same and different?
- What advice would I give myself right now?
- In what ways am I feeling successful, disappointed, challenged, and so on?

Reflection-for-Action

- What can this experience help prepare you for in the future?
- What did this experience teach you about yourself, your practice, the context or environment in which you work, and your impact on others and the environment?
- What is the big takeaway you can extract from this experience?
- How will you describe to others what you learned during this experience? What would be the title or headline if you were to write about what you learned?
- How will this situation help you think about other similar or different situations?

Invite participants to give advance thought to the questions before engaging in the personal theory-building process.

PROCESS Theory Building

Step 1

Provide a rationale for reflection.

Step 2

Guide the reflection process using your prepared questions.

PROCESS **Step 3**
(cont.) Debrief about the value of reflection. Use the following questions to guide the discussion.

- How did the reflection process contribute to your professional growth?
- What do you appreciate about yourself and others as staff or team members?
- What did you learn about your own and others' experiences with reflection?
- How might you integrate reflection into your practice even when you don't have an opportunity to reflect with a colleague or team?
- What aspect of the reflection process would you like to keep? Change? Stop?
- How might you use reflection in your classroom work with students?

Reference

Killion, J., & Harrison, C. (2017). Taking the lead: New roles for teacher and school-based coaches. *Oxford, OH: Learning Forward.*

Critical Events Analysis

Critical events analysis is a process individuals or teams can use to examine an experience with some significance, often because it was either highly successful or highly disappointing.

PURPOSE   To conduct an analysis of an event or experience and develop fluency and competence with the critical analysis of practice

PRODUCT   A record of the event or experience analysis

PARTICIPANTS   Any individual or team

MATERIALS   Critical Event Analysis Worksheet and available quantitative and qualitative data

TIME   Thirty to sixty minutes, depending on the complexity of the project

PREPARATION   Gather available quantitative and qualitative data.

PROCESS   **Step 1**

Select a significant situation that was particularly rewarding or challenging. It is best to select a meaningful situation likely to provide a rich opportunity for analysis and learning. Provide a brief description of it at the top of the critical event analysis worksheet (page 192).

Step 2

Describe the situation. When did it occur? Who were the actors? What were the circumstances? Note these on the worksheet.

Step 3

Complete the following using the chart in the worksheet.

- In the first column, map the sequence of events and the actions and reactions of the various players as part of your storyline.
- In the second column, add your feelings about each line in the first column. Your responses might be positive, neutral, or negative.
- In the third column, add reasons that did or might have contributed to your responses. What might have prompted your actions and how you feel about each line? What else is happening that isn't evident, yet was a part of this situation and influenced your actions? Keep the focus on your feelings and action.
- In the fourth column, note what you are learning about the relationship between your actions and feelings, and the possible reasons for your feelings.

Step 4

After completing the chart, look through all the lines of your story, your feelings, the possible reasons, and your insights to answer these questions.

- What did you discover when doing the analysis?
- What patterns and outliers are you noticing?
- What conclusions can you draw about this event and your actions and reactions?
- What hypotheses can you make about future events based on this one?
- How might you test those hypotheses? Which ones do you want to test?
- What will you tell others you learned from this event?
- As a result of the process, how will the new knowledge influence your future actions?
- What is an immediate next step based on this knowledge?

page 1 of 2

Critical Event Analysis Worksheet

Event (brief description): _____

When (date, time, duration): _____

Circumstances and context: _____

Sequence of Actions and Reactions (Note Names When Possible)	Your Feelings	Possible Reasons for These Feelings	Insights, Perspectives, and Learnings

Reference

Killion, J., & Harrison, C. (2017). Taking the lead: New roles for teacher and school-based coaches. *Oxford, OH: Learning Forward.*

PART 3

Preparing for Challenges

CHAPTER 10

Facing Challenges

Often, the greatest challenge facing an organization is recognizing and acting on opportunity rather than solving a problem.

—PETER GINTER

Professional learning can be challenging and exhilarating at the same time. Preparing to recognize challenges and addressing emerging challenges make the success of any learning-based initiative more likely. This chapter explores some of the common challenges school leadership and professional learning teams may face and offers practical strategies for addressing them. Of course, the best plan of action is to avoid the challenges altogether with careful planning responsive to clearly identified needs. However, even well-laid plans can go awry.

Imagine walking along a rocky coast with sea spray splashing up over you. The salty spray may be blinding and the wet rocks, sometimes covered in moss, make each step treacherous. Uncertainty and danger abound. Yet, stepping carefully with the proper footwear can minimize the danger of falling.

Many "slippery rocks" exist when leading a change initiative. For example, you can mandate attendance, but not mandate learners to learn. Some common "rocks" that disrupt any plan are resistance, complacency, compliance, conflict, competing priorities, leadership gaps, and resource deduction. In the following sections, we explore these challenges and offer some considerations for addressing each.

Dealing With Resistance

Among the knottiest challenges in any professional learning initiative is resistance. Resistance often devolves into power struggles. However, resistance to change is natural and constructive. Killion (2022) reports people are inherently wary or resistant to change because the brain perceives change as a threat to the status quo and what is comfortable and familiar. When people know change is coming, resistance is the likely response (Kantor, 2012; Pennington, 2018). Yet, when resistance occurs, it signals change is happening, which this is an opportunity for leaders to consider how to respond to resistance and influence people's response to achieve the goals. Leaders seek to recognize the signs of resistance, engage in honest conversation about its roots, and find agreement. After all, change is not about winning or losing. Change is about adapting and adjusting. Unfortunately, leaders often simply react to resistance rather than taking time to recognize its positive aspects.

Resistance can be overt, such as when people make negative statements publicly about the value of the change, how it is conducted, who exerts power over whom, or the resources expended. Another kind of resistance, sometimes harder to address, is *silent resistance*, the covert kind that occurs in parking lots, whispers in hallways, or secret meetings off campus.

Resistance can be about process—for example, staff feeling like they didn't have opportunities to share their suggestions or counterpoints. Sometimes, resistance is about the extra effort a leader asks staff to commit to learning and adapting. Occasionally, resistance is about power, such as who has power over another. Rarely is resistance about the nature of the change itself. Keeping this in mind is enormously helpful. If leaders fail to deal with resistance, it may eventually become sabotage, which is far more challenging to address.

During change, people (even those educators who commit to student success) care about themselves first, which is fundamental to human nature. People want to know what's in it for them. Unfortunately, staff are not asking what's in it for students. They do not want to hear the rationale or reason for the professional learning–based initiative. They want to know what it means for them as educators. What does it mean for their daily work routines? What does it mean in terms of extra time to prepare? What does it mean in terms of effort?

Staff also wonder if the change is a judgment about their existing performance. They often fear the change results from poor-quality work, effort, or results. Resisters often interpret the impending change through a filter of fear.

Control and power concerns drive many resisters and how others make decisions becomes a source of resistance. Resisters want to engage to influence and persuade others, but when they do not have a platform, their resistance grows. In addition, they want a voice; they want influence and want others to perceive them as influential. They value their status as voices of reason. Finally, they may be fighting to maintain the status quo or define the change in a way comfortable for them.

Resistance might not be all bad; it can have some positive qualities. In physics, *resistance* can mean exerting enough friction to cause movement. Without friction, shoes would slide on any surface and braking systems on vehicles would not work. Resistance can surface areas that need attention and show where change is disrupting the status quo. As Rosabeth Moss Kantor (2012), founding chair of the Harvard Advanced Leadership Initiative, notes, "The best tool for leaders of change is to understand the predictable, universal sources of resistance in each situation and then strategize around them." Leaders can influence how others respond to change if they listen fully to people, honor their reasons for resisting, and remain curious rather than judgmental (Killion, 2022). Hall and Hord's (2015) *Implementing Change: Patterns Principles, and Potholes* is one of many excellent resources on leading, facilitating, and managing change.

Whatever the reasons for resistance, and it is not always possible to know them all, leaders can take positive steps to manage and even minimize it. Early steps include reframing the behavior from detrimental to constructive then embracing the change as progress. Furthermore, leaders can engage people in the planning process and create opportunities for them to raise questions, share concerns, and contribute. Sometimes leaders who reach out and engage others in these actions are not school administrators but rather caring peers committed to relationships as well as professional learning. Leaders might consider one or more of these actions to address resistance.

- ▶ Invite individual conversations.
- ▶ Listen to understand.

- ► Acknowledge concerns.

- ► Seek commonalities at higher levels.

- ► Agree to temporary commitment.

- ► Reach temporary solutions and review their effectiveness often.

Leaders seek to add to and refine their conflict-management skills and strategies. By having multiple ways to work with conflict and resistant people, leaders can be effective in multiple situations. See the reproducible "Dealing With Resistance" (page 207).

Understanding Complacency

Complacency is a state of being too comfortable, too settled in, and too stuck in the status quo to imagine or even consider a change. Leaders often hear these statements: "I have been doing this for twenty years and my students are successful," "If it isn't broken, don't try to fix it," and "My students are among the highest-scoring students in the school."

Each of these statements may be true. However, if leaders are unable to explain the reason for the change in terms that connect with individuals, those individuals will not move from complacency. If no one is enthusiastic or curious about new approaches to teaching, new resources to use, or new opportunities to learn, complacency has set in. Complacency holds the whole school back if those others consider leaders are caught in its web or if the number of compliant staff raises significantly. According to author and consultant Sharon Lipinski (2021), complacency is one of the top issues related to safety in organizations, and you can address complacency by viewing it from the perspective of neuroscience. Lipinski (2021) writes that "complacency is actually rooted in which brain structures the brain activates while performing its activities." When complacency is reconceptualized from this perspective, there are multiple strategies (see page 198) you can use to address it and improve the safety of all learners. Rather than looking at the symptoms of complacency, Lipinski (2021) contends it is important to look at complacency from the perspective of changing habits. Doing this requires practice, reduced cognitive load, physical well-being, stress management, critical thinking, communication, and anomaly detection.

When complacency exists, there's no motivation for change. Without adult learner motivation, professional learning is futile. Disengagement is one of the most significant indicators of complacency. People stop participating or contributing to the team or school. They may opt for shortcuts or doing what is essential and little more. They consider learning or change unnecessary because they have a confirmed perception that what exists is good. Finally, they are usually polite and persistent in doing what they have always been doing.

What causes complacency may be life circumstances or resignation that results from comparing oneself to others. For example, more senior staff may notice that less-experienced staff attend extracurricular activities, volunteer to serve on various committees, or spend extra hours in planning and grading. Those senior staff will conclude they have been there and done that. Their eye is on the prize at the end of their day, week, or career. They consider the acts of the newer staff a part of their rite of passage.

Complacent people have a limited level of commitment to the organization, which restricts their level of enthusiasm and engagement. For some, complacency is a defensive mechanism. They reason that laying low will avoid attention on them. They may harbor a fear of what a change might mean and would rather not face it. For some who are complacent, this way of thinking may be temporary and leaders can shift this thinking by committing to connect personally and tap into the expertise of those who may be hiding in the shadows.

One way to address complacency is to create conditions to engage the disengaged. The ways to address complacency take time, effort, and commitment. The entire school leadership or professional learning team shares responsibility for these strategies. Some complacent staff will appreciate peers reaching out to them more than their supervisors. Leaders acknowledge that every staff member deserves the following recognition and support, so to address complacency, consider these strategies.

- ▸ Highlight successes.
- ▸ Acknowledge personal commitment.
- ▸ Build a sense of team.
- ▸ Create challenging and worthy work.
- ▸ Report progress frequently.
- ▸ Create unlikely alliances.
- ▸ Meet privately to check in and seek perspectives.
- ▸ Meet privately to ask staff about their individual vision, mission, and values.
- ▸ Compliment accomplished work privately and publicly.

Learning to Change Unnecessary Compliance

Compliance often occurs where there is complacency. Of course, compliance in some situations is essential, especially in legal, safety, or risk areas. However, in other situations, people comply with leadership's directives even when they disagree because they perceive they have no choice or the risks of noncompliance are too great. They acknowledge they "can't fight the machine" or "big boss." In these situations, people just go through the motions without the heart or will necessary to sustain results.

For leaders, compliance may be challenging to spot and even more challenging to address because the staff appear to be doing the tasks, but they are just going through the motions and have no investment in their actions. Compliance may produce limited results, but it also can lead to ill feelings. Compliance typically emerges from an *egocentric view* (a focus on self rather than the whole) because compliant staff members demonstrate little regard for others or the intended outcomes. Their motives focus on self-protection, survival, or avoidance of consequences.

Staff social-emotional well-being complicates their commitment to work responsibilities (Dodd, 2021). For example, in 2020–2021, the added challenges of continuous or periodic remote work and the overall uncertainty of the time (due to the COVID-19 pandemic) affected people's level of dedication. Many staff had expanded responsibilities at home and shifted their priorities away from full-time work and career pathways. Human resource functions in school systems were strained to hire and maintain a reliable employee base, especially in critical support roles. Grant (2021b) describes the state of mind during this time:

It wasn't burnout—we still had energy. It wasn't depression—we didn't feel hopeless. We just felt somewhat joyless and aimless. It turns out there's a name for that: languishing. Languishing is a sense of stagnation and emptiness. It feels as if you're muddling through your days, looking at your life through a foggy windshield. And it might be the dominant emotion of 2021.

When people resort to compliance, leaders initiate a campaign to shift the organization's culture. They can take the culture's main attributes, such as communication, decision making, rituals, taboos, and processes, and shift them to advocacy opportunities for reinforcing the school's vision, mission, and values and the goals of the professional learning initiative. *Shifting from a compliant culture* means directly linking each meeting, contact, decision, and action to the professional learning, so learning becomes the priority for educators and students.

To address compliance, leaders might take the following actions.

▸ Be clear about expectations by delineating precisely what you require and noting any flexibility or options, and keep the vision, mission, values, and goals at the forefront of all efforts.

▸ Communicate frequently about progress, successes, and challenges, and invite frequent input from all staff about their learning experiences and application in practice.

▸ Assess alignment between current practice and expected practice frequently (or at least monthly). Also, be willing to adapt and adjust requirements and expectations if necessary.

▸ Provide personalized support to close gaps between current practice and expected practice and meet individually with staff to examine motivation, seek perspectives, and explore individual needs.

▸ Provide clear guidance on the consequences and rewards of expected practice.

▸ Engage staff in collaborative teams to extend additional support as needed.

Diffusing Conflict

During change, conflict is inevitable. The sources and types of conflict will vary. For example, *interpersonal conflict* might erupt between staff members who support the learning initiative and those who do not. Bob Chadwick (n.d.), consensus facilitator and trainer, describes *conflict* this way:

Conflict is not good or bad—but it is just a normal, healthy part of our lives, like death and taxes. Conflict is an opportunity for growth, change and leads to progress, which leads to better decision making. Conflict is stimulating and an antidote to boredom. Conflict is the fuel for creativity and makes me able to shift my paradigm.

Conflict is an opportunity for growth, change and leads to progress, which leads to better decision making.

Conflict can emerge from multiple situations. Some of those situations include the following.

▸ Confusing or undefined roles

▸ Differing interests, values, or beliefs

▸ Communication barriers and lack of civility

- Dependence on one person
- Differentiation or segmentation in the school
- Lack of consensus
- Imbalance of power
- Lack of behavior regulations or agreed-on norms
- Scarcity of resources
- Unsolved prior tensions

Structural conflict about available resources might occur, particularly with limited physical resources and time. The following are some other types of conflict.

- *Value-based conflict* about intellectual or academic freedom
- *Procedural conflict* regarding decision making or allocation of support
- *Status conflict* regarding recognition and position
- *Psychological conflict,* such as when one party feels disempowered or devalued

In the best case, conflict is productive because it signals change is happening. *Disrupting the status quo* means there will be a period of discomfort and chaos. Without discomfort and chaos, change is not occurring. On the other hand, conflict can be destructive when staff take it underground or leaders do not address it constructively. The most common approach to conflict is compromise, but that leaves all parties without something important to them.

Interest-based conflict resolution invites all parties to enter conversations about the conflict without prior commitment to positions or predetermined solutions (Fisher & Ury, 2011; Oghenechuko & Godbless, 2018). It is based on the premise that the parties in conflict are open to creative solutions grounded in one another's interests. Often, it is helpful to have a neutral third party facilitate conflict resolution. The following process delineates how neutral facilitators can engage others in addressing conflict. People in conflict can also use this process themselves.

- Define the conflict jointly.
- Take time out to assess and adjust; get into the proper frame of reference.
- State interests.
- Form criteria for selecting solutions.
- Generate solutions.
- Analyze the feasibility and consequences of each solution.
- Select a solution.
- Develop and agree on a plan of action.
- Implement the plan.
- Evaluate the effectiveness of the plan.
- Revise or modify the plan.

The process works best when those in conflict approach the work with an intent to listen to understand and consider their needs and the needs of others. Sometimes setting norms for conflict conversations help create these conditions. For example, norms such as the following can be helpful for people in conflict.

▶ Listen and hear one another's viewpoints; one's perspective is one's truth.

▶ Say what you want while you are here in the room, not in the parking lot. If you do not say it here, forever hold your piece.

▶ Make it your responsibility to ensure your idea is in the room.

▶ Encourage equal "airtime" (or verbal participation) for fairness.

▶ Address issues, not personalities.

▶ Speak directly to the person with whom you have an issue.

Negotiating Competing Priorities

Competing priorities can derail any effort, and many occur in schools daily. To manage priorities, it is crucial to be clear about the priorities and plan to address each. While many tasks and responsibilities seem to be equally important, they may not be. When multiple competing priorities exist, people tend to lose focus and efficiency. In *Willpower: Rediscovering the Greatest Human Strength*, coauthors Roy F. Baumeister and John Tierney (2011) suggest the more people worry about what they feel obligated to do, the less likely they are to be efficient and effective, and the less they are likely to accomplish.

One helpful process is to use the approach to prioritizing tasks General Dwight Eisenhower used and carried into his presidency—the *Eisenhower matrix* (Krogerus & Tschäppeler, 2012; Zhu, Yang, & Hsee, 2018). Covey (1989, 2020) adapted this process as the *urgent-important matrix*. Regardless of the label, using a matrix like the one figure 10.1 (page 201) depicts encourages people to sort their tasks and responsibilities into four quadrants using the concepts of urgent and important and their opposites.

	Urgent	**Nonurgent**
Important	Urgent and important tasks clearly align with the school's vision, mission, values, and goals, have clear deadlines, and have significant consequences for not doing them. Leaders ensure staff accomplish these tasks.	Important yet nonurgent tasks relate to the school's vision, mission, values, and goals and are not time sensitive. If left undone, they will have a negative impact on the goal; however, leaders can postpone them without serious consequences. Leaders schedule these tasks.
Unimportant	Staff may handle urgent and unimportant tasks, but might consider them busy work. However, these tasks are essential to accomplish the goal and to stay aligned with the school's vision, mission, and values. Leaders might assign these tasks to others.	Tasks that are neither important nor urgent are distractions and may not align with the school's vision, mission, and values. They might be easy to accomplish, but take time and effort away from those tasks that have a greater impact on the goal. Therefore, leaders remove these tasks from the to-do list.

FIGURE 10.1: Urgent-important matrix

When competing priorities emerge, leaders review tasks and responsibilities and reassess their urgency and importance by considering the overall vision, mission, values, and goals. This assessment deserves thoughtful and deliberate attention to avoid *decision fatigue*, which happens when people have cognitive fatigue or too many choices. The Decision Lab (n.d.) states:

> The phenomena of decision fatigue can affect even the most rational and intelligent individuals, as everyone can become mentally exhausted. The more decisions made throughout the day, the harder each decision becomes for us. Eventually, the brain looks for shortcuts to circumvent decision fatigue, leading to poor decision-making.

Leaders take time to determine how to accomplish tasks they deem important and assess whether tasks they consider unimportant will negatively impact overall goal attainment. Sometimes they create *not-to-do lists* to remind themselves and others how to keep focused on the tasks they determine most important.

To address competing priorities, leaders might do the following.

- ▶ Review and prioritize all initiatives and routine work to identify top priorities.

- ▶ Seek input on challenges and barriers.

- ▶ Recognize when competing priorities emerge and clarify priorities quickly.

- ▶ Maintain open lines of communication for interacting about the priorities.

- ▶ If necessary, reprioritize initiatives and communicate the rationale.

Finding Leadership Gaps

Leadership gaps happen when leaders' efforts stray from the priority. This can happen to all leaders, not just the school's administrators. Their time and effort focus intensely on the goals. At each meeting, they take time to update the effort, review and assess their commitments and overall progress, and identify and promptly address any surfacing barriers. Leaders' behaviors are models and symbols for others to understand priorities. During change, leaders address any lack of communication and barriers that emerge.

Leaders' communication conveys what they consider important and urgent. What leaders talk about, with whom they talk, and how they talk matters. Communicate to all stakeholders who influence the culture and the success of professional learning. Staff and students constitute *internal* stakeholders. School-system staff, parents, community members, and community businesses constitute *external* stakeholders.

For example, how do leaders explain to students and parents the purpose of shortened school days they designate for professional learning? How do leaders relay to community members how professional learning contributes to the community's well-being? Are parents, students, or community leaders invited to participate in the same or a related learning experience that staff engage in? Professional learning can enrich the entire community, yet leaders often hold a narrow view of its role in student and staff success.

Addressing barriers is another core responsibility of leaders. Those barriers are likely to go unnoticed unless leaders make it a point to see, examine, and address them. Rather than pretending they don't exist, leaders look for ways to go around, over, under, or through barriers. Leaders adapt plans, realign resources, change tactics, redistribute responsibilities, extend or shorten timelines, coach people, remove barriers, and commit to listening deeply to understand others' experiences in learning to change.

Sometimes leaders are unclear about their decision-making processes and the lack of clarity confuses others involved in change. Staff may assume they have the prerogative to make some decisions on their own even when that is not the leaders' intent. When there is confusion about who decides what, implementation can falter. Increasing clarity about decision making is a key task for leaders and leadership teams (Groysberg & Abbott, 2020; Latham, 2015). Leaders may find the reproducible "Clarifying Decision Making" (page 208) useful to review decision-making processes when challenges arise.

When leaders' focus strays, the staff's level of effort, willingness, and progress wanes. Leaders are the linchpins of any change initiative. As such, leaders must be deliberate in how they demonstrate their belief in and commitment to staff learning goals. Leaders demonstrate their commitment in how they do the following.

> **When leaders' focus strays, the staff's level of effort, willingness, and progress wanes.**

- ▸ Celebrate and acknowledge learning.

- ▸ Name and address challenges publicly.

- ▸ Report on processes and progress in leadership, staff, and community meetings.

- ▸ Make their own goals transparent.

- ▸ Seek input from peers, supervisors, and staff about their goals.

Addressing Resource Reduction

Resources such as time and funding are finite. They often ebb and flow with governmental and community priorities. When professional learning initiatives launch, special funds from public or private sources may add to the baseline funding to purchase time for staff to engage in and apply their learning. Unfortunately, these resources are rarely permanent additions to a school's budget, and once expended, they are not renewed. Leaders can use these funds to initiate a professional learning program and rarely give thought to the resources necessary to fully implement, sustain, and upgrade it over time. The following fictional case, drawn from our experiences in school systems around the globe, describes what happens when leaders redistribute resources.

SCHOOL-BASED PROFESSIONAL LEARNING IN PRACTICE
Funding

The school system's middle schools implemented a new mathematics curriculum. The school system allocated special funds to each school to provide training to staff in using the curriculum and purchasing the classroom instructional resources needed to implement the curriculum in each mathematics class. Teachers had extra time to develop the daily instructional resources needed to use the curriculum with integrity and fidelity. The school system allocated a coach to each school one week per month to support teachers in using the curriculum and address any emerging classroom challenges.

The first year of implementation was rocky. Teachers worked diligently to be true to the curriculum structure and design. Coaches helped teachers solve the problems they encountered. Principals surfaced challenges with other school leaders and identified workable solutions. Overall, student performance increased slightly. The degree of implementation was about 50 percent, and teachers indicated they had much yet to learn to feel completely comfortable and confident using the curriculum.

The school year ended, and the following year, the school's focus shifted to middle school writing. The extra funds for the mathematics curriculum implementation shifted to the writing curriculum. The coaches returned to their classroom positions or found other positions, and leaders hired new writing coaches. Just as the mathematics teachers were on the precipice of making great leaps with the instruction and curriculum changes, they lost their support resources. Along with the resources, so too went their commitment, ability to solve problems with the integrity of the curriculum in mind, and consistency and fidelity to the curriculum. As a result, student scores in mathematics and teachers' use of the curriculum in the second year of the program decreased.

In the preceding case study, the school-system leaders focused on the short-term, initial steps of implementation, but failed to look beyond the initial year to the second year and beyond when deep change and fuller implementation are likely. As Fullan (1982, 2007, 2016) reminds leaders, initiation alone is insufficient to produce deep change; leaders must look beyond initiating to implementing and sustaining the change over the long term.

Resources alone cannot make or break the success of professional learning; however, they can leverage staff to engage and commit to it. The investment in resources signals the significance of the professional learning and conveys leaders' value of it. Resource allocation becomes a symbol by which staff judge value. A school system does not necessarily hold back the launch of the writing initiative until the mathematics initiative is fully and faithfully implemented, yet it does ensure sufficient resources are available and used appropriately to achieve the goals of both efforts.

To address resource reductions, leaders might take the following actions.

▶ Tap the expertise among staff.

▶ Repurpose existing resources to the high-priority areas.

▶ Rearrange the school day to provide time for professional learning.

▶ Repurpose meeting time for professional learning.

▶ Take advantage of *open educational resources* (or any type of educational material available free for teachers and students to use, adapt, share, and reuse).

▶ Partner with other schools or school systems to share costs.

Conclusion

Slippery rocks make the path dangerous and uncertain. The right footwear and attention to where one steps can eliminate some of the risk. This chapter identified some of the major challenges that can occur when implementing professional learning, and undoubtedly there are others.

The leadership team makes every effort to avoid many challenges through planning, foresight, and listening deeply to those responsible for the day-to-day work associated with professional learning initiatives. When unanticipated challenges appear, leaders pause to study their origins, consider the implications of not addressing them, and determine how to address them if necessary. Leaders remember that what one person deems important might not be important to another.

Leaders engage multiple, diverse stakeholders on a team to coordinate the professional learning initiative and facilitate implementation. Leaders are present in classrooms, hallways, and large- and small-group meetings to listen and reflect with implementers. They overcommunicate, using every interaction as an opportunity to illuminate the goals, outcomes, and rationale for learning and listen deeply to other perspectives. Leaders celebrate success and failure equally. In addition, they look outward and inward to understand before they act or speak. Finally, leaders place people first, acknowledging all change results from the learning people experience and their willingness to make the change. Using the reproducible "Working With People Who Have Different Styles" (page 210), leadership and professional learning teams can plan to focus on the needs of the adults learners while managing and facilitating professional learning to advance student learning.

Leadership Tips

Although many challenges arise when changing strategies for school-based professional learning, leaders have many tools to use to help staff face these challenges. The following tips will help you get started.

- ▶ Create a forum or process to facilitate identifying and handling challenges in a timely, transparent, and fair way.

- ▶ Invite staff and community members with diverse perspectives to contribute to identifying and handling challenges related to professional learning.

- ▶ Take a long view with any learning initiative so resources are available to support full and faithful implementation.

- ▶ Communicate (via print and electronic media) the rationale, process, and supports available for change, and correct erroneous messages that emerge through individual interpretations.

- ▶ Designate leadership responsibilities for professional learning to a wide array of staff who will make personal connections with implementers.

Reflection Questions

1. Of the "slippery rocks" (challenges) this chapter addressed, which is mostly likely to occur in your school? What other unnamed challenges might occur?

2. In past professional learning initiatives, what challenges surfaced most frequently and how did leaders address them?

3. As you look back on past professional learning initiatives, how did leaders contribute to their success or influence their challenges? What made a difference to staff?

4. In each school, there are likely to be compliant and complacent individuals. What might these individuals value from leaders as evidence of their commitment to success and as incentives to increase their willingness to support the effort?

5. How will your leadership team celebrate success and failure?

Dealing With Resistance

This tool helps school leadership or professional learning team members investigate the causes of resistance and plan how they will address those causes.

PURPOSE To uncover the causes of resistance and respond with honesty

PRODUCT Action plans to respond honestly to emerging resistance

PARTICIPANTS School leadership team members or any team

MATERIALS None

TIME Time varies, depending on the complexity of the issues being examined

PREPARATION Listen carefully to the issues change implementers share.

PROCESS **Step 1**
Listen to faculty concerns.

Step 2
Take each concern seriously.

Step 3
Talk about a plan.

Examples

For example, suppose some staff members do not know the *why*, *what*, or *how* of a new initiative. Therefore, leaders spend time deepening the understanding of the intended purpose of the work, what it will look like once implemented, and the professional learning to ensure everyone has the knowledge, skills, and behaviors to help students succeed.

If staff question the intention of the initiative because they are satisfied with the status quo, it may be time to analyze and discuss the disaggregated data (districtwide, schoolwide, by grade level or department, individual teacher, or individual student) for evidence of successes and challenges.

Clarifying Decision Making

This tool will help teams clarify the level of responsibility of various stakeholders for decisions related to professional learning in the school.

PURPOSE To determine the level of engagement of stakeholders with responsibility for initiating, implementing, and sustaining professional learning and related changes

PRODUCT A decision-making matrix outlining stakeholders' level of involvement in decisions

PARTICIPANTS School leadership or professional learning team representatives

MATERIALS A decision-making matrix (see chart)

TIME Ten minutes to discuss one issue (A team identifying several issues and discussing the decision-making authority for each issue may need forty-five to sixty minutes.)

PREPARATION Identify the decisions and list the stakeholders involved in any of the decisions.

PROCESS **Step 1**

In the left column, make a list of routinely made decisions. In the top row, add a list of the stakeholders (one in each column). Stakeholders could include board of education members, the superintendent, central office staff, the principal, school leadership team, department heads, grade-level chairs, teachers, parents, students, and others in the school or district.

Step 2

Once you identify the decisions and name the stakeholders, discuss the level of engagement for each stakeholder in the process. In the matrix (see page 209), make note of the *As*, *Rs*, *Cs*, *Is*, and *Os*. Use the chart to guide the discussion.

A *for Approve*
Who needs to approve the decision? There may be more than one stakeholder who needs to approve the decision.

R *for Responsible*
Who is responsible for making and implementing the decision? Try not to have more than one person or group responsible because it's more complicated when multiple people are responsible.

C *for Consult*
Who do you need to consult *before* making the decision? You may need to consult several groups.

I *for Inform*
Who do you need to inform about the decision *after* you make the decision? Many groups may want this information.

O *for Out of the Loop*
These are individuals or groups you do not need to consult or even inform about a decision.

Decisions to Make	Stakeholder: _____	Stakeholder: _____	Stakeholder: _____	Stakeholder: _____

Working With People Who Have Different Styles

This tool is designed to help people understand and work with others whose styles differ from their own.

PURPOSE To recognize and appreciate team members' different personal styles that demonstrate different preferences

PRODUCT List of challenges, styles, and preferences of each team member

PARTICIPANTS School leadership team, professional learning team, grade-level or department team, or any other team

MATERIALS A chart with notes about the styles or preferences of each team member and a list of the challenging behaviors each team member notes

TIME Thirty to ninety minutes, depending on the size of the team and team members' relationships with one another

PREPARATION Facilitator pays attention to the behaviors of team members and prepares for meetings with individuals, small groups, or the whole team to address styles and challenging behaviors.

PROCESS **Step 1**

Ask participants each to assess their preferences by describing their personal style. The following questions can guide them to think about their social interaction and cognitive-processing preferences.

Do I want or prefer to do the following.

- Get down to business and move through the work quickly?
- Be correct and confident that I know what I am talking about?
- Have time to think things over before deciding?
- Agree to maintain harmony?
- Believe others appreciate and value me?
- Be in control?
- Have time to socialize with colleagues?

Facilitate the discussion on how to focus on strengths and what each individual contributes to the team. Use the following questions to guide the discussion. Encourage each member of the team to appreciate the styles of other members.

- What strengths does each member bring?
- How can we capitalize on our unique strengths?
- What are the upsides and downsides of us all being the same?

Step 2

It's also good to observe different behaviors of your team members. Once you observe some behaviors that interfere with teamwork, it's important to consider what may be at the heart of the behavior and consider how to respond. Here is an example.

Behavior	Why	What to Do
Example: Silent person	Some people are more comfortable sharing in small groups.	Create opportunities for the larger group to divide into smaller teams for greater participation. Establish facilitation processes such as round robin, carousel brainstorming, four corners, and so on.

EPILOGUE

Adapt what is useful, reject what is useless, and add what is specifically your own.
—BRUCE LEE

Professional learning is a complex undertaking some often take far too lightly for the weight of its impact. However, the potential impacts of professional learning on student success, educator performance, career advancement, and workplace satisfaction are enormous. In addition, professional learning coalesces staff as a community, inspires excellence, and renews educators' moral purpose.

No longer can educators relegate decisions about professional learning without considering the school's overall goals. Instead, weave together a comprehensive approach to professional learning that begins with the students' learning needs, the school's vision, mission, and values, strategic priorities and improvement plan, and staff needs. If educators acknowledge that the quality of teaching is the single factor with the highest impact on student success (Leithwood, Seashore-Louis Anderson, & Wahlstrom, 2014), then they concomitantly accept that the quality of professional learning can directly influence the quality of teaching.

We have explored key questions about planning, implementing, and evaluating professional learning. In addition, we answered the following questions.

- ▶ **Why is the locus of control for professional learning best in schools?** Classrooms are the center of teaching and learning and the most common place for leaders to implement teacher professional learning. Professional learning at the school level accelerates the application of learning, personalizes the learning process for the school's specific needs, and builds collective responsibility for student and educator learning. Professional learning begins and ends with students. It begins with understanding student needs and what educators require to meet them. It ends with measuring the success of professional learning by student progress.

- ▶ **What are the roles and responsibilities of stakeholders?** From those in the school-system office to those in schools, every educator has a role and responsibility for effective professional learning. School-system staff, administrators, leadership or professional learning teams, teacher leaders, and coaches contribute to identifying needs and planning, implementing, and evaluating the professional learning.

- ▶ **Where do you start?** Start with examining student, educator, and system data. Gathering and analyzing data brings all voices into decision making about professional learning. Data about student learning needs to narrow the focus for professional learning. Data about educators contribute to the design decisions. Data about the system contribute to implementation and support decisions. The quality, validity, and reliability of the data improve decisions about professional learning. Using data establishes a clear and compelling reason for the work and connects the work with school and school-system priorities.

▶ **Where are you going?** Establishing the school's vision, mission, values, and goals keeps a tight focus on the intended results so professional learning aligns with these results. After establishing goals, school leadership or professional learning teams identify the essential knowledge, attitudes, skills, aspirations, and behaviors (KASABs) necessary to achieve the goals. Then, leaders allocate effort and resources to achieve the desired results.

▶ **How do you get there?** To effectively, efficiently, and adequately meet learners' needs and align with context and learning content requires careful attention to selecting the professional learning designs. From among the many learning designs available, leaders consider various areas related to the content, learners, resources, and intended goals. In addition, consider the appropriate designs for individual, team, and schoolwide professional learning, and how to collaborate to build talent density across the school.

▶ **How do you implement and support professional learning?** Professional learning occurs over time. Therefore, it requires substantial resources and ongoing support to achieve deep implementation. Building efficacy and mastery with new practices require coaching individuals, teams, and administrators; peer coaching; learning walks within and across schools; and other processes at all stages of implementation. Resources such as time, staff, budget, policies, and materials create the conditions for success.

▶ **How do you assess and evaluate progress?** Measuring progress and results and keeping the school leadership or professional learning team informed about the status of the professional learning helps members monitor progress, adjust the plan as needed, and analyze results to identify success and opportunities. In addition, using formative and summative evaluation processes helps members understand the current state and refine professional learning.

▶ **How do you face the inevitable challenges?** Change generates challenges such as resistance, leadership gaps, conflict, complacency, and compliance. Addressing these challenges is a twofold task. First, plan to avoid them; second, if challenges occur, be responsive and quick in addressing the underlying causes. An effective tool for identifying challenges and finding viable ways to handle them is open, honest, and direct communication.

▶ **How do you recognize and celebrate success?** Communicate progress and results regularly to staff and community members. In addition, school leadership and professional learning teams use a variety of ways to celebrate, report, and use the findings to make improvements. Recognizing and appreciating success conveys to those implementing professional learning you value their efforts. Building a strong communication system, frequently communicating about the work to stakeholders, and soliciting input from the community and staff members contribute to a sense of ownership and engagement in the learning and results.

▶ **How do you reflect on your work?** Reflection is an attribute of an accomplished professional. Three types of reflection—*in*, *on*, and *for practice*—provide opportunities for school leadership and professional learning team members to learn from their experiences and make tacit knowledge explicit so members can integrate it into future planning. In addition, reflection guides school leadership teams to think about the components of each step of their work.

Hargreaves and Fullan (2013) acknowledge the importance of committing to the learning and growth of staff and students, which they describe as *human capital*:

> Systems that invest in professional capital recognize that education spending is an investment in developing human capital from early childhood to adulthood, leading to rewards of economic productivity and social cohesion in the next generation. . . . Continuous professional development pays off in Finland, Singapore, Alberta, and Ontario. The best way you can support and motivate teachers is to create the conditions where they can be effective day after day, together. And this isn't just about intraschool collaboration. It's about interschool and interdistrict collaboration. It's about the whole profession. (Hargreaves & Fullan, 2013, p. 36–37)

When the adults in a school learn and grow, students are also more likely to learn and grow. Acknowledging the important role of professional learning in a school's efforts to strengthen student learning will start committed educators on the path to building the structures, culture, conditions, and opportunities for professional learning.

As we conclude this book, we want to offer these reminders, which have served us well throughout our careers.

- ▶ Professional learning is about committing to continuous improvement among adults to benefit student learning.

- ▶ The future of education depends on the adaptability of educators to meet the emerging trends that influence schools, whether they are technological, structural, political, fiscal, physiological, sociological, or environmental.

- ▶ Professional learning requires trust to create safety in the community. You build trust through collaboration within the school, across teams, between individuals, and with the community the school serves. You build trust by being *trustworthy* (I model personal integrity by doing what I say I will do; keeping my word; maintaining my confidences; and supporting others to learn and grow) and by *trusting* (I listen to understand with curiosity rather than judgment; I value the contributions of others; I take a risk with you; I am vulnerable; I am honest; and I seek to grow and learn).

- ▶ Open school and classroom doors encourage and facilitate learning with, from, and on behalf of one another. Each staff member has talents and gifts to share with others. Observing how others do their work is a powerful way to build schoolwide capacity, trust, and a culture of continuous improvement.

- ▶ Encourage school leadership and professional learning teams to "Do all the good you can, by all the means you can, in all the ways you can, in all the places you can, at all the times you can, to all the people you can, as long as ever you can" (attributed to John Wesley and others). Students' lives depend on it.

REFERENCES AND RESOURCES

Abbajay, M. (2018). *Managing up: How to move up, win at work, and succeed with any type of boss*. Hoboken, NJ: Wiley.

Abrahamson, E. (2004). *Change without pain: How managers can overcome initiative overload, organizational chaos, and employee burnout*. Boston: Harvard Business School Press.

Akbar, M. (2020). *Beyond ally: The pursuit of racial justice*. Hartford, CT: Publish Your Purpose Press.

Alegre, I., Berbegal-Mirabent, J., Guerrero, A., & Mas-Machuca, M. (2018). The real mission of the mission statement: A systematic review of the literature. *Journal of Management and Organization, 24*(4), 456–473. https://doi.org/10.1017/jmo.2017.82

Alessandra, T. (n.d.). *Tony Alessandra quotes*. Accessed at https://azquotes.com/quote/807100 on August 12, 2022.

AllThingsPLC. (n.d.). *Tools & resources*. Accessed at www.allthingsplc.info/tools-resources/page,1/filtered,0 /categories,/type on June 28, 2022.

Ambrose, D. (1987). *Managing complex change*. Pittsburgh, PA: Enterprise.

American Institutes for Research. (2010, December 8). *Innovation configurations | Concerns-Based adoption model*. Accessed at https://air.org/resource/innovation-configurations-concerns-based-adoption-model on August 8, 2022.

Anderson, C. (2016). *TED talks: The official TED guide to public speaking*. Boston: Houghton Mifflin Harcourt.

Anthony, S. B., Gage, M. J., & Stanton, E. C. (1876, July 4). *Declaration of rights of the women of the United States - July 4, 1876* [Speech transcript]. Accessed at https://awpc.cattcenter.iastate.edu/2017/03/21/declaration-of -rights-of-the-women-of-the-united-states-july-4-1876 on August 8, 2022.

Archibald, S., Goggshall, J. G., Croft, A., & Goe, L. (2011, February). *High-quality professional development for all teachers: Effectively allocating resources* [Research & policy brief]. Washington, DC: National Comprehensive Center for Teacher Quality.

Audisio, A., Taylor-Perryman, R., Tasker, T., & Steinberg, M. P. (2022, June). *Does teacher professional development improve student learning? Evidence from leading educators' teacher fellowship model*. (EdWorkingPaper: 22-597). Providence, RI: Annenberg Institute at Brown University. https://doi.org/10.26300/ah2f-z471

Australian Institute for Teaching and School Leadership. (2014). *Designing professional learning*. Victoria, Australia: Author.

Bailey, K., & Jakicic, C. (2017). *Simplifying common assessment: A guide for Professional Learning Communities at Work*. Bloomington, IN: Solution Tree Press.

Ball, S. J. (2003). The teacher's soul and the terrors of performativity. *Journal of Education Policy, 18*(2), 215–228.

Ball, S. J. (2015). Education, governance and the tyranny of numbers. *Journal of Education Policy, 30*(3), 299–301.

Barbee, G. E. L. (2018, February 13). *Two simple concepts to free up innovation* [Blog post]. Accessed at www .strategy-business.com/blog/Two-Simple-Concepts-to-Free-Up-Innovation on May 9, 2022.

Barker, E. (2017). *Barking up the wrong tree: The surprising science behind why everything you know about success is (mostly) wrong*. New York: HarperOne.

Barth, R. S. (1990). *Improving schools from within: Teachers, parents, and principals can make the difference*. San Francisco: Jossey-Bass.

Barth, R. S. (1997, March 5). The leader as learner. *Education Week*. Accessed at https://edweek.org/leadership/opinion-the-leader-as-learner/1997/03 on May 9, 2022.

Baumeister, R. F., & Tierney, J. (2011). *Willpower: Rediscovering the greatest human strength*. New York: Penguin Press.

Bernhardt, V. L. (2018). *Data analysis for continuous school improvement* (4th ed.). New York: Routledge, Taylor & Francis.

Blazar, D., & Kraft, M. A. (2017). Teacher and teaching effects on students' attitudes and behaviors. *Educational Evaluation and Policy Analysis, 39*(1), 146–170. https://doi.org/10.3102/0162373716670260

Blythe, T., Allen, D., & Powell, B. S. (2015). *Looking together at student work* (3rd ed.). New York: Teachers College Press.

Borko, H. (2004). Professional development and teacher learning: Mapping the terrain. *Educational Researcher, 33*(8), 3–15.

Bossidy, L., & Charan, R. (2002). *Execution: The discipline of getting things done*. New York: Crown Business.

Boyd, V., & Hord, S. M. (1994). Schools as learning communities. *Issues About Change, 4*(1) Accessed at https://sedl.org/pubs/catalog/items/sch11.html on May 9, 2022.

Braddock Middle School. (n.d.). *Vision and mission statements*. Accessed at www.acpsmd.org/Page/1446 on June 28, 2022.

Branch, G. F., Hanushek, E. A., & Rivkin, S. G. (2012, February). *Estimating the effect of leaders on public sector productivity: The case of school principals* [Working paper 17803]. Cambridge, MA: National Bureau of Economic Research. Accessed at https://nber.org/system/files/working_papers/w17803/w17803.pdf on May 9, 2022.

Brookfield, S. D. (2013). *Powerful techniques for teaching adults*. San Francisco: Jossey-Bass.

Bryk, A. S. (2020). *Improvement in action: Advancing quality in America's schools*. Cambridge, MA: Harvard Education Press.

Bryk, A. S., Gomez, L. M., Grunow, A., & LeMahieu, P. G. (2015). *Learning to improve: How America's schools can get better at getting better*. Cambridge, MA: Harvard Education Press.

Bryk, A. S., & Schneider, B. (2002). *Trust in schools: A core resource for improvement*. New York: Sage Foundation.

Bryk, A. S., Sebring, P. B., Allensworth, E., Luppescu, S., & Easton, J. Q. (2010). *Organizing schools for improvement: Lessons from Chicago*. Chicago: University of Chicago Press.

Buczynski, S., & Hansen, C. B. (2010). Impact of professional development on teacher practice: Uncovering connections. *Teaching and Teacher Education, 26*(3), 606.

Buffum, A., Mattos, M., & Malone, J. (2018). *Taking action: A handbook for RTI at Work*. Bloomington, IN: Solution Tree Press.

Bush, R. N. (1984, June). Effective staff development. In *Making our schools more effective: Proceedings of three state conferences* (pp. 223–238). San Francisco: Far West Laboratory for Educational Research and Development. Accessed at https://files.eric.ed.gov/fulltext/ED249576.pdf on May 9, 2022.

Calhoun, E. F. (2002). Action research for school improvement. *Educational Leadership, 59*(6), 18–24.

Cantrell, S., & Kane, T. J. (2013, January). *Ensuring fair and reliable measures of effective teaching: Culminating findings from the MET Project's three-year study* [Policy & practice brief]. Seattle, WA: Bill & Melinda Gates Foundation.

Caro-Bruce, C. (2000). *Action research facilitator's handbook*. Oxford, Ohio: National Staff Development Council.

Center for African Studies. (n.d.) *Swahili proverbs: methali za kiswahili*. University of Illinois at Urbana-Champaign. Accessed at http://swahiliproverbs.afrst.illinois.edu/proverbs.htm on August 8, 2022.

Chadwick, B. (n.d.). *Beyond conflict to consensus: An introductory learning manual*. Accessed at https://managingwholes.com/chadwick.htm on May 9, 2022.

Chetty, R., Friedman, J. N., & Rockoff, J. E. (2014). Measuring the impacts of teachers II: Teacher value-added and student outcomes in adulthood. *American Economic Review, 104*(9), 2633–2679.

Cleveland Clinic. (2022). *Endorphins.* Accessed at https://my.clevelandclinic.org/health/body/23040-endorphins on July 12, 2022.

Clifford, M. A., Larsen, S. E., & Chiang, E. (2017, April 27–May 1). *Preparing future principals: Results of an impact analysis of four innovative preparation programs.* AERA Online Paper Repository. Paper presented at the Annual Meeting of the American Educational Research Association, San Antonio, TX.

Clifford, M., Menon, R., Gangi, T., Condon, C., & Hornung, K. (2012, April). *Measuring school climate for gauging principal performance: A review of the validity and reliability of publicly accessible measures* [Issue brief]. Washington, DC: American Institutes for Research. Accessed at https://air.org/sites/default/files/downloads/report/school_climate2_0.pdf on May 9, 2022.

Colorado Department of Education. (n.d.). *Renew a professional teacher license.* Accessed at www.cde.state.co.us/cdeprof/checklist-renewprofessionalteacher on July 8, 2022.

Conzemius, A. E., & O'Neill, J. (2014). *The handbook for SMART school teams: Revitalizing best practices for collaboration* (2nd ed.). Bloomington, IN: Solution Tree Press.

Covey, S. M. R. (2006). *The speed of trust: The one thing that changes everything.* New York: Free Press.

Covey, S. R. (1989). *The seven habits of highly effective people: Restoring the character ethic.* New York: Simon & Schuster.

Covey, S. R. (2020). *The seven habits of highly effective people: Powerful lessons in personal change* (30th anniversary ed.). New York: Simon & Schuster.

Cravens, X., Drake, T. A., Goldring, E., & Schuermann, P. (2017). Teacher peer excellence groups (TPEGs): Building communities of practice for instructional improvement. *Journal of Educational Administration, 55*(5), 526–551.

Cruse, A. V. (2021). *An analysis of the relationship between school culture and teachers' professional learning* [Doctoral dissertation, Youngstown State University] OhioLINK. https://etd.ohiolink.edu/apexprod/rws_etd/send_file/send?accession=ysu1619470476923736&disposition=inline

Dam, M., Janssen, F. J. J. M., & van Driel, J. H. (2020). Making sense of student data in teacher professional development. *Professional Development in Education, 46*(2), 256–273. https://doi.org/10.1080/19415257.2018.1550104

Darling-Hammond, L., Hyler, M. E., & Gardner, M. (2017, May). *Effective teacher professional development.* Palo Alto, CA: Learning Policy Institute.

Datnow, A., & Park, V. (2015). Five (good) ways to look at data. *Educational Leadership, 73*(3), 10–15. Accessed at www.siprep.org/uploaded/ProfessionalDevelopment/Minutes/Five_(Good)_Ways_to_Talk_About_Data.pdf on May 9, 2022.

The Decision Lab. (n.d.). *Why do we make worse decisions at the end of the day? Decision fatigue, explained.* Accessed at https://thedecisionlab.com/biases/decision-fatigue on May 9, 2022.

De La Rosa, S. (2021, February 1). *Eliminating microaggressions key to creating a more equitable school culture.* Accessed at https://k12dive.com/news/eliminating-microaggressions-key-to-creating-a-more-equitable-school-cultur/594260 on August 1, 2022.

Delehant, A., & Easton, L. B. (2015). Systems: The context for learning. In L. B. Easton (Ed.), *Powerful designs for professional learning* (3rd ed.; pp. 29–46). Oxford, OH: Learning Forward.

Delehant, A. M. (2007) *Making meetings work: How to get started, get going, and get it done.* Thousand Oaks, CA: Corwin Press.

Dewey, J. (2009). *How we think.* Hawthorne, CA: Barnes & Noble.

Dodd, V. (2021, July 18). *Ten top compliance challenges in 2021* [Blog post]. Accessed at https://skillcast.com/blog/top-10-compliance-challenges-2021 on May 9, 2022.

Drago-Severson, E., & Blum-DeStefano, J. (2016). *Tell me so I can hear you: A developmental approach to feedback for educators.* Cambridge, MA: Harvard Education Press.

Drew, C. (2022, July 5). *79 examples of school vision and mission statements*. Accessed at https://helpfulprofessor .com/school-vision-and-mission-statements on August 3, 2022.

DuFour, R., DuFour, R., Eaker, R., Many, T. W., & Mattos, M. (2016). *Learning by doing: A handbook for Professional Learning Communities at Work* (3rd ed.). Bloomington, IN: Solution Tree Press.

DuFour, R., DuFour, R., Eaker, R., Mattos, M., & Muhammad, A. (2021). *Revisiting Professional Learning Communities at Work: Proven insights for sustained, substantive school improvement* (2nd ed.). Bloomington, IN: Solution Tree Press.

DuFour, R., & Eaker, R. (1998). *Professional Learning Communities at Work: Best practices for enhancing student achievement*. Bloomington, IN: Solution Tree Press.

DuFour, R., & Reeves, D. (2016). The futility of PLC lite. *Phi Delta Kappan, 97*(6), 69–71.

Duhigg, C. (2016). What Google learned from its quest to build the perfect team. *The New York Times Magazine*. Accessed from https://nytimes.com/2016/02/28/magazine/what-google-learned-from-its-quest-to-build-the -perfect-team.html on July 13, 2022.

Dyer, W. G. (1995) *Team building: Current issues and new alternatives* (3rd ed.). Reading, MA: Addison-Wesley.

Easton, L. B. (2009). *Protocols for professional learning*. Alexandria, VA: ASCD.

Easton, L. B. (Ed.). (2015). *Powerful designs for professional learning* (3rd ed.). Oxford, OH: Learning Forward.

Edmondson, A. C. (2019). *The fearless organization: Creating psychological safety in the workplace for learning, innovation, and growth*. Hoboken, NJ: Wiley.

Edmondson. A. C., & Lei, Z. (2014). Psychological safety: The history, renaissance, and future of an interpersonal construct. *Annual Review of Organizational Psychology and Organizational Behavior, 1*(1), 23–43.

Elliott, J. (1998). *Requisite organization: A total system for effective managerial organization and managerial leadership for the 21st century* (Rev. 2nd ed.). Arlington, VA: Cason Hall.

Feeney, E. J. (2016). How an orientation to learning influences the expansive-restrictive nature of teacher learning and change. *Teacher Development, 20*(4), 458–481.

Ferlazzo, L. (2020, September 1). *Educators must challenge racist language & actions* [Blog post]. Accessed at https://edweek.org/teaching-learning/opinion-educators-must-challenge-racist-language-actions/2020/09 on August 1, 2022.

Fisher, D., & Frey, N. (2014). Using teacher learning walks to improve instruction. *Principal Leadership, 14*(5), 58–61.

Fisher, R., & Ury, W. (2011). *Getting to yes: Negotiating agreement without giving in* (B. Patton, Ed.; Rev. 3rd ed.). New York: Penguin.

Fixsen, A. A. M., Aijaz, M., Fixsen, D. L., Burks, E., & Schultes, M-T. (2021). *Implementation frameworks: An analysis*. Chapel Hill, NC: Active Implementation Research Network. Accessed at https://activeimplementation .org/wp-content/uploads/2021/04/AIRN-AFixsen-FrameworksAnalysis-2021.pdf on May 9, 2022.

Fixsen, D., Blase, K., Naoom, S., & Duda, M. (2015). *Implementation drivers: Assessing best practices*. Chapel Hill, NC: National Implementation Science Network.

Frank, C. J., & Magnone, P. F. (2011). *Drinking from the fire hose: Making smarter decisions without drowning in information*. New York: Portfolio Penguin.

Fredrickson, B. (2009). *Positivity*. New York: Crown.

Frey, N., Hattie, J., & Fisher, D. (2018). *Developing assessment-capable visible learners, grades K–12: Maximizing will, skill, and thrill*. Thousand Oaks, CA: Corwin Literacy.

Fritz, R. (1989) *The path of least resistance: Learning to become the creative force in your own life* (Rev. and expanded ed.). New York: Fawcett Columbine.

Fullan, M. (1982). *The meaning of educational change*. New York: Teachers College Press.

Fullan, M. (2007). *The new meaning of educational change* (4th ed.). New York: Teachers College Press.

Fullan, M. (2016). *The new meaning of educational change* (5th ed.). New York: Teachers College Press.

Fullan, M. (2020). *Leading in a culture of change* (2nd ed.). San Francisco: Jossey-Bass.

Garet, M. S., Heppen, J. B., Walters, K., Parkinson, J., Smith, T. M., Song, M., et al. (2016, September). *Focusing on mathematical knowledge: The impact of content-intensive teacher professional development*. Washington, DC: National Center for Education Evaluation and Regional Assistance. Accessed at https://files.eric.ed.gov/fulltext/ED569154.pdf on May 9, 2022.

Garet, M. S., Porter, A. C., Desimone, L., Birman, B. F., & Yoon, K. S. (2001). What makes professional development effective? Results from a national sample of teachers. *American Educational Research Journal, 38*(4), 915–945.

Garrett, R., Zhang, Q., Citkowicz, M., & Burr, L. (2021, December). *How Learning Forward's Standards for Professional Learning are associated with teacher instruction and student achievement: A meta-analysis*. Washington, DC: Center on Great Teachers and Leaders at the American Institutes for Research. Accessed at https://gtlcenter.org/sites/default/files/LF-2022-Standards-for-PL-Meta%20Analysis%20Report_Final.pdf on August 9, 2022.

Garmston, R., & McKanders, C. (2022). *It's your turn: Teacher as facilitators—A handbook*. Burlington, VT: MiraVia.

Glaser, J. E. (2014). *Conversational intelligence: How great leaders build trust and get extraordinary results*. Brookline, MA: Bibliomotion Books + Media.

Glaser, J. E. (2015, December 28). *Celebration time: A cocktail each executive should know how to mix* [Blog post]. Accessed at www.psychologytoday.com/us/blog/conversational-intelligence/201512/celebration-time on May 9, 2022.

Goddard, R. D., Hoy, W. K., & Hoy, A. W. (2000). Collective teacher efficacy: Its meaning, measure, and impact on student achievement. *American Educational Research Journal, 37*(2), 479–507.

Goldsmith, M., & Silvester, S. (2018). *Stakeholder centered coaching: Maximizing your impact as a coach*. Cupertino, CA: THINKaha.

Gordon, J. (2018). *The power of a positive team: Proven principles and practices that make great teams great*. Hoboken, NJ: Wiley.

Grant, A. [@AdamMGrant]. (2021a, November 5). *Many "best practices" were created for a world that no longer exists. In the face of change, the routines that* [Tweet]. Twitter. Accessed at https://twitter.com/adammgrant/status/1456612007524900866?lang=en on May 9, 2022.

Grant, A. (2021b, April 19). There's a name for the blah you're feeling: It's called languishing. *The New York Times*. Accessed at www.nytimes.com/2021/04/19/well/mind/covid-mental-health-languishing.html?smid=em-share on May 9, 2022.

Green, G., & Ballard, G. H. (2010–2011). No substitute for experience: Transforming teacher preparation with experiential and adult learning practices. *Southeastern Regional Association of Teacher Educators Journal, 20*(1), 12–20.

Grissom, J., Egalite, A., & Lindsay, C. (2021). *How principals affect students and schools: A systematic synthesis of two decades of research*. New York: The Wallace Foundation. Accessed at www.wallacefoundation.org/knowledge-center/Documents/How-Principals-Affect-Students-and-Schools.pdf on September 6, 2022.

Groysberg, B., & Abbott, S. (2020, July 9). It's time to reset decision-making in your organization. *Harvard Business School*. Accessed at https://hbswk.hbs.edu/item/it-s-time-to-reset-decision-making-in-your-organization on July 13, 2022.

Hall, G. E., & Hord, S. M. (2015). *Implementing change: Patterns, principles, and potholes* (4th ed.). Boston: Pearson.

Hall, P., & Simeral, A. (2008). *Building teachers' capacity for success: A collaborative approach for coaches and school leaders*. Alexandria, VA: ASCD.

Hallam, P. R., Smith, H. R., Hite, J. M., Hite, S. J., & Wilcox, B. R. (2015). Trust and collaboration in PLC teams: Teacher relationship, principal support, and collaborative benefits. *NASSP Bulletin, 99*(3), 193–216.

Hargreaves, A., & Fullan, M. (2012). *Professional capital: Transforming teaching in every school*. New York: Teachers College Press.

Hargreaves, A., & Fullan, M. (2013). The power of professional capital: With an investment in collaboration, teachers become nation builders. *Journal of Staff Development, 34*(3), 36–39.

Hargreaves, A., & O'Connor, M. T. (2018). *Collaborative professionalism: When teaching together means learning for all.* Thousand Oaks, CA: Corwin Press.

Harrison, C., & Bryan, C. (2008). Data dialogue: Focused conversations put evidence to work in the classroom. *Journal of Staff Development, 29*(4), 15–19.

Hastings, R., & Meyer, E. (2020). *No rules rules: Netflix and the culture of reinvention.* New York: Penguin Press.

Hattie, J. (2015). *What works best in education: The politics of collaborative expertise.* London: Pearson.

Hattie, J., & Timperley, H. (2007). The power of feedback. *Review of Educational Research, 77*(1), 81–112.

Hauge, K. (2019). Teachers' collective professional development in school: A review study (P. Wan, Reviewing ed.). *Cogent Education, 6*(1). https://doi.org/10.1080/2331186X.2019.1619223

Heath, D. (2020). *Upstream: The quest to solve problems before they happen.* New York: Avid Reader Press.

Herzberg, F. (2008). *One more time: How do you motivate employees?* Boston: Harvard Business Press.

Hord, S. M. (1997a). *Professional learning communities: Communities of continuous inquiry and improvement.* Austin, TX: Southwest Educational Development Laboratory.

Hord, S. M. (1997b). Professional learning communities: What are they and why are they important? *Issues About Change, 6*(1). Accessed at https://sedl.org/change/issues/issues61.html on May 9, 2022.

Hord, S. M. (Ed.). (2004). *Learning together, leading together: Changing schools through professional learning communities.* New York: Teachers College Press.

Hord, S. M., & Roussin, J. L. (2013). *Implementing change through learning: Concerns-based concepts, tools, and strategies for guiding change.* Thousand Oaks, CA: Corwin Press.

Hord, S. M., & Sommers, W. A. (Eds.). (2008). *Leading professional learning communities: Voice from research and practice.* Thousand Oaks, CA: Corwin Press.

Horseheads Central School District. (n.d.). *Horseheads central school district mission, vision, value statements.* Accessed at https://horseheadsdistrict.com/hcsdmission.cfm#:~:text=Our%20Vision%3A,student%2Dcentered%2C%20 nurturing%20environment on June 28, 2022.

Huguet, A., Holtzman, D. J., Robyn, A., Steiner, E. D., Todd, I., Choi, L., et al. (2020). *The intensive partnerships for effective teaching: A comparison of school outcomes* [Research brief]. Santa Monica, CA: RAND. Accessed at https://rand.org/pubs/research_briefs/RBA124-1.html on July 8, 2022.

Huysman, J. D. (2014, May 29). *Emotional safety: What does it really mean?* [Blog post]. Accessed at https://psychologytoday.com/us/blog/life-in-the-recovery-room/201405/emotional-safety-what-does-it-really-mean on August 9, 2022.

Hyatt, M. (2020). *The vision-driven leader: 10 questions to focus your efforts, energize your team, and scale your business.* Ada, MI: Baker Books.

International Coach Federation. (2022). *All things coaching.* International Coaching Federation. Accessed at https://coachingfederation.org/about on May 9, 2022.

Iqbal, M. Z. (2017). Reflection-in-action: A stimulus reflective practice for professional development of student teachers. *Bulletin of Education and Research, 39*(2), 65–82.

Johnson, B. (1992). *Polarity management: Identifying and managing unsolvable problems.* Amherst, MA: HRD Press.

Johnson, B. (2020). *And: Making a difference by leveraging polarity, paradox or dilemma, Volume one—Foundations.* Amherst, MA: HRD Press.

Joyce, B. R., & Showers, B. (2002). *Student achievement through staff development* (3rd ed.). Alexandria, VA: ASCD.

Joyce, B. R., Weil, M., & Calhoun, E. (2015). *Models of teaching* (9th ed.). Boston: Pearson.

Kantor, R. M. (2012, September 25). *Ten reasons people resist change* [Blog post]. Accessed at https://hbr.org/2012/09/ten-reasons-people-resist-chang on July 13, 2022.

Katz, S., & Dack, L. A. (2013). *Intentional interruptions: Breaking down learning barriers to transform professional practice.* Thousand Oaks, CA: Corwin Press.

Kennedy, J. F. (1961). *President John F. Kennedy's inaugural address (1961)* [Speech]. Accessed at https://archives .gov/milestone-documents/president-john-f-kennedys-inaugural-address on August 9, 2022.

Killion, J. (2012a). Coaching in the K–12 context. In S. J. Fletcher & C. A. Mullen (Eds.), *The Sage handbook of mentoring and coaching in education* (pp. 273–294). Los Angeles: SAGE.

Killion, J. (2012b). *Meet the promise of content standards: Investing in professional learning.* Oxford, OH: Learning Forward.

Killion, J. (2018). *Assessing impact: Evaluating professional learning* (3rd ed.). Thousand Oaks, CA: Corwin Press.

Killion, J. (2019). *The feedback process: Transforming feedback for professional learning* (2nd ed.). Oxford, OH: Learning Forward.

Killion, J. (2022). Facing change. In J. Keating & J. K. Kullar (Eds.), *Women who lead: Insights, inspiration, and guidance to grow as an educator.* (pp. 33–52). Bloomington, IN: Solution Tree Press.

Killion, J., & Harrison, C. (2006). *Taking the lead: New roles for teacher and school-based coaches.* Oxford, OH: Learning Forward.

Killion, J., & Harrison, C. (2017). *Taking the lead: New roles for teacher and school-based coaches* (2nd ed.). Oxford, OH: Learning Forward.

Killion, J., Harrison, C., Colton, A., Bryan, C., Delehant, A., & Cooke, D. (2016, November). *A systemic approach to elevating teacher leadership.* Oxford, OH: Learning Forward. Accessed at https://learningforward .org/wp-content/uploads/2017/08/a-systemic-approach-to-elevating-teacher-leadership.pdf on May 9, 2022.

Killion, J., & Hirsh, S. (2012). The bottom line on excellence. *Journal of Staff Development, 33*(1), 10–16.

Killion, J., & Roy, P (2009). *Becoming a learning school.* Oxford, OH: National Staff Development Council.

Killion, J., & Todnem, G. R. (1991). A process for personal theory building. *Educational Leadership, 48*(6), 14–16.

King, M. L., Jr. (1963). *Read Martin Luther King Jr.'s 'I have a dream' speech in its entirety.* NPR. Accessed at https://npr.org/2010/01/18/122701268/i-have-a-dream-speech-in-its-entirety on August 9, 2022.

Kise, J. A. G., & Watterston, B. K. (2019). *Step in, step up: Empowering women for the school leadership journey.* Bloomington, IN: Solution Tree Press.

Kolb, D. A. (1984). *Experiential learning: Experience as the source of learning and development.* Englewood Cliffs, NJ: Prentice-Hall.

Kraft, M. A., & Blazar, D. L. (2017). Individualized coaching to improve teacher practice across grades and subjects: New experimental evidence. *Educational Policy, 31*(7), 1033–1068.

Kraft, M. A., Blazar, D. L., & Hogan, D. (2018). The effect of teacher coaching on instruction and achievement: A meta-analysis of the causal evidence. *Review of Educational Research, 88*(4), 547–588.

Krogerus, M., & Tschäppeler, R. (2012). *The decision book: Fifty models for strategic thinking* (J. Piening, Trans.). New York: Norton.

Landry, L. (2020 March 5). *Why managers should involve their team in the decision-making process* [Blog post]. Accessed at https://online.hbs.edu/blog/post/team-decision-making on July 16, 2022.

Lasater, K., Albiladi, W. S., Davis, W. S., & Bengtson, E. (2020). The data culture continuum: An examination of school data cultures. *Educational Administration Quarterly, 56*(4), 533–569.

Latham, A. (2015, November 15). 12 reasons why how you make decisions is more important than what you decide. *Forbes Careers.* Accessed at https://forbes.com/sites/annlatham/2015/11/15/12-reasons-why-how -you-make-decisions-is-more-important-than-what-you-decide/?sh=6e8a203b7db8 on July 13, 2022.

Learning Forward. (2011). *2011 standards.* Oxford, OH: Author.

Learning Forward. (2022). *Standards for professional learning.* Oxford, OH: Author.

Leithwood, K., Louis, K. S., Anderson, S., & Wahlstrom, K. (2004). *How leadership influences student learning.* New York: Wallace Foundation. Accessed at www.wallacefoundation.org/knowledge-center/documents /how-leadership-influences-student-learning.pdf on May 9, 2022.

Leithwood, K., & Louis, K. S. (2012). *Linking leadership to student learning.* San Francisco: Jossey-Bass.

Lencioni, P. (2000). *Obsessions of an extraordinary executive: The four disciplines at the heart of making an organization world class*. San Francisco: Jossey-Bass.

Lencioni, P. (2016). *The ideal team player: How to recognize and cultivate the three essential virtues*. Hoboken, NJ: Wiley.

Lipinski, S. (2021, September). *The biological basis of complacency: Implications for improving safety performance—Special report*. Bethesda, MD: Habit Mastery Consulting. Accessed at https://habitmasteryconsulting.com /wp-content/uploads/2020/09/Biological-Basis-of-Complacency.pdf on July 13, 2022.

Little, J. W. (1982). Norms of collegiality and experimentation: Workplace conditions of school success. *American Educational Research Journal, 19*(3), 325–340.

Little, J. W. (2003). Inside teacher community: Representations of classroom practice. *Teachers College Record, 105*(6), 913–945.

Love, N., Stiles, K. E., Mundry, S., & DiRanna, K. (2008). *The data coach's guide to improving learning for all students: Unleashing the power of collaborative inquiry*. Thousand Oaks, CA: Corwin Press.

Mann, A., & Dvorak, N. (2016, June 28). Employee recognition: Low cost, high impact. *Gallup*. Accessed at https://gallup.com/workplace/236441/employee-recognition-low-cost-high-impact.aspx on May 9, 2022.

Many, T., & Butler, B. (2018). Moving schools from PLC lite to PLC right. *Texas Elementary Principals and Supervisors Association (TEPSA) News, 75*(2). Accessed at https://tepsa.org/resource/moving-schools-from -plc-lite-to-plc-right on May 9, 2022.

McLaughlin, M. W., & Talbert, J. E. (2001). *Professional communities and the work of high school teaching*. Chicago: University of Chicago Press.

McLeod, S. (2019). What does effect size tell you? *Simply Psychology*. Accessed at https://simplypsychology.org/effect -size.html on May 9, 2022.

Mendy, A., Stewart, M. L., & VanAtkin, K. (2020, May). A leader's guide: Communicating with teams, stakeholders, and communities during COVID-19. In McKinsey & Company (Ed.), *The path to the next normal: Leading with* resolve *through the coronavirus pandemic* (pp. 24–31). Accessed at https://mckinsey.com/~/media /McKinsey/Featured%20Insights/Navigating%20the%20coronavirus%20crisis%20collected%20works/Path -to-the-next-normal-collection.pdf on May 9, 2022.

Michigan Department of Education. (2022). *Law, rule, policy: Educator certification*. Accessed at https://michigan.gov /mde/services/ed-serv/ed-cert/law on July 8, 2022.

Mike, B. (2020, June 25). *Bridge the gap between corporate training and real work outcomes* [Blog post]. Accessed at www.mentorworks.ca/blog/business-strategy/bridge-the-gap-between-corporate-training-and-real-work -outcomes on May 9, 2022.

Miller, H. H., & Miskimon, K. (2021, March 4). *Microaggressions and microinterventions in the classroom* [Blog post]. Accessed at https://education.fsu.edu/microaggressions-and-microinterventions-classroom on August 1, 2022.

Model Teaching. (2022). *Louisiana teacher professional development*. Accessed at www.modelteaching.com/professional -development-requirements/louisiana-teacher-professional-development#:~:text=Once%20you%20hold%20 a%20Level,system%2Dapproved%20professional%20development%20activity on July 11, 2022.

Modoono, J. (2017). The trust factor. *ASCD*. Accessed at www.ascd.org/el/articles/the-trust-factor on July 13, 2022.

Muir. J. (n.d.). *Prescription without diagnosis is malpractice*. Accessed at https://puremuir.com/prescription-without -diagnosis-malpractice on May 9, 2022.

National Institute for Excellence in Teaching. (2021). *Using learning walks to improve feedback and schoolwide success*. Accessed at https://niet.org/assets/Resources/learning-walks-improve-feedback-schoolwide-success.pdf on July 11, 2022.

National School Reform Faculty. (n.d.a). *NSRF protocols and activities . . . from a to z*. Accessed at https://nsrfharmony .org/protocols on June 24, 2022.

National School Reform Faculty. (n.d.b). *Success analysis protocol with reflective questions*. Accessed at https:// nsrfharmony.org/wp-content/uploads/2017/10/success_analysis_reflective_0.pdf on July 7, 2022.

National School Reform Faculty. (2015). *Tuning protocol.* Accessed at https://nsrfharmony.org/wp-content/uploads/2017/10/Tuning-N_0.pdf on July 7, 2022.

New York State United Teachers. (2022). *Fact sheet 21-14: Registration and CTLE—Teachers.* Accessed at https://nysut.org/resources/all-listing/research/fact-sheets/fact-sheet-registration-and-ctle-teachers on July 11, 2022.

Nickols, F. (2010, May 29). *The knowledge in knowledge management.* Accessed at https://nickols.us/knowledge_in_KM.pdf on August 8, 2022.

Nietzsche, F. W. (2019). *Thus spake Zarathustra: A book for all and none* (Rev. ed.; T. Common, Trans.). Ingersoll, Ontario, Canada: Devoted.

Ning, H. K., Lee, D., & Lee, W. O. (2016). The relationship between teacher value orientations and engagement in professional learning communities. *Teachers and Teaching, 22*(2), 235–254.

Norton Public Schools. (n.d.) *Mission, vision, goals & core values.* Accessed at www.norton.k12.ma.us/about-us/mission-vision-core-values-statement on June 28, 2022.

Odden, A. R., Goetz, M. E., & Picus, L. O. (2008). Using available evidence to estimate the cost of educational adequacy. *Education Finance and Policy, 3*(3), 374–397.

Oghenechuko, O. J., & Godbless, E. E. (2018). Interest-based conflict management systems: Beyond traditional and ADR systems of conflict resolution. *European Journal of Business and Management, 10*(17), 80–91. Accessed at https://core.ac.uk/download/pdf/234628443.pdf on July 13, 2022.

Opfer, V. D., & Pedder, D. (2011). Conceptualizing teacher professional learning. *Review of Educational Research, 81*(3), 376–407. https://doi.org/10.3102/0034654311413609

Pascale, R. T., Sternin, J., & Sternin, M. (2010). *The power of positive deviance: How unlikely innovators solve the world's toughest problems.* Boston: Harvard Business Press.

Patton, M. Q. (2015). *Qualitative research and evaluation methods: Integrating theory and practice* (4th ed.). Thousand Oaks, CA: SAGE.

Patton, M. Q., & Campbell-Patton, C. E. (2022). *Utilization-focused evaluation* (5th ed.). Thousand Oaks, CA: SAGE.

Pennington, C. (2018, April 3). We are hardwired to resist change. *Emerson Human Capital.* Accessed at https://emersonhc.com/change-management/people-hard-wired-resist-change on July 13, 2022.

Pfeffer, J., & Sutton, R. I. (2000). *The knowing-doing gap: How smart companies turn knowledge into action.* Boston: Harvard Business School Press.

Postholm, M. B. (2018). Teachers' professional development in school: A review study (M. Boylan, Reviewing ed.). *Cogent Education, 5*(1). https://doi.org/10.1080/2331186X.2018.1522781

P.S./M.S. 5 Port Morris School of Community Leadership. (2021). *Vision statement.* Accessed at www.psms5.com/our_school/vision_statement on May 9, 2022.

Quintero, D. (2019, January 25). *Instructional coaching holds promise as a method to improve teachers' impact* [Blog post]. Accessed at https://brookings.edu/blog/brown-center-chalkboard/2019/01/25/instructional-coaching-holds-promise-as-a-method-to-improve-teachers-impact on May 9, 2022.

Ranosa, R. (2019, November 5). What is tall poppy syndrome? *Human Resources Director Magazine.* Accessed at https://hcamag.com/au/specialisation/employee-engagement/what-is-tall-poppy-syndrome/190607 on May 9, 2022.

Ratcliffe, S. (Ed.). (2017). *Oxford essential quotations* (5th ed.). England: Oxford University Press.

Regional Educational Laboratory Program West. (n.d.). *Using inquiry cycles in PLCs to improve instruction* [Infographic]. Accessed at https://ies.ed.gov/ncee/edlabs/regions/west/relwestFiles/pdf/REL-West-4-2-3-4-Literacy-Improvement-Partnership-Inquiry-Cycles-Infographics-508.pdf on August 9, 2022.

Research for Better Teaching (2019). *Coaching high-impact teacher teams.* Accessed at www.rbteach.com/our-services/core-programs/courses/17 on November 15, 2022.

Richlands High School. (2022). *Vision.* Accessed at https://www.onslow.k12.nc.us/domain/503 on August 9, 2022.

Rios, J. A., Ling, G., Pugh, R., Becker, D., & Bacall, A. (2020). Identifying critical 21st-century skills for workplace success: A content analysis of job advertisements. *Educational Researcher, 49*(2), 80–89.

Robbins, P., & Alvy, H. B. (2009). *The principal's companion: Strategies for making the job easier* (3rd Ed.). Thousand Oaks, CA: Corwin Press.

Rogers, M. G. (2017). *You are the team: Six simple ways teammates can go from good to great.* Scotts Valley, CA: CreateSpace.

Saphier, J. (2015, June 22). *12 observable features of a strong adult professional culture* [Blog post]. Research for Better Teaching. Accessed at www.rbteach.com/blogs/12-observable-features-strong-adult-professional-culture on May 9, 2022.

Saphier, J. (1989). *School culture survey.* Acton, MA: Research for Better Teaching.

Save the Children. (n.d.). *Who we are.* Accessed at https://savethechildren.net/about-us/who-we-are on July 22, 2022.

Schein, E. H. (2012). Foreword. In A. C. Edmondson (Ed.), *Teaming: How organizations learn, innovate, and compete in the knowledge economy*, pp. xi–xiii. San Francisco: Jossey-Bass.

Schön, D. A. (1983). *The reflective practitioner: How professionals think in action.* New York: Basic Books.

Schön, D. A. (1987). *Educating the reflective practitioner: Toward a new design for teaching and learning in the professions.* San Francisco: Jossey-Bass.

School Reform Initiative. (2021). *Collaborative assessment conference: Overview.* Accessed at https://schoolreforminitiative.org/download/collaborative-assessment-conference/?wpdmdl=12768&refresh=62f2ca4175aba1660078657 on August 9, 2022.

Sheridan, R. (2018). *Chief joy officer: How great leaders elevate human energy and eliminate fear.* New York: Portfolio.

Shirley, D., & Hargreaves, A. (2021). *Five paths of student engagement: Blazing the trail to learning and success.* Bloomington, IN: Solution Tree Press.

Showers, B. (1982, December). *Transfer of training: The role of coaching.* Eugene, OR: Center for Educational Policy and Management, College of Education, University of Oregon. Accessed at https://files.eric.ed.gov/fulltext/ED231035.pdf on May 9, 2022.

Showers, B. (1987). The role of coaching in the implementation of innovations. *Teacher Education Quarterly, 14*(3), 59–70.

Showers, B., Joyce, B., & Bennett, B. (1987). Synthesis of research on staff development: A framework for future study and a state-of-the-art analysis. *Educational Leadership, 45*(3), 77–87.

Sinek, S. (2011). *Start with why: How great leaders inspire everyone to take action.* New York: Portfolio.

Sommers, W. A. (2021). *Creating talent density: Accelerating adult learning.* Lanham, MD: Rowman & Littlefield.

Studin, I. (2021). To find and reintegrate the world's "third bucket kids" by September. *21CQ.* Accessed at https://i21cq.com/publications/to-find-and-reintegrate-the-worlds-third-bucket-kids-by-september on May 9, 2022.

Summit Hill School District 161. (n.d.) *ELL mission and vision statements.* Accessed at https://summithill.org/Documents/Ctrl_Hyperlink/ELL_uid10282014241332.pdf on July 22, 2022.

Surowiecki, J. (2004). *The wisdom of crowds: Why the many are smarter than the few and how collective wisdom shapes business, economies, societies, and nations.* New York: Doubleday.

SurveyMonkey. (n.d.a). *How to create surveys.* Accessed at https://surveymonkey.com/mp/how-to-create-surveys on June 23, 2022.

SurveyMonkey. (n.d.b) *What is a Likert scale?* Accessed at https://surveymonkey.com/mp/likert-scale July 22, 2022.

Three Village Central School District. (2022). *Setauket Elementary: Mission statement.* Accessed at http://threevillagecsd.org/schools/principals_message_-_setauket on July 22, 2022.

Tooley, M., & Connally, K. (2016). *No panacea: Diagnosing what ails teacher professional development before reaching for remedies.* Washington, DC: New America.

Tooley, M., & White, T. (2018, August). *Rethinking relicensure: Promoting professional learning through teacher licensure renewal policies—Executive summary*. Accessed at https://s3.amazonaws.com/newamericadotorg /documents/Executive_Summary_-_Rethinking_Relicensure_FINAL.pdf on May 9, 2022.

Tschannen-Moran, M. (2014) *Trust matters: Leadership for successful schools* (2nd ed.). San Francisco: Jossey-Bass.

Tupper, H., & Ellis, S. (2021). Make learning a part of your daily routine. *Harvard Business Review*. Accessed at https:// hbr.org/2021/11/make-learning-a-part-of-your-daily-routine?utm_medium=email&utm_source=newsletter _daily&utm_campaign=mtod_notactsubs https://hbr.org/2021/11/make-learning-a-part-of-your-daily-routine on May 9, 2022.

United Nations. (1989). *Convention on the Rights of the Child text*. Accessed at https://unicef.org/child-rights -convention/convention-text on July 22, 2022.

Watson, K. M. (2013, April 29). *Wesley didn't say it: Do all the good you can, by all the means you can . . .* [Blog post]. Accessed at https://kevinmwatson.com/2013/04/29/wesley-didnt-say-it-do-all-the-good-you-can-by-all -the-means-you-can on May 9, 2022.

Watson, S. (2021). Feel-good hormones: How they affect the mind, mood and body. *Harvard Health*. Accessed at https://health.harvard.edu/mind-and-mood/feel-good-hormones-how-they-affect-your-mind-mood-and -body on July 12, 2022.

Wei, R. C., Darling-Hammond, L., Andree, A., Richardson, N., & Orphanos, S. (2009). *Professional learning in the learning profession: A status report on teacher development in the U.S. and abroad* [Technical report]. Dallas, TX: National Staff Development Council.

Wellman, B., & Lipton, L. (2017). *Data-driven dialogue: A facilitator's guide to collaborative inquiry* (2nd ed.). Burlington, VT: MiraVia.

Wenger, E. (1998). *Communities of practice: Learning, meaning, and identity*. New York: Cambridge University Press.

Weston Public Schools. (n.d.) *Vision statement*. Accessed at https://westonschools.org/district/vision-statement on June 28, 2022.

Wiseman, L. (2014). *Rookie smarts: Why learning beats knowing in the new game of work*. New York: Harper Business.

Woolfolk, A., Winne, P., & Perry, N. (2012). *Educational psychology* (5th Canadian ed.). Toronto, Canada: Pearson.

World Vision. (2022). *Our vision statement*. Accessed at https://wvi.org/our-vision-statement on July 22, 2022.

York-Barr, J., Sommers, W. A., Ghere, G. S., & Montie, J. (2016). *Reflective practice for renewing schools: An action guide for educators* (3rd ed.). Thousand Oaks, CA: Corwin Press.

Zhu, M., Yang, Y., & Hsee, C. K. (2018). The mere urgency effect. *Journal of Consumer Research, 45*(3), 673–690. https://doi.org/10.1093/jcr/ucy008

INDEX

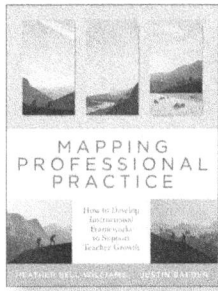

Mapping Professional Practice
Heather Bell-Williams and Justin Baeder
Put into action, instructional frameworks help teachers locate their current level of fluency, focus on the key dimensions of professional judgment, and take their practice to the next level. Discover how to accelerate teacher growth by taking the "insider's view" of practice, articulating key dimensions of professional judgment to create clear growth pathways for teachers at every level of fluency.
BKG054

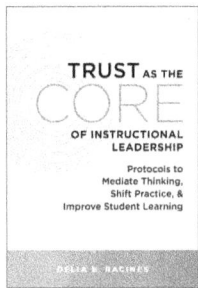

Trust as the Core of Instructional Leadership
Delia E. Racines
Be visible and approachable. Unpack necessary conversations with care. Build capacity based on strengths. Author Delia E. Racines offers these powerful protocols and more to support instructional leaders in building a community of trust in which positive change can occur. All current and aspiring instructional leaders ready to work collaboratively to improve teaching and learning will value this book.
BKG047

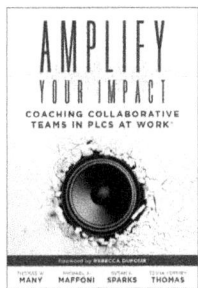

Amplify Your Impact
Thomas W. Many, Michael J. Maffoni, Susan K. Sparks, and Tesha Ferriby Thomas
Amplify Your Impact presents K–12 educators with a framework for improving collaboration in their PLCs. The authors share best practices and processes teams can rely on to ensure they are doing the right work in a cycle of continuous improvement. Discover concrete action steps your school can take to adopt proven collaborative coaching methods, fortify teacher teams, and ultimately improve student learning in classrooms.
BKF794

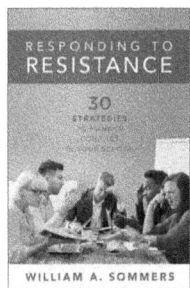

Responding to Resistance
William A. Sommers
Educational leadership is never conflict free. In *Responding to Resistance*, author William A. Sommers presents school and district leaders with a set of wide-ranging response strategies. Whether a conflict involves staff, students, parents, or other stakeholders, this book will help you address it openly, decisively, and efficiently, so you have more time to focus on what matters most: improving learning in your school community.
BKF955

Leadership at Every Level
Janelle Clevenger McLaughlin
Leadership is a mindset, not a position. Rely on this resource as you nurture your leadership skills and grow as a lifelong learner. Ideal for book studies, *Leadership at Every Level* shares real-world examples and research-based strategies for strengthening leadership capacity at the classroom, school, and district levels. You'll learn to foster authentic relationships, build a culture of innovation, and more.
BKG014

9 781954 631397